EDUCATION AND TEACHING

A publication in the
Merrill Coordinated Teacher Preparation Series
under the editorship of Donald E. Orlosky

Education
and
Teaching

21 Performance-Based Units for an
Introduction to Education

Robert G. Packard
The University of Missouri

Charles E. Merrill Publishing Company

A Bell & Howell Company

Columbus, Ohio

Published by
Charles E. Merrill Publishing Company
A Bell & Howell Company
Columbus, Ohio 43216

International Standard Book Number: 0–675–08837–2

Library of Congress Catalog Card Number: 73–91451

Printed in the United States of America

3 4 5 6 7 8 — 79 78 77 76 75

To Sally and Randy
Carine and Rollin

CONTENTS

Part III: Extensions and Projects

PREFACE

Many texts simply present information. This text is designed to teach. If you work through each unit as suggested, you will be able to talk intelligently about many basic and crucial aspects of American education, you will acquire skills that are very basic to teaching, and you will learn enough about the teaching profession and yourself to make intelligent decisions about your future as a teacher.

The topics in this text were chosen primarily for their usefulness to a prospective teacher or to a student who is trying to decide whether to pursue the teaching profession. The content is designed to serve as a broad overview of the past, present, and future of American education—an advance organizer for a program of education courses. The text will not make you an expert in any of the topics. Much of the depth and detail which you expect in later education courses, as well as some of the topics, are not to be found in this text. But most of what you do find you can expect to master and retain.

Part I considers some basic factors in the enterprise of education: the story of the development of elementary, secondary, and teacher education from colonial times, and how its successes and failures still influence the schools of today; the organization of schools today as state functions, governed by state and national laws, and financed in a variety of ways (some of which are being challenged today); and the social patterns and cultural systems that inevitably color the way in which teachers and students, communities and schools interact. Finally, the current teaching profession is described: what a teacher does, what a teacher gets paid, how difficult it is to get a job, and what the chances are that you would be satisfied and effective as a teacher.

Part II focuses on the science of teaching: how a student learns; what the factors are that determine whether he will want to learn; how a teacher keeps discipline; how a teacher decides when and whether a change in methods should be made; and how a teacher states the objectives clearly enough that the change can be measured. In treating such topics as writing behavioral objectives, asking questions effectively, and analyzing and changing behavior (including your own when necessary), Part II teaches you skills that are basic enough to be useful to you even if you do not continue in education. Parts I and II both conclude with a review and application unit, the purpose of which is not simply to review the previous units, but to integrate the information and to provide further practice in applying it to contemporary situations.

Part III adds enrichment units and projects, including a statistical picture of the American teacher and a summary of several dozen current issues and spokesmen in American education. Optional projects relate to research, to live observation in a classroom, to changing your own study behavior, and to learning with others how to listen to and express deeply felt feelings with clarity and empathy.

In working with each successive unit, you will find the following suggestions helpful:

1. Before studying, skim through the unit to get an overview. Focus on the paragraph headings, diagrams, italicized words, and particularly the study-guide questions interspersed throughout the unit. These questions represent the objectives for the unit—statements of precisely what you are expected to do or say when you have finished the unit.

2. Begin studying the unit until you come to the first set of study guide questions. Test yourself on these questions by checking your answers against the preceding pages and by checking especially to see if your details are exact and complete and your examples appropriate.

3. Continue working through the unit in this way. If you have doubts or problems with any point, be sure to check with your instructor immediately. It is very important that you master all the objectives before proceeding to the next unit.

Several thousands of students have worked through these units in a self-paced, individualized way, with short mastery quizzes after each unit. The successes and problems, comments and critiques of each student, incorporated in three revisions of this text, have contributed immensely to the clarity and effectiveness of the units.

The author is also indebted to many others who, like the students who helped develop these units, have been careful and patient teachers, particularly Jack Michael, Wells Hively, Marv Daley, Bill Franzen and Hans Olsen. Elizabeth Watson and Paul Travers made helpful contributions to several units of the original version, and Doris Knight and Sandy Laham made innumerable contributions to the subsequent versions.

EDUCATION AND TEACHING

Part I

INTRODUCTION TO EDUCATION IN AMERICA

Unit 1

SHORT HISTORY OF AMERICAN EDUCATION

> I thank God there are no free schools, and I hope we shall not have them these hundred years; for learning has brought disobedience and heresy and sects into the world. (Governor Berkeley of Virginia, 1670)

Obviously, things have changed in 300 years. While history doesn't tell us who should be thanked (or cursed), we do have "free schools" of a sort that Governor Berkeley never envisioned. And he would agree that they have produced not only learning but also many forms of "disobedience and heresy." The story of how today's education developed over this period is one of a remarkable revolution. Even without going into detail, it can be fun to look at some stages in this revolutionizing process, at some of the men who helped "invent" the education we have today, at the national fights that developed, at how attitudes like Governor Berkeley's changed over the years, and at some questions that have remained unsolved for 300 years. Furthermore, in order to know what teaching is today, it helps to know the effect of past events on today's practices and attitudes. Many features of today's schooling are still being influenced by this historical past.

Education in Colonial America
(1600–1776)

The first immigrants to the New World did not bring universal public education with them; they couldn't because it hadn't been invented yet. For most children in *Asia and Africa,* education was an informal apprenticeship within the family and community, where they learned a basic trade skill (usually farming) as well as attitudes about life and social class. In this kind of informal system, education was a loose process by which a culture transmitted itself from generation to generation. In *Europe* formal education was regarded as a privilege of the wealthy few. Prep schools and universities were available to the children of the landed aristocrats and some of the new industrialists, to train them as elite leaders of society. Other European children learned some basic skills in a formal apprenticeship to a craftsman. But for the masses, lack of formal education was assumed to be inevitable. Beginning about 1600, England and a few other European countries established some "charity schools" to provide a minimum degree of literacy for the masses. But these charity schools were a far cry from the free public elementary schools that were to develop first in the United States and later in Europe.

As you might expect, colonial life in the United States was primarily an extension of European social and educational systems. But there were important differences, caused by special religious, political and social forces at work in the colonies. And these forces had different effects in different sections of the colonies, thereby preventing the development of a single unified educational system in the New World.

In the *New England Colonies* (Plymouth, Massachusetts Bay, New Haven, and Connecticut) education and religion were inseparable twins. Puritan theology, the state religion of these colonies, defined adults and children as sinners whose salvation was uncertain. Naturally, then, the "perfecting of the saints" was the primary and often harsh business of the schools. The Puritans respected education, especially reading skills, as a means of developing reason, of making man a more willing instrument in the hands of God, of counteracting the wiles of Satan, of providing a learned clergy and a literate congregation, and of allowing the people to read the Bible from older Latin translations. Consider this excerpt from the *New England Primer* on the purpose of reading:

> I shall praise the Lord in a more cheerful strain, that I was taught to read
> his Word, and have not learnt in vain.

In 1635, only fifteen years after Boston had been founded, its citizens started the first "public" *Latin grammar school* for boys eight to fifteen years old. As the name implies, these schools included instruction in the classical languages of Latin and Greek, essential instruction for the few colonial boys who went on to a university. The school boys—only boys were admitted—who attended the grammar schools spent most of their time memorizing and then reciting to the schoolmaster. One graduate recalled:

> At ten years of age I committed to memory many rules of syntax, the meaning of which I had no notion of, although I could apply them in a mechanical way. For instance, the rule for the ablative absolute—'A noun and a participle are put in the ablative, called absolute, to denote the time, cause or concomitant of an action, or the condition on which it depends'—I could rattle off whenever I encountered a sample of that construction, but it was several years after I learnt the rule that I arrived at even the faintest conception of what it meant.

Several years later (1636), *Harvard college* began operating in Cambridge, Massachusetts, with one professor, one building, and some public and private funds. Harvard's entrance requirements of that time specified:

> When any scholar is able to read fully, or such like classical Latin author extempore, and make and speak true Latin in verse and prose, and decline perfectly the paradigms of nouns and verbs in the Greek tongue, then may he be admitted into the College, nor shall any claim admission before such qualifications.

These college admission requirements became the basic curriculum of the existing Latin grammar schools.

In addition to the Latin grammar schools, so-called *"dame schools"* operated on a tuition basis. This type of school was kept by a "teacher" who was usually an object of disguised charity. The teacher might be a widow who couldn't provide a livelihood for her family, or a bond servant who was indentured to someone for several years in return for his passage to America, or an apprentice entering the trade of school master. Usually the teacher of a "dame school" taught in her own home. Though the curriculum emphasized religion and the three R's, she was considered successful if she kept the youngsters quiet and disciplined while she went about her household tasks.

Remember, however, that for many years most colonial children received little or no formal education at all. The *family* was the primary agent for the informal transmission of culture and a labor skill. The colonial family, unless it was wealthy and urban, assumed responsibility for socialization of the young and also for vocational training. Frequently the family would draw up a contract with a local tradesman, under which the master provided vocational training in his own family atmosphere, in exchange for the personal services of the apprentice for several years. Indentures of apprenticeship were also drawn up for poor, orphaned, and illegitimate children who were involuntarily assigned to master craftsmen in order to learn a craft and hopefully to learn to read. Apprenticeship was probably the most successful type of elementary school in all the colonies.

The first general education law in New England, called the *Massachusetts Law of 1642,* was in part an apprenticeship law requiring basic skills in reading and religion:

> This court, taking into consideration the great neglect in many parents and masters in training up their children in learning and labor and other employment which may be profitable to the commonwealth, do hereupon order and decree that in every town the chosen men appointed for managing the prudential affairs of the same shall henceforth stand charged with the care of the redress of this evil, and for this end they shall have power to take account from time to time of their parents and masters, and of their children, concerning their calling and employment of their children, especially of their ability to read and understand the principles of religion and the capital laws of the country, and to impose fines upon all those who refuse to render such account to them when required; and they shall have power to put forth apprentice the children of such as they shall find not to be able and fit to employ and bring them up.

Another interesting law, passed in Massachusetts five years later, was the first to require towns of a certain size to establish schools:

> It being one chiefe project of that old deluder, Satan, to keepe men from the knowledge of the Scriptures . . . it is therefore ordered that every township in this jurisdiction, after the Lord hath increased their number to 50 householders, shall then forthwith appoint one within their towne to teach all such children as shall resort to him to write and reade, whose wages shall be paid either by the parents or masters of such children, or by the inhabitants in general . . . and it is further ordered that where any towne shall increase to the number of 100 families they shall set up a grammar schoole, the Master thereof being able to instruct youth so farr as they shall be fitted for the University.

Some historians feel that these laws were simply religious laws designed to extend the influence of Calvinism; others see in these laws the foundation for such principles as the necessity of education and the right of the state to require it, tax for it, and establish minimum standards, without defining the curriculum completely. Though it was more than 100 years before the Colonies as a whole were to really begin to comply with such laws, they represent the beginning of the decline of the family as the major educational agent. The colonists gradually became convinced that transmitting a past culture was not enough for the present and the future.

Education in the *Middle Colonies* was different in several important ways from that of the New England colonies. In contrast to the North's homogeneous allegiance to Calvinism, the Middle Colonies were the "colonial melting

---

Before continuing, check yourself to see if you can:

1. Describe the major and minor forms of education received by immigrants to America before they left their native lands (Europe, Asia and Africa).

2. Briefly describe the four kinds of education available in the New England colonies. (Hint: Latin grammar and college, dame, family, apprentice.)

3. Summarize one objective contained in each of the Massachusetts education laws of the 1640s.

4. Explain why the Massachusetts laws are regarded as significant, although colonial adoption and compliance was slow.

---

pot" (or vegetable stew, if you prefer), settled by people of many different national origins and religions. Since the state could hardly legislate a common religion and curriculum on such divergent groups, the responsibility for education was left with a variety of private institutions, including families, churches, and philanthropic organizations. Furthermore, the churches were highly suspicious of the state's intentions.

The Dutch Reformed Church established Puritan-like schools in New York, and the Quakers did the same in Pennsylvania, though with less severity. William Penn said that children should "be making tools and instruments of play, shaping, drawing, framing, and building, rather than getting some rules of propriety of speech by heart; those would follow with more judgment, and less trouble and time." Later other religious and national groups would conduct their own schools also. Notice that the basic problem of educational systems for divergent cultures and religions is still a part of our challenge today. But the Middle Colonies' determination to separate church and state left its influence on the Constitution in 1787.

The *Southern Colonies* were again a different scene, consisting of large plantations and very few towns, a few wealthy plantation owners and a mass of poor black slaves and indentured white servants who worked the plantations. A plantation owner might explain his outlook on education this way:

> We don't need schools here in the South because, in the first place the workers do not need any education at all, and in the second place because our children live too far apart to make a central school practical. So I hire a tutor to live here on my plantation and teach my children. When my boys get old enough I'll send them back to Europe to attend a university.

The poorer white settlers in the South taught their children what they themselves knew, and indentured their boys out as apprentices to a master craftsman, as was frequently done in the North. But in contrast to the New England and Middle Colonies, the South had no reason or intrinsic force urging public schools. The system of slavery required an elitist education for the sons of white gentry who would themselves become slave masters. A society that prohibited teaching slaves to write, under fine of $100 for each offense, depended on a *tutorial* system of classical education for its leaders.

The *eighteenth century* brought some radical ideas from Europe to the colonies: appeals to human reason rather than divine law, to natural rights rather than supernatural rights, to scientific method rather than to established truths, and to democratic faith rather than aristocratic privilege. This shift in thinking had its effect on education. One result was the establishment of the *Philadelphia Academy* in 1751. This school, founded by Ben Franklin (one of the new humanists) had a curriculum that included practical training in areas such as surveying, navigation, and printing, as well as courses in English, geography, history, logic, rhetoric, Latin and Greek. The language emphasis was on English, a critical event in the making of a one-language nation. And the Academy's focus on practical skills served a real need in the colonies for technically trained citizens. Until the early 1700s, the only form of secondary education was the Latin grammar school. After Franklin, other private (and usually coed) academies were quickly established, and this type of secondary school flourished for over a hundred years, to be replaced by the new English public high school. Ironically, the Academy then became a college preparatory school like the Latin grammar school it had replaced.

> 5. Summarize in your own words several education-related *differences* between the New England and the Middle Colonies; how did the South differ from both?
>
> 6. Briefly describe the *origins* and *nature* of the school that replaced the Latin grammar school.

Education for All

After the *Revolution* from England, the new nation, committed to democracy, had the great problem of welding a nation of diverse political and religious convictions into a nation of informed voters. This meant, first of all, that the citizens must be able to read in order to keep informed on the critical issues. The need was not unrecognized. Two very significant educational events occurred shortly after the Revolution: *Northwest Ordinances* of 1785 and 1787, each of which contained a provision to reserve section 16 of each township of public land for educational purposes. Consider this quote from the Northwest Ordinance: "religion, morality, and knowledge being necessary to good government and happiness of mankind, schools and the means of education shall forever be encouraged."

There began a relentless trend in American society toward education for all people. Thomas Jefferson introduced a bill to the Virginia Assembly in 1779, entitled "A Bill for the More General Diffusion of Knowledge." It called for three years schooling for all children, tuition free; the superior students would then be selected and sent to regional grammar schools; the best of them would be sent to the College of William and Mary for a full college education, all of which would be paid for by the public. However selective his plan was, it was a milestone in the slow move toward universal public education. The Virginia Assembly decided that education was a private matter; but 15 years later, they legislated a comprehensive system of elementary schools. Essentially what Jefferson wanted was the three R's for all, plus the opportunity for advanced education for the brighter boys, extending even to the university. That was about 200 years ago.

From about 1780 to 1820 the expansion of educational opportunity was a slow, unofficial, but steadily increasing movement. Schools and colleges began to multiply, in spite of the fact that newspapers of those years opposed free public schools and there was very little tax support for schools. It was quite common for townsmen to build a school house with their own hands, chip in to hire a teacher, and then design a course of instruction for their children.

But then the movement became official. *Andrew Jackson's* election in 1824, signalled the beginning of what is called "the age of the common man." Jackson was elected through support of the "common people"—the small farmers, the immigrants, and the urban laborers, and these were the people most vigorous in their demand for public schools for their children. Encouraged by the democratic promise and by this new sign of their power to effect change, they began to insist not only on more schools but also that the educational system drop its aristocratic selectivity which was "locking the common child in the bonds of ignorance and poverty."

It's not that there were no schools. There were, but they were a hodgepodge of public, semiprivate, private, and religious institutions with little common direction or uniform quality. The following is an excerpt from a teacher's description of her 1810 New England public school. While getting a first-hand picture of what a public school was like at that time, see also if you notice parallel problems facing us today.

> The school house stood near the center of the district, at the junction of four roads. Except in the dry season the ground was wet. Neither was there any such thing as an outhouse of any kind, not even a wooden shed. The size of the building was 22 × 20 feet. From the floor to the ceiling it was 7 feet. Around the sides of the room were connected desks. Attached to the sides of the desks nearest to the instructor were benches for small pupils. The instructor's desk and chair occupied the center. On this desk were stationed a rod or ferule. These, with books, writings, ink-

stands, rules, and plummets, with a fire shovel, and a pair of tongs (often broken) were the principal furniture.

The windows were five in number, of twelve panes each. They were situated so low in the walls as to give full opportunity to the pupils to see every traveller as he passed, and to be easily seen. The places of the broken panes were usually supplied with hats, during school hours.

The school was not infrequently broken up for a day or two for want of wood. The instructor or pupils were sometimes compelled to cut or saw it to prevent the closing of the school. The wood was left in the road near the house, so that it often was buried in the snow, or wet with rain. At the best, it was usually burnt green. The fires were to be kindled about half an hour before the time of beginning the school. Often, the scholar whose lot it was neglected to build it. In consequence of this, the house was frequently cold and uncomfortable about half of the forenoon, when, the fire being very large, the excess of heat became equally distressing. Frequently, too, we were annoyed by smoke.

The winter school usually opened before the first week of December and continued from 12 to 16 weeks. The summer term commenced about the first of May. Males have been uniformly employed in winter, and females in summer. The instructors have usually been changed every season, but sometimes they have been continued two successive summers or winters. A strong prejudice has always existed against employing the same instructor more than once or twice in the same district. I have not been able to ascertain the number of instructors who have been engaged in the school during the last thirty years, but I can distinctly recollect 37. Many of them, both males and females, were from 16 to 18 years of age, and a few over 21.

Good moral character, and a thorough knowledge of the common branches, formerly were considered as indispensable qualification in an instructor. But for 15 or 20 years these things have not been so much regarded. They have indeed been deemed desirable, but the most common method now seems to be to ascertain, as near as possible, the dividend for that season from the public treasury, and then fix upon a teacher who will take charge of the school three or four months for this money. He must indeed be able to obtain a license from the Board of Visitors; but this has become nearly a matter of course, provided he can spell, read and write. It gives me great pleasure, however, to say that the moral character of almost every instructor, so far as I know, has been unexceptional (sic).

Instructors have usually boarded in the families of their pupils. Their compensation has varied from 7 to 11 dollars a month for males and from 62 and a half cents to one dollar a week for females.

Two of the Board of Visitors usually visit the winter schools twice during the term. In the summer, their visits are often omitted. These visits usually occupy from one hour to an hour and a half. They are spent merely in hearing a few hurried lessons and in making some remarks, general in their character. The parents seldom visit the school, except by special invitation. The greater number pay very little attention to it at all. The school books have been about the same for 30 years. *Webster's Spelling Book,* the *American Preceptor,* and the New Testament have been the principal books used. Until within a few years, no studies have been permitted in the day school but spelling, reading and writing. Arithmetic was taught by a few instructors, one or two evenings in a week, but, in spite of the most determined opposition, arithmetic is now permitted in the day school, and a few pupils study geography.

The period from Jackson's election to the Civil War witnessed the *Common School Crusade,* an all-out crusade for free, tax-supported, nondenominational, state-controlled elementary schools for all. The arguments for universal education were varied: we need an educated citizenry; we must unify the various groups in our nation and acculturate the immigrants; our economic growth requires skilled businessmen and workers; each man has a desire and a right to improve himself socially and economically. The opponents of public education, however, argued: a breakdown of class distinctions will reduce the country itself to a low common denominator; secular concerns will come to destroy religious values; the distinctive languages and life-styles of our ethnic groups and sects will disappear; why should we pay taxes to educate another man's child. Not unlike today, an affluent minority felt unwilling to pay for the education of the majority.

With great difficulty, the country gradually abandoned its ideas of elitist and charity schools. The movement was carried forward by educators, humanitarians, and political leaders, with an enormous amount of rhetoric and propaganda, citations of foreign examples, and warnings of doom. The movement succeeded in several *stages.* At first, several states agreed to *permit* communities to organize a school district and to tax the property of those consenting and residing in that district. Later some states began *encouraging* the formation of school districts by passing incentive legislation granting state funds to those districts which agreed to tax themselves. In the third state, states *required* public education, but not necessarily free education. The mandatory public schools were partly tax supported, with the rest of the support coming from "the rate"—a levy charged to the parents by the school district. This compromise with tuition gradually was discontinued, partly because the nation's growing economy provided increased sources of revenue, and partly because many parents kept their children out of school to avoid paying "the rate." The final stage, therefore, established *mandatory* and completely *tax-supported* public schools. Not every state went through all stages, of course; some states entered the union with such a law in their constitution. By 1850, all states had at least some "common" schools. Massachusetts passed the first compulsory attendance law in 1852, and by 1900 thirty-two states had similar laws. Mississippi was the last state in 1918.

The man who led the fight for mandatory and completely tax-supported schools was *Horace Mann,* a Massachusetts legislator, and later the first Superintendent of Schools in that state. Because of his work in these two capacities, as well as his writing and speaking, Mann earned the title "Father of the Common School." Another prominent promoter was Henry Barnard, Superintendent of Schools in Connecticut and later in Rhode Island, and the first United States Commissioner of Education (1867). He was succeeded by William Harris, and both men worked to entrench the common school in American tradition.

The Common School Crusade was very successful, but in an ironically selective way. In accord with the democratic ideal, equal educational opportunities were greatly increased for all citizens—if they were white, but not if they were black. In fact, educational opportunities for blacks actually decreased. After the slave rebellions in Haiti and the Nat Turner Rebellion of 1831, more southern legislatures passed laws prohibiting the teaching of Negroes, free or slave. In the north, as well as on the frontier, there was increased opposition to Negroes and whites attending the same schools.

> 7. What was the special significance of the Northwest Ordinances for national education? What was their connection with Andrew Jackson forty years later?
>
> 8. Summarize the arguments for and against universal education in the 1830s, and the four stages through which the movement passed. Was it successful?

Secondary Education

As we saw earlier, the first secondary school was the *Latin grammar school,* eventually replaced by the *academy,* the prototype of the secondary school. The academies were the best available, but their selectivity was not in the spirit of the democratic ideal, nor were they under public control, or free. In the 1820s, a new form of secondary school, unique to the United States, was begun in Boston under the name *"English High School."* Its curriculum emphasized mathematics, social studies, science and English.

A Massachusetts law of 1852 required school attendance of children eight to fourteen years old. By 1860 there were about 300 high schools across the nation. The movement for publicly supported secondary schools met heavy resistance, as had the common school fifty years earlier. Now, however, the question was not to get education laws on the books, but whether these laws provided a legal basis for extending public education to the secondary level. The first conclusive answer came in the *Kalamazoo Case* of 1874. A group of taxpayers challenged the right of the Kalamazoo School District to collect taxes for support of a high school. The Michigan Supreme Court ruled that since the state had already provided for a tax-supported elementary system and a state university, it was inconsistent to exclude secondary education.

Though this decision clarified the legal status of secondary education, and set the stage for national expansion of public high schools, the expansion was slow to develop. By 1890 there were only 200,000 students in public high schools—about forty students in each of the 60,000 high schools. Contrast this with the twelve and a half million students in elementary public schools at that time. Clearly, universal secondary education was not a reality by the turn of the century.

Furthermore, everyone had his own ideas about what a high school should be and do. Some were two-year schools, others three or four; some were "college prep," others terminal institutions; some weeded out all but the "best" students. This diversity of goals and procedures led to attempts at standardization by professional committees set up to investigate and recommend. In 1892 the National Education Association (NEA) set up its *Committee of Ten,* which later recommended eight years of elementary and four years of secondary schooling, four separate curricula for the high school (classical, Latin-scientific, modern language and English); intensive study of fewer subjects for longer periods of time; and the teaching of every subject in the same way to every pupil "no matter what the probable destination of the pupil may be or at what point his education may cease." Whatever their intentions, the effect of the Committee's recommendations was to gear secondary education primarily for the college-bound student.

Three years later, another NEA committee recommended six years of secondary schooling beginning with grade seven; a few free electives; and the definition of the "unit" as a subject studied four or five periods per week for one year. This "unit," later called the *"Carnegie unit"* after it was endorsed by the Carnegie Foundation for the Advancement of Teaching, is still used as a basic measure. The report also paved the way for the development of junior high schools during the 1920s, designed to provide a gradual transition from elementary to secondary education.

In 1918, another NEA committee issued a famous report, "Cardinal Principles of Secondary Education," which noted: "Secondary education should be determined by the needs of the society to be served, the character of the individuals to be educated, and the knowledge of educational theory and practice available. These factors are by no means static. . . . Failure to make adjustments when the need arises leads to the necessity for extensive reorganization at irregular intervals." For their time, they recommended seven objectives for education: health, command of fundamental processes, worthy home-membership, vocation, citizenship, worthy use of leisure, and ethical character.

From 1900 to 1950, these *committee reports* were the most effective change agents in education. They were effective in emphasizing vocational education and in securing federal funds to the states for this purpose, and in other ways they contributed greatly to the diversification of the curricula of the high school. They also helped in breaking down the selective upper-class character of its focus, so that it served adolescents from a variety of backgrounds and offered a wide range of subjects. Later committees prompted extension of secondary education to include grades thirteen and fourteen, through the establishment of *junior colleges*.

During this period the United States was undergoing major economic and social changes, caused by a major war and a catastrophic depression. "The Crash" seemed to generate a national social conscience and a renewed effort to include a variety of minority groups into the public educational system. Hundreds of special schools were established to care for the blind, deaf, and retarded children. Child labor laws were enacted, and the federal government began to send surplus food for school lunches into the hardest-hit states.

Then came the *Second World War*. The unbelievably high draft rejection rate for illiteracy illustrated that a high school diploma was no guarantee of achievement, and the fact that young men from some regions of the country scored consistently lower on military exams proved both embarrassing and stimulating. After the War, the increasing mobility of Americans made these disparities in educational quality a national problem; the dropout from St. Louis became the welfare problem of New York, and the military reject from New York became a criminal problem in California. As a result, most states began to require more years of education, broader curricula, and higher standards for teacher certification.

But how could educators emphasize quality of schooling in the face of the postwar *"baby boom"* and the massive influx of veterans? The tension between quality and quantity of education was a factor in sharply increasing the federal government's involvement in all phases of education. This involvement was further affected by an increasingly militant black movement for the justice promised them for 100 years. *Selma* forced the nation to attend to the inferior status of blacks, and the inferior education that kept them at the bottom of the national ladder. And finally there was *Sputnik*. The 1957 launching frightened Americans, and critics began charging that education had gone too far

9. Summarize in your own words the stages in the development of our secondary school system. (Hint: grammar, academy, English High, Kalamazoo, expansion, standardization through committees.)

10. What was the major effect on education of: the depression, Second World War, mobility, baby boom, Sputnik, Selma? (If you are not familiar with these or other terms used in the units of this course, be sure to look them up in a dictionary or encyclopedia.)

toward "life adjustment" to the neglect of intellectual training. A major result of this protest was the National Defense Education Act (*NDEA*) of 1958, designed to improve the teaching of science and math in schools and colleges.

Teacher Education

Despite this history of education expansion and improvement, the country was very slow to realize that good education requires good teaching. Until about 1850, teachers were very poorly prepared for their jobs, and teaching itself was considered unimportant and even menial.

The widow who operated a dame school frequently was a semiliterate, as were many of the *itinerate teachers* who moved from one community to another, setting up short-term schools on the basis of local support. Success was usually measured by the colonists in terms of maintaining discipline, so there was little incentive for educated people to teach. Since education in the colonies had a strongly religious motive, the schools were often conducted by the *minister*. When the job got too big for him, he would hire a layman who, in addition to teaching, would also act as court messenger, serve summonses, conduct some services in the church, lead the Sunday choir, ring the bell for public worship, dig the graves, and perform other occasional duties.

Since apprenticeship was a well-established way of learning in those days, some boys became teachers by serving as apprentices to a schoolmaster. Here is an example of an apprenticeship agreement from 1772:

> This indenture witnesseth that John Campbel, Son of Robert Campbel of the City of New York, with the consent of his father and mother, doth voluntarily put and bind himself apprentice to George Brownell of the same city Schoolmaster to learn the art, trade, or mystery for and during the term of ten years . . . and the said George Brownell doth hereby covenent and promise to teach and instruct or cause the said apprentice to be taught and instructed in the art, trade, or calling of a Schoolmaster by the best way or means he or his wife may or can.

When Ben Franklin established his *Academy* in 1751, he suggested that the poorer graduates of his academy would make good teachers—an indication of the low esteem for teachers at that time.

> A number of the poorer sort of graduates will be hereby qualified to act as Schoolmasters in the Country . . . and may be recommended from the Academy to Country Schools for that purpose; the Country suffering at present very much for want of good Schoolmasters, and obliged frequently to employ in their schools vicious imported servants, or concealed papists, who by their bad examples and instructions often deprave the morals and corrupt the principles of the children under their care.

Early in the 1800s, a system of teaching, developed in London by *Joseph Lancaster,* was imported to America. The method was simple and economical. A group of older and able students was taught a particular lesson by the master and given some ideas on how the lesson should be taught. Then each monitor took over a group of younger students and taught the same lesson to them. In this way, one master was in effect handling up to a thousand students, and the monitors learned something about teaching through supervised practice.

The first *normal school* for the training of teachers was established as an adjunct to an academy operated by the Reverend Samuel Hall at Concord, Vermont, in 1823. Basically, students took the same training as other academy students, with some additional work in teaching methodology and discipline. Since there was no text for this, Hall wrote his own, entitled *Lectures on Schoolkeeping.* The curriculum in Hall's private normal school included "mental philosophy," the forerunner of educational psychology, and "general criticism" (presumably of the student's practice teaching). Incidentally, the word "normal" comes from the Latin word meaning model or rule; "normal" schools were originally designed to give teachers training in the rules for good teaching.

In 1838, in the face of strenuous opposition, Horace Mann and James Carter succeeded in establishing the first public tax-supported teaching training school in Lexington, Massachusetts, and others quickly followed. At first, normal schools offered a two-year program to prepare its students (many of whom had not attended secondary school) to teach elementary school. Eventually they moved to four-year programs, and required a high school diploma for entry. During the 1920s, they changed their names to *State Teachers' Colleges.*

In recent years, most teachers colleges have changed to *liberal arts colleges,* thus becoming multipurpose institutions. Some have begun offering graduate programs and have changed their names to State Universities. Since 1900, the trend has been for major universities of the country to develop teacher education programs of their own. While there was considerable opposition to this trend, such programs are now an integral part of most universities and have made a major contribution to teacher education.

In recent years, *in-service* programs have contributed immensely to teacher education. Teacher institutes and workshops, summer schools, and extension programs have reached millions of teachers, with the result that experienced teachers have been able to upgrade their skills, and new teachers have begun teaching in a more flexible and innovative environment.

The American Dilemma

One feature which has run throughout the history of American Education, and is still with us, is what the Swedish sociologist Gunnar Myrdal called the

"American dilemma"—the *conflict* between our regard for freedom, liberty, and dignity, and our jealousies, prejudices, wants, and impulses. Our constitution, our public documents and our stated ideals have usually been vigorously opposed in educational practice. The most striking, but not the only example is the matter of racial discrimination in education. Prior to the civil war there simply was no form of education for blacks, and it was legally prohibited in some states. Though there had been scattered interest in educating the Negro during the colonial and early national periods, for the most part the slave was mere property to be used for personal gain. To educate the Negro was to threaten the entire social and economic system of the South.

Reconstruction after the Civil War forced reorganization of education, and this was the beginning of free public schools for blacks and whites in the South. Whatever slow progress there was at that time can be credited to the educational programs of the Freedmen's Bureau, various church groups, the support of some northern philanthropists, and the concern of civic leaders in the North. Ultimately, real progress had to await the emergence of Negro leaders such as *W.E.B. DuBois, Mary McLeod Bethune,* and *Charlotte Hawkins-Brown. Booker T. Washington,* founder of Tuskegee Institute (1881), had a profound effect on black education. He regarded equality as a commendable but distant goal. In his "Atlanta Compromise" speech of 1895, he said: "in all things that are purely social we can be as separate as the five fingers, yet one as the hand in all things essential to mutual progress." The fateful idea of "separate but equal" was born, despite the opposition of men like DuBois, and the following year the Supreme Court made it law in their *Plessy* v. *Ferguson* decision. Separate school systems were established for the two races, but they were far from equal. Although this decision was invalidated in 1954 by the *Brown* v. *Topeka* decision, de facto segregation and inequality has continued as a major challenge and an obvious example of the American dilemma.

To quote the United States Office of Education, "the American School is still trying to bridge the gulf between the intellectual elite and the functional illiterate. Education, which brought us into the atomic age, has yet to rescue some of our citizens from a near-medieval helplessness in the face of a world which they neither made nor understand. The school is still the basic selector of the winners and losers in our society. In virtually every study of schools made since 1900, more children have failed (dropped out or fallen below 'normal' grade level) than succeeded, both in absolute and in relative numbers. For too many of our children, Batman—the pop-art farce of the decade—remains the most accessible cultural experience."[1]

Still, there has been impressive progress. The average citizen completes 12 years of school, and half continue their education beyond high school. Millions

---

[1] U.S. Office of Education, "Three Hundred Years at a Glance," *American Education,* March 1967, p. 13.

of adults continue their education in one way or another throughout much of their life. And the best of these schools and instructional programs are indeed effective.

---

11. Summarize the stages in the development of teacher education. (Hint: widows and itinerates, apprentices, academy graduates, Lancaster system, normal schools, teachers college, universities.)

12. Describe the "American Dilemma" and give several original examples.

13. Can you identify the following?
    Philadelphia Academy
    Northwest Ordinances
    Age of the Common Man
    Common School Crusade
    Horace Mann
    Kalamazoo Case
    Committee of Ten
    Carnegie Unit
    NDEA
    Joseph Lancaster
    Samuel Hall
    DuBois
    Booker T. Washington
    Plessy v. *Ferguson*
    Brown v. *Topeka*

Unit 2

SCHOOL ADMINISTRATION, LAW, AND FINANCE

Schooling in the United States has become a massive enterprise. Today there are about fifty million elementary and secondary children in the nation's public and private schools. The operation of this enterprise requires management of vast amounts of money and personnel according to basic policies and procedures. School personnel, school funds, school buildings and resources, and school laws all exist for the single purpose of providing excellent instruction for each of the fifty million students. The massiveness of the enterprise sometimes makes this point difficult to remember in practice.

State

Unlike many countries, the United States does not have a federal school system. The management and control of education in this country is *primarily a function of the state*. The State *Legislature* formulates state educational law—some mandatory, some optional—which directs and guides the school boards responsible for public education. Because such legislation deals with children and with money, legislators are subject to considerable lobbying by a variety of interested groups.

Each state has some type of *department of education* which certifies school personnel, disburses funds, provides consultative assistance to local schools,

19

and in general implements the state's policies regarding education. All but two states (Illinois and Wisconsin) also have a state board of education whose purpose it is to develop further policies and guidelines for the operation of the state's public schools. In most states, the Board members are appointed by the Governor, though in fifteen states the members are elected by the people or their representatives.

Each state has a chief school officer (usually called the state *Superintendent of Education*) who heads the Department of Education. In about half the states, the Superintendent is elected by popular vote; in most other states, he is appointed by the Board of Education. The Superintendent's official and real duties and powers vary from state to state. He may be primarily a supervisor of the Department's enforcement and assistance functions, or he may be the state's chief spokesman for education, and have considerable power in defining policy.

Local

To citizens and teachers, the most visible agency of educational control is the *local school district,* a political subdivision of a state (perhaps a city or a county or a part thereof) created to provide a system of public education for that area. Despite their similar major purposes, local school districts have vastly differing characteristics regarding size, enrollment, organization and homogeneity. Almost half of the nation's local school districts enroll less than 300 pupils each, and the total enrollment of such districts represents only two percent of the total national enrollment. The trend has been to reduce the number of districts (100,000 districts in 1945 down to 16,000 in 1973) in order to improve efficiency and effectiveness, and to include both elementary and secondary levels (primary through twelfth grade) within one district. But consolidation of districts has created other problems in such very large cities as New York, Chicago, and Pittsburgh, where immense enrollment and massive agencies have tended to distort communication and smother local influence.

Despite the differences, a local school district is generally operated by a board of education, which is headed by a full-time superintendent, and whose members serve part time by election or appointment. The local board determines the specific policies and procedures under which the district's schools operate. Although education is a *legal* function of the state, in actual practice much of the operational responsibility for the schools is *delegated* to the local school district. The local board's functions must, of course, conform to the policies of the state board. For example, in hiring, the state board sets the certification requirements, and thus sets minimum standards for the local schools, but it is the local school board and its superintendent who make day-to-day hiring and retaining decisions.

Each district school has an administrator (principal) who is responsible to the superintendent. Under the principal are his assistants, directors of various departments, teachers, and various nonteaching personnel. Though a teacher may contact the principal or superintendent for employment, the local school board is the actual employer as a delegate of the State. In practice, however, the administrators have a major influence on the board's decisions regarding issuing or renewing a contract, promoting, granting tenure, and dealing with special requests or suggestions a teacher may submit.

School Law

As with most professions, there is a body of laws and legal principles that determines the rights, duties, obligations, and status of members of the teaching profession. Such law is especially important for teachers to know, since they are usually government employees and creatures of the law. Whether *statutory* (including the statutes and school laws from the legislature) or decisional or *common* (whereby the source is judicial, as in court decisions which interpret or apply statutes and rule on their constitutionality), school law is a statement of public policy regarding the conduct of education. Statutory law frequently varies from state to state, but decisional or common law usually has national application when no statute covers the situation. There are some basic principles underlying the specifics of school law:

1. Under our federal form of government, education is a function of *state* government, not local or federal.
2. School districts are state (not local) agencies, school buildings, school money, and school taxes are the property of the state (not the local community), and school employees in any capacity are state employees (not local government employees).
3. The state legislature can enact any legislation regarding education that it desires, limited only by the state and federal constitution. Future state legislative sessions can amend, alter, or repeal past educational legislation.
4. The state legislature can *delegate* authority to administer, monitor, and enforce school law, but it can never delegate authority to enact *new* laws regarding education unless that authority is limited and controlled by very specific guidelines from the legislature.

THE TEACHER AND THE LAW

There are a variety of specific laws relating to the teacher. The states require all public school teachers to hold *certificates* indicating that the holder meets certain minimum qualifications required by the state. Legally there is no such thing as a permanent certificate, because the state has the right to alter the requirements or impose additional qualifications on those holding certificates. The local school board, while it cannot employ teachers who do not meet these minimum requirements, may also impose *additional* requirements from its local teachers.

A *contract* with a teacher can be entered into only by the local board of education acting as a whole. The board cannot be bound by a contract issued by one of its members or by a school administrator. The contract can, however, be an oral one, unless this violates an existing law (such as the law requiring certification or a law prohibiting oral contracts). Any contract between a teacher and a school board is binding on both parties, but it can be broken by mutual agreement. Therefore, a teacher may resign but it is not effective until the resignation is approved by the board, and it may be withdrawn anytime before board approval.

Usually the laws are specific and exhaustive in regard to the reasons for which a teacher may be *dismissed* and a school board may not dismiss a teacher for a reason not included in these laws. A teacher may be dismissed for lack of competence, but competence here means a reasonable degree of skill, not a maximum degree. This applies in a limited way to a teacher's conduct outside the classroom as well as in. A teacher does not lose the rights of citizenship, and may engage in all legal political activities in the community, although he may not use the classroom as a forum for political effort.

Only the board of education has the right to dismiss a teacher, just as it is the only hiring agency, and it cannot delegate this authority to an administrator. A dismissed teacher may appeal to the courts for breach of contract when there is evidence that the board acted contrary to law, arbitrarily, or in bad faith.

1. Outline the administrative structure and roles of the typical state and local school system.
2. Differentiate between statutory and common law.
3. Identify several specific implications of the fact that education is a state function.
4. Who certifies teachers, contracts with teachers, dismisses teachers, establishes minimum requirements and additional requirements? Are there exceptions?

The state or district may grant a teacher *tenure* (an official assurance of some degree of permanency in employment), based usually on length of service with the district and sometimes also on the quality of that service. Many states have tenure laws designed to provide teachers with some degree of employment security. Tenure laws are not guarantees; a school board may dismiss teachers or reduce their salaries for reasons of economy, decrease in enrollment, change in curriculum offerings, or other reasonable administrative purposes. But such decisions must not be arbitrary; they must be part of a general revision program affecting all teachers similarly, and wherever possible tenured

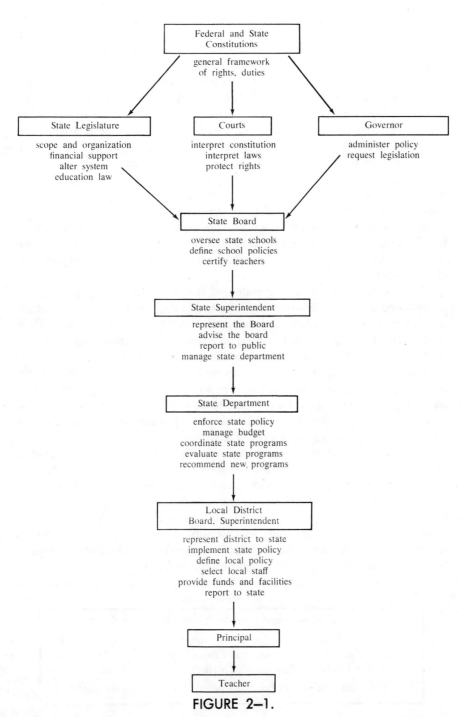

FIGURE 2-1.

SCHEMATIC OUTLINE OF THE FUNCTIONS AND RELATIONSHIP OF STATE AND
EDUCATIONAL UNITS.

teachers must still be given priority if their skills are appropriate. Nor does tenure guarantee a teacher the right to continue teaching the same grade or subject; the board is free to reassign a tenured teacher to work of equal status and salary for good cause.

Most state laws also indicate the manner in which a teacher may be dismissed. Generally, the specific reasons for the dismissal action must be stated to the teacher, who is given the opportunity for a hearing. Frequently the hearing must be conducted in a very specific way, and if the board violates the statute's specified steps in handling a dismissal, the dismissal action can be voided in court if the teacher brings suit for reinstatement.

Most states also have legislated teacher *retirement* programs, and a teacher may be required to contribute part of his salary to this retirement or pension fund. If the teacher is required to do so, then subsequent legislatures can change or even repeal the program and teachers have no legal complaint. If, however, the teacher is not required to contribute but elects to do so, then this becomes a kind of contract and the law cannot be changed subsequently to his detriment.

The general labor laws of the state and the nation do not apply to school districts and boards, unless this is so specified in the law. Less than half of the states have enacted legislation covering the *collective bargaining* of teachers (i.e., teachers acting as a single body in negotiating contract terms with the district board), but more and more states are considering such matters. Where the matter is covered, of course, the law applies. Unless specific law indicates otherwise, teachers may organize if they so choose, and school boards may bargain with such groups if they choose to do so. But teachers may not strike unless permitted by law, and legislatures may penalize those who do. This applies also to picketing in support of a strike.

In negotiating with teachers, the school board may not agree to binding arbitrations (bringing in a third party to mediate or arbitrate between the teachers' group and the board, and rendering a final decision binding on both parties), since this would in effect delegate the board's authority to an arbitrator—though of course it can agree to arbitrate differences. Furthermore, the board cannot agree to something which limits the authority of future boards to make policy; such an agreement can only be valid for a limited period of time, after which it is subject to change by the board. Of course, teachers and other state employees do strike and picket on occasion, in violation of the law,

---

5. Specify the purpose and some limitations of tenure for teachers.

6. Can teachers organize? Can they engage in collective bargaining? Can the school board do likewise? Must they do so if asked by the teachers? May teachers strike? May they picket?

7. Why can't the school board agree to compulsory arbitration?

and they are frequently penalized by the courts for doing so. Many state legislators now consider the "no-strike" laws unworkable and are pondering a
variety of alternatives, particularly regarding binding arbitration.

THE STUDENT AND THE LAW

School law also covers students as well as teachers and school boards. Until
recently, it seems to have been assumed that minors were not covered by the
Bill of Rights, and most cases involving students were heard only in state
courts. But since the famous 1954 *Brown* v. *Topeka* decision by the Supreme
Court, in which racial segregation in the schools was ruled unconstitutional
because it violated the equal protection clause of the Fourteenth Amendment,
the rights of students have become an increasingly important concern. Recent
cases indicate that a student does have *basic rights* guaranteed by the Consti-
tuition, and cannot be deprived of these rights without due process of law,
including the right to be represented by counsel in a hearing regarding his
dismissal from a school.

Furthermore, court action is beginning to define the student's right to
freedom of expression. For example, in the *Tinker* case (1969), when a Des
Moines school board expelled students for wearing black armbands as a protest of the Vietnamese war, the Supreme Court ruled that vague fear of dis-
turbance was not enough reason to curb freedom of expression of views. The
court also emphasized, however, that students are not protected to the same
degree as adults; the degree of maturity evidently modifies the freedom of
expression to some extent. The exact conditions and manner in which boards
of education may limit certain rights of students is yet to be clarified by the
courts and legislatures. But in the *Tinker* decision, the Court did say that
"students in school as well as out of school are 'persons' under our Constitution . . . students may not be regarded as closed-circuit recipients of only
that which the state wishes to communicate. They may not be confined to the
expression of those sentiments that are officially approved."

But a student's right to attend school is not absolute. The school board may,
therefore, *expel* a pupil for disobeying any reasonable rule without violating
his rights. The teacher does not have this right, however; the teacher may only
exclude such a student from class until the board can rule on the matter.

TEACHER LIABILITY

Most state law regards the teacher as having some of the parent's authority
over the student. This includes the general right to regulate the student's conduct while under his supervision, and the responsibility to take whatever

measures are necessary to guarantee a pupil's safety, health, and welfare in the absence of the parents. The teacher also has the general right to administer all reasonable punishment (including corporal), unless specifically prohibited by law, for offenses the student commits on or off school property, during or after school hours, as long as the offense has a direct relationship to the welfare of the school. The law presumes that a teacher is innocent unless it can be proven that the punishment was unreasonable, excessive, or motivated by spite, hatred or revenge.

The laws regarding teacher liability (legal responsibility) vary widely from state to state and are very complicated. In general, school districts are immune from liability since they are agencies of the state. But about a dozen states have abrogated or limited this immunity and now hold districts at least partly liable for injuries resulting from negligence. However, an individual teacher does not share a district's immunity and can be held liable even if the district is not.

In no case can a teacher be held liable without proven *negligence*. The teacher is the guarantor of a student's safety. Negligence means that a teacher neglects his duty to use care by taking unreasonable risk. A teacher's duties include supervising the students from the time they arrive until they leave (not including travel to and from, though the district may have responsibility here). A teacher's conduct is considered negligent if a reasonably prudent person would or could have foreseen that injury would be likely to occur as a result of such conduct. For example, a teacher is not liable if a student is injured at a dangerous intersection near the school, but a teacher might be liable for this injury if the student was on an errand for the teacher at the time. The teacher might also be liable for providing improper first-aid to an injured student in an emergency, or for not providing any treatment in the same situation. Getting parents to sign permission slips before allowing students to go on field trips may be good public relations, but this does not absolve the teacher from possible liability, because the law does not allow a parent to waive a student's right to recover damages received as the result of someone else's negligence.

Because certain aspects of school law are changing rapidly through legislation and court decision, some of the above principles and particulars may quickly become obsolete. No law is static, and interpretations of old laws are usually not made by the standards of past eras. However school law evolves, the results of this evolution will quickly reach the classroom, and the teacher must stay on top of new developments.

8. Identify several common law rights of students.

9. In general, under what circumstances is a teacher liable for a student's welfare? State several examples.

10. Why is parental permission not an absolution from teacher liability?

School Finance

Education in our country is a big business. Current operating expenses for elementary and secondary schools run over fifty billion dollars per year. About fifteen cents out of every tax dollar goes for public education, which means we spend about as much for education as we do for recreation, tobacco, and alcohol. While it is impossible to say what proportion of our wealth we should allocate to education, it does seem that we are limited more by our unwillingness than by our inability to pay.

Most of the funds which finance the educational enterprise come from *taxes*. Recall that in colonial days and even into the nineteenth century, schooling was financed primarily through contributions from lotteries and patrons or by churches of various denominations. The movement for free public schools began in the early 1800s, and culminated in the *Kalamazoo* decision supporting taxation for public high schools. By the end of the century, public schools were financed almost entirely by local funds from local taxation.

Today local school taxes are supplemented by a variety of state and federal taxes, which are distributed to the local school districts for the operation of their schools. In general, local governments use property taxes, state governments use sales and income taxes, and the federal government relies on income taxes to raise funds for education. The percentage of financial support contributed by federal, state, and local sources varies widely from state to state. The national average for 1973 was about 8 percent federal, 41 percent state, and 52 percent local; but for some states like California and Illinois the federal

TABLE 2–1

CURRENT EXPENDITURES PER PUPIL IN AVERAGE DAILY MEMBERSHIP, 1972–73.

1.	New York	$1424
2.	Alaska	1398*
3.	New Jersey	1216
4.	Vermont	1151†
5.	Connecticut	1141
6.	Pennsylvania	1100
7.	Minnesota	1089
8.	Delaware	1083
9.	Maryland	1082
10.	Rhode Island	1075
11.	Wisconsin	1071
12.	Massachusetts	1060
13.	Illinois	1058

	South Carolina	6.2
14.	Iowa	6.1
	Maine	6.1
	Mississippi	6.1
	Oregon	6.1
	South Dakota	6.1
	Wisconsin	6.1
20.	Colorado	6.0
	Michigan	6.0†
	North Dakota	6.0
23.	California	5.9
	Hawaii	5.9†
	Idaho	5.9
	Washington	5.9
27.	Indiana	5.8
28.	Connecticut	5.7
	North Carolina	5.7
	Pennsylvania	5.7
	UNITED STATES	5.6
31.	New Jersey	5.5
	Virginia	5.5
	West Virginia	5.5
34.	Nevada	5.4
	Texas	5.4
36.	Kansas	5.2
	Missouri	5.2
38.	Illinois	5.1
	New Hampshire	5.1
40.	Rhode Island	5.0
	Tennessee	5.0
42.	Florida	4.9
	Kentucky	4.9
	Ohio	4.9
	Oklahoma	4.9
46.	Arkansas	4.8
47.	Massachusetts	4.6
48.	Alabama	4.5
	Georgia	4.5
50.	Nebraska	4.1

NEA, *Estimates of School Statistics, 1972–73*, p. 32. Reprinted by permission.
Survey of Current Business, August 1972, p. 25.

*Reduce 30% to make purchasing power comparable to figures for other areas of the United States.

† NEA Research estimate.

percentage is much lower and the local percentage higher, and states like Mississippi and Alaska receive higher federal percentages. One reason for this variation in federal funds to schools of different states is that federal aid is usually specific aid for a specific need, or resolves a specific problem related to equality of educational opportunity.

For example, the nation as a whole spends about $970 per pupil (elementary and secondary) per year of education (see Table 2–1). At least fifteen states spend over $1000 per pupil per year, while at least seven states spend $600 or less per pupil. Such large differences can make large differences in the quality of education a student receives in one state or another.

Of course, some states have many more students to educate than do other states. For example, California has four-and-one-half million elementary and secondary students, and New York has three-and-one-half million, but over thirty states have less than one million students. Furthermore, some states have more citizens, business, and taxable revenue than others do. And finally, some states have higher tax rates than others and can therefore afford to spend more on education than other states.

It is difficult to balance these factors out in comparing states. One way is to compare the state's total personal income (before taxes) with the state's total public-school revenue (see Table 2–2). This shows that on the average, a state spends about 5½ percent of its personal income on education, with eleven states spending no more than 5 percent, and several states spending 7 percent or more.

In Kansas, for example, some wealthy districts have an assessed valuation per pupil that is 182 times greater than that of poorer districts within the same state. Typically it's the urban areas that have the poorest tax bases. It is rea-

TABLE 2–2

PUBLIC SCHOOL REVENUE, 1971–72, AS PER CENT OF PERSONAL INCOME, 1971.

1.	Alaska	9.1
2.	Vermont	8.2†
3.	Minnesota	7.3
4.	New Mexico	7.0
	Wyoming	7.0
6.	Utah	6.6
7.	Maryland	6.5
8.	Arizona	6.4
	Delaware	6.4
	Louisiana	6.4
11.	Montana	6.2†
	New York	6.2

UNITED STATES		966
14.	Arizona	1022
15.	Iowa	1007
16.	Texas	974
17.	Hawaii	970†
18.	Oregon	939
19.	California	937
20.	Wyoming	909†
21.	Nevada	904
22.	Colorado	895
	Montana	895†
24.	Ohio	883
25.	Kansas	870
26.	Virginia	866
27.	Louisiana	855
28.	Florida	841
	New Hampshire	841
30.	Missouri	837
31.	Indiana	833†
32.	North Dakota	825
33.	South Dakota	803
34.	New Mexico	799
35.	Maine	789
36.	North Carolina	753
37.	Georgia	722
38.	South Carolina	702
	West Virginia	702
40.	Nebraska	700
41.	Utah	698
42.	Tennessee	692
43.	Oklahoma	663
44.	Mississippi	651
45.	Kentucky	649
46.	Arkansas	619
47.	Alabama	556
	Idaho	NA
	Michigan	NA
	Washington	NA

NEA *Estimates of School Statistics, 1972–73*, p. 35. Reprinted by permission.

* Reduce 30% to make purchasing power comparable to figures for other areas of the United States.

† NEA Research estimate.

sonable to predict that such widely differing local tax bases will simply widen the gap between good and poor schools.

The need for overhauling the way in which we pay for our schools has long been critical; now it is being required by law. In the summer of 1971, the California Supreme Court, in the *Serrano* case, ruled that California's system of relying heavily on local real property taxes to finance its schools resulted in wide disparities in school revenue and violated the equal protection clauses of the Fourteenth Amendment. Within two years, the Supreme Courts of many other states, from Minnesota to Texas to New Jersey, handed down similar rulings.

The United States Supreme Court, in the *Rodriguez* case (1973), refused to declare the local property tax unconstitutional as a basis for public school financing. However, most of the state court rulings have indicated that the property tax method violates the state constitutions, even though the national constitutionality of this method remains in doubt. By 1973, every state except Vermont was at least moving officially toward sweeping reform of school financing in order to remedy inequalities. A gallup poll (1972) indicates that the public supports (55 to 34 percent) shifting the school tax burden to the state and federal levels. The intent of these moves is not to reduce all schools to common mediocrity, but to guarantee a quality education for all.

The property tax as a source of school revenue is not dead; the courts have merely ruled that the unequal way in which it is distributed is unconstitutional. But it is clear that additional sources of revenue will have to be found. The legal decisions have not made the pie bigger, they have only changed the manner in which it must be cut. It is highly unlikely that large cities and other truly poor school districts can be bailed out unless additional appropriations for public education are identified. This increased burden must be assumed by the states and the federal government together.

---

11. How are local, state, and federal monies raised?

12. Nationally, what percentage of educational money comes from local, state and federal sources?

13. What's the national average expenditure per pupil? How much does your state spend? What's the range per pupil (highest and lowest) among the states?

14. What has changed to make the property tax questionable as a base for educational funding?

FEDERAL AID

Despite the fact that currently only about 8 percent of local school funds are collected and dispersed by the nation as a whole, the federal government has often played a crucial role in the development and support of local schooling. Even before the Constitutional Convention convened, the Continental Congress had passed the Northwest Ordinances of 1785 and 1787, which were in part designed to stimulate the growth of "schools and the means of education." The earlier ordinance of 1785 was essentially a land selling gimmick to encourage migration westward, and the later ordinance of 1787 established the principles of government for the new territories. Principles such as freedom of religion, no slavery, the right of habeas corpus, the right of trial by jury, and the requirements for statehood were outlined.

Crucial to the educational question of these ordinances was the stipulation that in every township of the western lands, one section of land (640 acres) was set aside for the support of schools. A township was a rectilinear area of land six miles by six miles, and further subdivided into thirty-six sections, each section a one-mile square. So the amount of land earmarked for schools was considerable.

What makes these ordinances very important is that most of the new states of the nineteenth century got a decent start in educational matters because the land was available. At a time when taxation for schools was either nonexistent or embryonic, the federal lands were helpful. These lands have been given as late as 1959 in the cases of Alaska and Hawaii. Approximately thirty-three states have come into the Union utilizing the township principle of organization, of which at least one section was reserved for the support of public schools.

From 1787 until 1862, the federal government continued to build nominal support for education in a general way by occasionally returning a surplus of funds to the states for educational purposes. It was not until 1862, however, that federal aid became categorical in the sense that the states had to use the assistance in designated ways.

The famous *Morrill Land Grant Act* of 1862 provided land for the states in the amount of 30,000 acres per senator and representative in Congress, if the states would agree to broaden higher education so that agricultural and engineering studies would be included. This meant that within five years the states would have to erect a new school for such purposes or adapt an existing state college or university to the tenets of the Morrill Act. Included also in this broader curriculum was the opportunity to take R.O.T.C. courses, since military study had to be a stipulated part of the curriculum.

It is interesting to note that not only has professional study broadened immeasurably since the first passage of the Morrill Act, but also the leading or near-leading public college or university in over thirty states is the land-grant school. Schools like Michigan State, the University of Illinois, Purdue, Ohio State, Cornell, and Pennsylvania State, are all good examples of how the federal government has provided a needed impetus for educational improvement.

The role of the federal government has continued unabated for the last century. Witness, for example, the first and subsequent congressional acts concerning eduational benefits for veterans. These famous *G.I. Bills* have resulted in multibillion dollar expenditures since 1944. The money goes to the veteran, not the school, yet it indirectly bolsters both public and private educational institutions.

Other important examples of federal contributions have been the National Defense Education Act (NDEA, 1958) and the Elementary-Secondary Education Act (ESEA, 1965). Both laws have aided education below the college level. Even though the latter act has never been fully funded, it still holds great possibility for alleviating the hardships of poverty.

From the above discussion, one may infer that the federal government greatly supplements the states in their management of educational endeavors. The truth is that it does not. Recall that less than ten percent of all revenue for public schools comes from the federal government, despite the fact that about seventy percent of the taxes collected go to that level. Furthermore, much of the federal assistance comes to avert a last minute crisis and is often given in the name of defense—the Morrill Land Grant Act (ROTC), and the National Defense Education Act (keep up with Russia).

In 1972, federal funding began for a National Institute of Education which was given major responsibility for coordinating research and development programs in education. And the U.S. Office of Education has given high priority funding to the development of teacher renewal centers throughout the country. But several major funding bills passed by Congress (e.g., child welfare legislation) have been vetoed. And the value-added tax is increasingly being viewed as a regressive method of solving financial problems.

Federal aid to education has been traditional. It will probably continue to be. However, the argument surrounding such aid focuses on what form of aid it should be—revenue sharing (general) or categorical (specific). Categorical aid smacks of control, which scares many people because state and local control is seen by many to be more democratic, and to some more legal because of the Tenth Amendment which gives states control over public education.

Whatever the compromise, it still is urgent that schools receive assistance, for both the state and local tax bases need to be greatly supplemented. Great differences can exist in wealth per pupil from one school district to another. If education is to contribute to the solution of our nation's social and economic problems, this is going to require—among other things—more money than can be raised on a local level. A local school district's problems with providing quality education are frequently reflections of broader state and national problems. A suburb that mushrooms overnight, or a city that finds most of its affluent residents moving out, has school problems that it cannot adequately handle by itself.

Yet it is crucial to all of us that *all* students receive an education of high quality. You may not want to contribute to the education of children in another district or state, but when you take a teaching job (probably not in your present district) you will want to work in good schools with well-trained teachers and students, live with well-educated neighbors, buy commodities made by competent employees, vote with well-informed citizens, etc. Local school districts cannot solve state and national problems, using only local resources. Equalization of per pupil expenditures is a first step toward achieving equality of opportunity in education.

15. Briefly describe how the Morrill Land Grant Act, the Northwest Ordinances, and the G.I. Bills each contributed to education.

16. What is the main argument for increased federal support of education?

Unit 3

INTRODUCTION TO
THE SOCIOLOGY
OF EDUCATION

Different social sciences study education from different perspectives, and each new viewpoint can contribute to our understanding of education. History is one of those perspectives. Sociology, Social Psychology, and Anthropology are other valuable points of view.

In this unit, you will get a brief introduction to the ways in which Sociology and Anthropology look at education. You will learn to describe the school as a social system and as one among many important socialization agents for the student, and to describe some general research results and related areas of concern for teachers and others interested in education today.

Systems and Social Systems

From a *social* point of view, education is carried on in an organized social environment, largely through *interpersonal* processes. How a student responds in the classroom, for example, might depend on such factors as the organizational structure of the school, the procedures of the classroom, the objectives of the teacher and of the student, the reactions a student gets from his fellow students, his parents and friends. A social scientist would probably try to arrange all possible factors into a *model* which could be used to explain the interrelationships of factors in a specific classroom or school and the causes of individual student responses and response patterns.

One such model views the school as a special type of social system. The arrangement goes like this: A system is a set of elements in mutual interaction; a social system is a type of system with a patterned set of activities which are interdependent and organized for a specific product; and a school is one type of social system with special types of inputs and objectives. Let's backtrack and consider each step in some detail.

A *system* is a set of elements or events in mutual interaction. Every system has definite boundaries which distinguish it from its environment. You are a system, as is a car, a blood cell, and a school. Some systems, like a car or a battery-operated casette player, are relatively closed systems, because they do not relate to or make exchanges with their outside environment. Other systems, like people and plants, are relatively open systems in that they need input from their environment and they give output. (e.g., temperature changes affect a person's body functions; if a child gets good things after telling a lie, chances are he will try it again.) The school is also an example of an open system. Notice, however, that probably no system is completely closed or open. At some point in their development or operation, all systems need input and produce output and thus are influenced and influence the environment. A car, for example, affects people's lungs. A person or a school can be set up as a relatively closed system, cut off from many important environmental inter-actions. Just think of the social recluse or the "backward" school. An open system functions by recurrent cycles of energy input, transformation of that input, and output. According to this model, a *school* is a structured interaction between the staff, materials, and the students. Students are the input which is transformed, the teachers and materials are the input that does the transform-ing, and the output is socialized and skilled young adults who return to the environment to enter other systems, such as families and occupational organizations.

A *social system* (think of General Motors, the Republican Party, the University of Missouri) is a type of system with special defining characteristics: (1) It has a formal way of maintaining itself through the selection, training, and adequate rewarding of its personnel; (2) it has a formal role pattern; the division of labor and the function of each role is clearly specified; (3) it has a clear authority structure that defines how the control and management functions are carried out; (4) it has a well-developed feedback mechanism to tell it how effective it is and how its products should be adjusted; (5) it has an explicit philosophy, ideology, and criteria, as norms against which its output and functions can be measured.

Social systems have both a formal and informal structure. The formal structure of a school, for example, is made up of the roles and duties of all the various personnel, including the principal, teacher, student, nurse, counselor, etc. It is formal because the role requirements for each person are spelled out, as well as the expected interaction behaviors, the sanctions, and the rules. But there is also an informal structure in social systems. For instance, though the theory of a school calls for information to move from the school board to the principal to the teacher and then to the student, the school grapevine may carry information to the teachers before the principals know. A school secretary or a teacher's spouse may have an influence that is not evident in the formal structure of a school.

THE SCHOOL AS A SOCIAL SYSTEM

Let's look more closely at the *school,* as viewed through this social system model. While the school shares certain properties with all other organized social systems, it does have special properties. For example, the school is what has been called a domesticated organization. It is protected and cared for much like a household pet; unlike economic organizations, the school doesn't concern itself much with recruiting clients or finances, with struggling to survive (since funds are not closely tied to performance), or with its potential competitors. As a result, the school is not overly interested in change and adjustment; its survival does not really depend on its performance. Besides, there are few yardsticks to measure the efficiency or quality of the school's product. In contrast to most social organizations, schools reward their personnel on the basis of seniority or of criteria other than actual quality of performance. And the potential rewards for students are either hazy (a good job later on) or ineffective (an A to a student who will never earn one) or altogether absent, except for the avoidance of punishment.

There are several other interesting differences between schools and typical social systems, as seen in the light of this model. (1) The goals of schools are ambiguous (some say unmeasurable); therefore role specifications and reward criteria are also ambiguous. (2) The input to schools has immense variation, since schools accept children and teachers with a wide range of experiences, motivation and skill, causing considerable stress and inefficiency. (3) The performance of a teacher is (compared to other organizations) relatively invisible to other teachers or superiors, and students can't say much about what they see. (4) Schools have a low interdependence of personnel; what one teacher does or doesn't do has little effect on what another teacher does; thus the behavior of a teacher can become routine and unproductive. (5) Public schools are criticized and controlled by the outside environment and the lay community, to a greater extent than is the local factory; this reduces a school's autonomy and allows innovation only in the absence of community opposition.

Although your local school board might insist that its schools are locally controlled, analysis will usually reveal a somewhat different picture. Actually there is a national educational system which greatly influences the functioning of the public schools and their personnel. This national system consists of formal educational organizations (public schools, parochial schools, universities), informal educational organizations (ROTC, Boy Scouts, summer camps), governmental agencies (United States Office of Education, National Science Foundation, National Institute of Mental Health), commercial organizations (publishers, builders, research organizations), and nonprofit organizations (foundations, testing organizations, accreditation agencies, professional organizations). Each of these systems serves its own interests as well as those of the school. The interrelationships between the schools and these systems lead to a great deal of standardization of both curriculum and teaching procedures.

Looking at the school as a special kind of social system has several advantages. It helps teachers, students, and parents organize their thinking and expectations about what schools do and how they operate. This perspective also helps the sociologist analyze real schools and organize his findings in a systematic way.

Using this model (see Figure 3–1), sociologists have conducted some useful and interesting studies about schools in operation. As we have seen, though the social system model works well in understanding many aspects of business organizations, the school displays a variety of important deviations from this

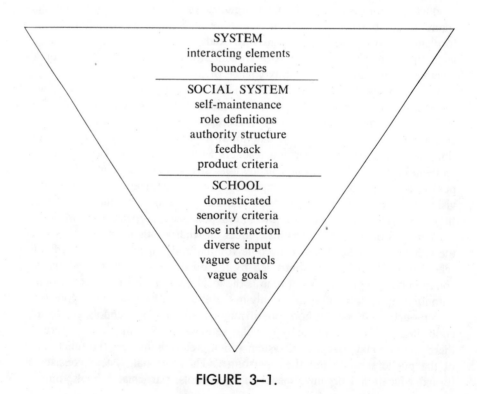

SYSTEM
interacting elements
boundaries

SOCIAL SYSTEM
self-maintenance
role definitions
authority structure
feedback
product criteria

SCHOOL
domesticated
senority criteria
loose interaction
diverse input
vague controls
vague goals

FIGURE 3–1.

model. For example, the *purpose* of the school system is to educate children—a vague and essentially indefinable goal. The specification of this goal is, of course, attempted by teachers, principals, superintendents, school boards, parents, and students. But a variety of studies have shown dramatic differences among all these school personnel and patrons about the specific objectives proper for the schools. Frequently these differences constitute a fundamental source of conflict that blocks effective action for all involved.

The same kind of discrepancy seems to exist regarding *role assumptions*. Though in this ideal model a social system calls for well-defined roles and responsibilities for each staff position, research indicates that many school personnel do not share the same views on the rights and responsibilities each other has. For example, superintendents usually feel that the school board should hire teachers and choose textbooks solely on the recommendation of the superintendent; most school board members feel otherwise. The same kinds of discrepancies are common between teachers and principals, students and teachers, parents and teachers.

These conflicting expectations (which sociologists call intra-role conflicts) appear from the research to be fairly common and predictable in school systems and frequently constitute major organizational barriers to their effective functioning.

---

1. Describe, with your own examples, the essential characteristics of a system, and of a social system.
2. List several special properties of schools as opposed to the typical social system.
3. Can you think of other intra-role conflicts in which you as a teacher could possibly find yourself?
4. Can you think of organizations which participate in the control of your local school district?

Socialization

Just as there are many organizations participating in the formal education of a student, so there are many social systems that contribute to his total learning. The school is only one of these systems, and in some cultures it plays a very small role.

Sociology and anthropology attempt to view formal schooling in the larger perspective of what is called *socialization;* that is, the process by which a person learns to adequately perform the social roles expected of him by his society. Culture is the name given to what he learns in this socialization process. Culture is the total way of life of the people of a particular society, and it includes knowledge and skills, beliefs, morals, values, laws, languages, tools, institutions, family-living and child-raising practices, and political, social, and economic arrangements.

Notice that socialization is not a biological process and should be distinguished from what we call maturation, the biologically determined process by which the organism grows up and changes. Socialization is a sociological process; it is a process of *learning by interaction* with social systems and individual agents of those systems. Since culture is learned, not inherited, each successive generation must learn it from the preceding generation. The social systems and organizations for teaching culture vary from one culture to the next. In Western societies, social institutions such as the family, the church, the school, government, business, and a variety of other formal and informal social systems share the responsibility for passing on the culture, in an attempt to assure the survival of the culture, the society, and the individual. The improperly socialized individual is unable to satisfy himself or his society.

Interaction is necessary for socialization. The people with whom one interacts in a significant way are the chief agents for socialization; they bear the culture, represent society, levy the sanctions and dispense the rewards. For a child, his parents and teachers are specifically responsible for this learning. Later an adolescent's peer group becomes a main socialization agent. In adulthood, a variety of adult social systems continue the process.

But socialization is more than just immediate interactions, since the web of social interaction is infinite. A child learns the culture from his parents and later his teachers; but they in turn are being influenced by their interactions with many other people—representatives of the culture—who in turn are being socialized by many others. So the child is indirectly interacting with a large segment of his society, and indirectly learning from all of them. In our society, multiple interaction is enhanced by TV, radio, books, newspapers, rapid transportation, and mobility.

But these factors also allow variants in our culture to spread and be learned by many in the society. Obviously, no one member of a complex society such as ours learns all elements of the culture. To put it another way, not all members possess exactly the same culture. All members have many cultural properties in common, but there is considerable variation resulting from immigration, religious freedom, and especially from economic and social differences.

The result is a number of identifiable *subcultures*. We speak, for example, of upper, middle, and lower social classes. And we tend to associate subculture traits with each class. We say that middleclass people are dependable and respectable, and that lower-class people are unambitious and lethargic. Of course, these are overgeneralizations, yet they represent patterns of behavior that are apt to be learned in subcultures. A child of a middle-class subculture will probably learn the kinds of behavior patterns we call industriousness and dependability and respectability, because these are the traits that his subculture rewards; they are also, therefore, the behaviors that he will find most rewarding. On the other hand, a child of the ghetto is apt to learn that hard work gets you no place, because that is what his parents have learned and that is what the particular subculture reinforces. Until very recently, at least, the middle class dominated our country's public schools, and their culture provided the basis for the formal and informal curriculum. The so-called WASP (white, Anglo-Saxon, Protestant) culture, which emphasized hard work and making something of oneself, was featured in the McGuffey readers and the Horatio Alger books, and is still presented as the culture on which this country was built into greatness.

Frequently, symbols (objects, styles, actions, even people) come to be adopted generally as representing a culture or subculture. Think of the crucifix as a cultural symbol of Christianity. Nations frequently use their flags and national anthems as cultural symbols. But subcultures also have their cultural symbols; think of the Confederate flag, the peace symbol, blue jeans, the family swimming pool, long hair, cadillac, McCarthy (Joe and Gene), the Afro, the braless look, etc. Whether or not the generalizations are accurate, these are symbols for many people of the values, beliefs and life-styles of specific subcultures.

A teacher who understands that this whole complex of behaviors and behavior probabilities which we call culture is *learned* is in a better position to see her teaching as but one part of the child's total socialization. Such a teacher can see the child in a much broader social context than that of the classroom. Most children come to school having already learned the fundamentals of a specific subculture; each child's subculture differs in some respect from the teacher's and from the WASP norm, and for many children the differences are enormous. Such cultural diversity further complicates the educational questions of what to teach and how to teach each individual student.

---

5. Describe socialization and culture in your own words, with an example from your own experience.

6. How is socialization achieved? How do subcultures arise?

7. Can you list several agents of socialization in this country, including some not mentioned in the text?

8. Briefly describe the WASP culture.

9. Identify several original cultural symbols and the subculture which each represents.

10. Why is it important for a teacher to know that a student's culture is *learned?* Cite an original example.

THE SCHOOL AS SOCIALIZER

In this country, whatever the real effect of school may be on subculture children, the formal purposes of the school include *socialization* and *selection.* By the age of five or six, when the child is normally sent to school, he is expected to have learned some basic skills such as feeding himself neatly and dressing himself, and controlling certain bodily functions such as walking, talking, and elimination. He is also expected to be able to identify the letters of the alphabet, to count to ten, and to use tools for eating, writing, coloring, cutting, etc. The dominant culture considers these reasonable expectations. A child who is not prepared for school in these ways is considered inadequately socialized and culturally disadvantaged, and the family is usually blamed for the failure. The school is expected to compensate for their shortcomings in whatever way it can, with programs such as headstart.

The elementary school's main socialization purpose is to teach the basic skills portion of the culture. At the same time there is a good deal of informal learning taking place as a result of interaction with the child's peer group and its social systems, and with the social systems of the school and the teacher. The child who is best able to adapt to these new cultures, different from the child's family culture in significant ways, is the child who will be regarded as the ideal student. Through the feedback a child gets from his peers and teacher, he learns which of his behaviors are acceptable to the cultural norm of the school. His questions, for example, and his investigative behaviors may be supported or punished by a confident or a threatened teacher. The teacher, who is like a parent in many ways, may modify a child's attitude toward his familial parents.

The child either learns new behaviors and modifies other behaviors to a degree acceptable to the dominant culture, or he is given a reserved seat on the dropout train. In this sense, the elementary school serves as a *selection* agency. Society expects schools to select students for allocation to future adult roles. The selection is based on achievement, which is based on how well each individual was taught. In the first grade, reading is the most important criterion for distinguishing between children. Children are usually divided into reading groups (red readers and blue readers, etc.), and on this basis evaluations (letter grades or their equivalent) are assigned. IQ tests are also used to measure the students' basic intelligence. Though such tests assess only what one has learned from particular kinds of experiences assumed to be common, the results are used to make conclusions about inborn intelligence. From the very beginning of schooling, therefore, the child's achievement rests largely on his entry skills.

When he moves on to secondary school, the child's achievement record is commonly used as a basis for assigning him to a general, vocational, or college prep curriculum. And, of course, this selection largely determines whether, several years later, he will continue on to college, and if so, to which college, and even later, which kinds of employment will be open to him and the subcultures he may join.

Students who drop out of this schooling process are among the poorest achievers. But achievement is not to be confused with ability. Though most measures of ability are generally unreliable, and probably invalid, we do have many examples of low school achievers who demonstrate remarkable ability later in life, despite the failure of the school to socialize them. For such students, school becomes a source of punishment, frustration, and failure; they predictably seek an escape.

When the student reaches secondary school, his school experiences have interacted with a variety of experiences with his family, neighborhood, peer group, and with many other social systems. At this time the peer group becomes a primary socializing agent for many young people. Cliques appear quickly, sometimes encouraged by school policies such as ability grouping. The cliques further stratify students and frequently dominate both school social life and school learning. Several decades ago, the primary factor affecting the composition of cliques seemed to be social class divisions. More recently it appears that the degree of independence from adult control is also an important influence in the formation of patterns of informal adolescent group activities and attitudes. Today there is evidence that some young people form distinct youth subcultures with their own values, requirements and attitudes— which are often at variance with those of the adult cultures. Often called the "generation gap," this difference in culture has begun to question the appropriateness of the dominant culture's values, of standard curriculum, and of traditional educational procedures.

In any social or group situation, an individual is always aware of others, and is to some extent concerned about their approval or disapproval because he has, through socialization, come to rely to some extent on their approval for his satisfaction. The classroom situation is liable to increase this peer pressure, especially if group procedures are used in instruction. A group of students can give or withhold approval, provide friendship and inclusion in the group's activities, or ostracize the individual if his behavior and school achievement differ from the norms of the group. Some groups, whose cultural norms are compatible with the schools, will reinforce academic effort and achievement; others will resist formal learning and criticize the curve busters and teachers' pets.

This effect has been illustrated in many experiments, as well as in the experience of all of us. If, for example, each member of a group is asked to choose one of four alternatives in a series of choice situations where the correct choice is fairly obvious, and all the individuals except one are instructed to not choose the correct item, the uninstructed individual will at first choose the correct item. But when he sees that the group chose differently, the uninstructed individual almost invariably changes his choice on later trials, so that it conforms to the group's choice. The individual may come to mistrust his own judgment or he may decide to avoid the disapproval of the others. However, if the uninstructed individual is given support from just one other individual in the group, the likelihood of his conforming is greatly decreased.

Sociometry attempts to define the structure of a particular class by identifying the cliques, the leaders, the isolates, and the rejected individuals. Techniques must then be developed and tested for dealing with the learning and social problems of individual students, and for capitalizing on or changing the group dynamic. Much research has been devoted to analyzing the effect of a teacher's authoritarian or democratic technique in teaching and discipline. Though the democratic climate is usually praised as being the more productive and harmonious approach, the procedures and behaviors that make up this general approach are difficult to pinpoint. Furthermore, a variety of cultural factors influence the results of such research. The behavior of individuals (student, teacher) and of groups of individuals (students, school systems) will depend primarily on how each of the individuals involved sees the situation of the moment interacting with the total of his past learning experiences. Many teachers have been shown to misread these interaction patterns, allowing their own biases toward individual students to block a correct assessment.

Such research has special meaning in regard to the unaccepted child in the classroom. Studies indicate that the powerful forces acting on such a child are group and classroom forces, rather than forces within the child himself. This questions the assumption of many teachers and counselors that individual counseling is the best way to change a child's behavior.

The fact that schools do not exist in a vacuum suggests another sociological point of view—that a school's functioning depends in part on the dynamics of the community in which it exists. We are all aware of the fact that migrations of people from one part of the country to another and from one part of a metropolitan area to another can drastically affect the composition of the student body, the effectiveness of the curricula and instructional methods, and the availability of resources. Demographic studies have suggested critical and continuing review of a school system's ability to meet the needs of each school's changing clientele. Specifically, many city and state systems are considering the advisability of a larger metropolitan approach to school organization.

Equally important is the *social class* structure of the students' families and of the school personnel. Studies in this area reveal that most aspects of school functioning are greatly influenced by the social class of the students and the teacher. The teacher typically determines criteria and expectations and grades partly on the basis of socioeconomic status. Other variables, such as the dropout rate, the vocational ambitions and academic confidence of the students,

---

11. Summarize several ways in which the elementary school serves to socialize and to select; what are several differences at the secondary level?

12. How does a child learn to adjust to the new cultures of school, teacher, and peers?

13. Describe how the factors of peer influence, community dynamics, and social class can each differentially affect the achievement of individual students.

dating behavior, and participation in extracurricular activities are influenced significantly by the socioeconomic status of the student's family.

Anthropology and Education

Anthropology, which studies the cultures of mankind, gives us valuable background information toward a perspective, if not a solution, for questions concerning what and how to teach individual students. Though we know that our educational system is largely a product of our history and particular social conditions, we still find it difficult to be critical and objective. Information about other societies and other educational systems can help us to see our own more clearly. All cultures are different, yet all are essentially similar. To know something of the range of possible educational systems can be interesting and useful.

Anthropology views education as a "program" for the learning of culture, a lifetime process that includes far more than the acquisition of technical competence. Western cultures emphasize the teaching of physical skills and vocational and professional knowledge, and they set up a formal educational program to teach them, leaving the teaching of cultural symbols, values, sanctions, and beliefs, to an informal program carried out by parents, friends, and counselors. Preliterate cultures usually do not separate these various aspects of the total educational process. This difference is due partly to the fact that in our society social mobility is valued; a man's progress through life is ideally measured by his acquisition of new and higher positions and status. In preliterate societies, very little importance is attached to social mobility; rather, recognition is attached to predefined formal status. Furthermore, in a society which changes rapidly, it is difficult to be sure about what are the best values, assumptions and beliefs.

Consider, as an example, education in rural *Guatemala,* which is in many respects intermediate between a simple tribe and a modern city. These people have schools, but they are of small cultural importance. Yet they do become educated in the cultural sense. The society consists of two main groups, the *Indian* and the *Ladino*. Indian culture is transmitted by the learning of moral values through myth and folktale, elaborate religious ceremonies, and dance-dramas. The Ladinos, however, rely on informal and unsystematic means such as story-telling, informational comments from parent to child, and complimentary or critical comments from others; that is, through a multitude of daily situations in which, by word and gesture, some part of the tradition is communicated from one individual to another, without any formal institution or any deliberate plan to teach. Most of the children go to school, however. Some learn to read and write and calculate; others do not. These skills have many practical uses and their possession gives some prestige; in some cases they provide the means for more profitable employment and lead the person to seek his fortune in the big city. But as an institution helping to preserve the local culture, the role of the school is small. If the schools were abolished, the culture would probably remain much as it is, because little of their heritage depends on literacy. In religion, for instance, a few individuals are needed to read the mass; but the pagan rituals, which the people practice conjointly with Catholicism, are stored unwritten in the memories of a small number of professionals.[1]

Another example from southern rural *Mexico* may provide some direct comparison with our own public schools. Southern Mexico has two social segments, the closed Indian villages, and Mestizos, who represent the national culture. The Indian is a subsistence peasant who grows crops to feed his family, hires himself out to the Mestizos for money, and funnels the money back into the village (raising his prestige with the rest of his villagers and reducing him back to subsistence). The Mestizos dominate the agriculture system, invest their surplus in wealth-producing ways, and adopt outward signs of status differential which are based on wealth. The Indian is highly democratic, subordinating his desires and profits to those of the community; the Mestizo is authoritarian and regards every office as a profit-making opportunity for personal exploitation.

Each of these groups, with its own culture, social structure, value system, and life-style, regards the other as immoral, and they try to avoid each other as much as possible. And, each benefits emotionally from his perception of the differences. A Mestizo sees himself as decent, clean, civilized and Christian, while the Indians are dirty, drunken, brutal, ignorant, savage pagans. To the Indian, however, the Mestizo is arbitrary and selfish, dictatorial, and exploits others, while he sees himself as morally responsible, hardworking and civic-minded. Despite these ethnic attitudes, each is largely ignorant of the nature and workings of the other segment. In addition, membership in each segment is publicly proclaimed by highly visible markers. For example, Indians speak an Indian language, and dress in clothing distinctive of their villages. Mestizos speak and read only Spanish, and dress in ordinary western tailored clothing.

Interactions between the two groups occur through "brokers" (official go-betweens) such as government inspectors and merchants. Brokers may come from either segment, but are usually Mestizos or Indians who migrated to the Mestizo segment. The teacher is an excellent example of such a broker. He is an employee of a large, urban-centered bureaucracy with a distinctive style of life, a representative of the Mestizo culture to himself, to other Mestizos, and to the Indians, and he has to somehow get along with the Indian population, whose cooperation is necessary if his career is to advance. Ever since the era

---

[1] Based on the work of Robert Redfield, as reported in the *American Journal of Sociology,* 1943, *48,* 640–648.

of Porfirio Diaz (c. 1900), Mexican education has been strongly directed toward progress, which means opening the Indian community and integrating the Indian into the national state. So it has tried to teach the Indians Spanish, Mexican history, geography, modern farming, etc. Of course, these goals are directly opposed to most of the goals of the local populace.

The teachers find themselves in a difficult situation. Their Indian students are not interested in learning about the Mestizo world and ways, and the teachers themselves have been taught to regard the Indian as stupid and incapable of learning anything. Furthermore, many teachers in these rural Indian towns are either newcomers to the Mestizo lower-middle class or are upwardly mobile Indians whose objective in becoming teachers is to raise themselves in ethnic terms. Both types are typically unsure of their own ethnic class identities. If they were to be successful in carrying out the national program of acculturating the Indian—which is their main responsibility—they would be violating the demands of the local Mestizos as well as their own outlook. Thus they have more of a stake than anyone else in preserving the distance and the difference between the Indian and the Mestizo. So they usually treat the Indians as unalterably stupid and lazy, tolerate them in the classroom while letting them and their parents know in a variety of ways that they are unworthy of Mestizo society, and concentrate their teaching efforts on the more rewarding Mestizo students. Curiously, the upper-class big-city Mexican tends to idealize the Indian as a Rouseauean primitive.[2]

14. Can you anthropologically distinguish between western and preliterate cultures? How does anthropology define education?

15. Think of some examples of cultural symbols in our society.

16. Distinguish between the cultural processes of the Indians and of the Ladinos in Guatemala, on the basis of how the culture is transmitted. How relevant is formal education for these peoples?

17. Cite several cultural differences between the Indians and Mestizos in Mexico.

18. What is meant by saying "The Mexican teacher is a broker of Mestizo culture?" Cite one reason why this role is usually difficult for the Mexican teacher.

Now consider, as an anthropologist might, the American inner-city school system. You will find some interesting similarities to the Mexican system. Our public school system is a bureaucracy largely staffed by middle-class personnel and is designed to provide the children with the technical and psychological skills and the information about society as a whole which he will need as an

---

[2] Based on the work of Robert and Eva Hunt, as reported in *Midway*, 1967, *8*, 99–109.

adult in this society. This includes certain bodies of myth and knowledge, the three R's, the abilities to perform an intellectual task in which there is no great interest and to be bored without rebellion, and the ability to divide the working part of a day into small and inflexible periods of time to meet the demands of externally imposed timetables. This is very consistent with the family background and later job life of middle-class youngsters; but not with those of inner-city children. For them, school is intended to represent an effective route for cultural migration, with school acting as the broker institution. For most of them, it doesn't work.

The reasons are not unlike those applying in rural Mexico. Both segments remain largely ignorant of each other, and what each perceives (or projects), it despises. The Negro inner-city child is told he speaks a corrupt and deficient version of English. Whereas the Mexican Indian knows that he can use school to move into the Mestizo world by learning some skills and then changing his group markers, for the Negro inner-city child, the major marker is his skin color. It is not surprising, therefore, that the Negro home does not always support the objectives of the middle-class public school, since the experience is painful and irrelevant to adult Negro life. And finally, the teachers have proved they can meet the demands of the middle-class world (they went through college); and if only recently arrived in the middle-class, they tend to hold rather rigidly to middle class values and behavior patterns. Like the teacher in Mexico, if there is some danger of being identified with his pupils (especially if the teacher is a Negro himself), he will reject the pupils and what they stand for. Teachers who were raised in a middle-class environment feel right and justified in making middle-class demands (regarding, for example, respect and attention, obedience, cleanliness, language, "acceptable" hair and clothing) of their pupils. Those who were not are forced to do so to avoid threats to their own change of identity. We have, then, a school which is middle class in subject matter, in expectations, and in staff—but not in pupils. And our teachers, as their Mexican counterparts, are trapped in a net of cultural oppositions where the wrong choice is personally threatening.

In our country, the cultural conflict is not limited to blacks and whites. For example, The United States Civil Rights Commission, in its Fifth Report (Mexican-American Education, 1972) presented convincing evidence that most teachers in the Southwest tend to hold back Chicano students by ignoring them. One can easily imagine the same kind of process happening to Indians, Puerto Ricans, "poor white trash," or students from differing religious, political or life-style families.

For a practical illustration, let's look more closely at just one feature of the current black subculture. Examine this situational dialogue:

> "Cmon, man, les git goin!" called the boy to his companion.
> "Dat bell ringin. It say, 'Git in rat now'!"
> "Aw, fget you," replied the other. "Whe Richuh?"

"Whe da muvvuh? He be goin to school. He in de now, man!" was the answer.

Inside the classroom, they tried to read a story. It went: Come, Bill, come. Come with me. Come and see this. See what is here.

The first boy poked his friend. "What da wor?"

"Da wor is, you dope."

"Is? Ain't no wor is. You jivin me? Wha da wor mean?"

"Ah dunno. Jus is."

Many (most?) teachers would not understand this dialogue, especially if they heard it rather than read it; they speak and understand *Standard* English. Yet it's normal speech for thousands of children in our schools. Though the books these children use are written in Standard English, they themselves speak *Black* English, a dialect typically viewed as bad English, or sloppy grammar and lazy pronunciation. Whether the children learn Standard English or not, they do learn that the black dialect is bad and so are those who use it. Some will withdraw and stop talking in school; others say "Fget you, honky." In either case, the results are disastrous.

Yet Black English is a language, a rather rigidly constructed set of speech patterns, with the same sort of specialization in sounds, structure, and vocabulary as any other language. For example, substituting "dis" for "this" is not carelessness; it is a characteristic of the dialect. The *th* sound is almost non-existent in the West African languages which most black immigrants brought with them to America; similarly, the only Germans who use this sound are the ones who lisp.

Another surprising difference is that black dialect words leave off some consonant sounds at the end of words, similar to Italian and Japanese. Boot is boo, sure is sho, your is yo, what is wha. There's the story of a white teacher who asked a black child to use *so* in a sentence—not "sew a dress" but the other *so*. The child said: "I got a so on my leg." A related feature of the dialect is not to use sequences of more than one final consonant sound. Just is jus, past is pas, mend sounds like men, and hold sounds like hole. Why? Perhaps because West African languages, like Japanese, have almost no clusters of consonants in their speech.

There are also differences in vowel sounds. A black child asks his teacher how to spell rat. "R-A-T," she replied. "Ah don mean rat mouse," he said, "Ah mean rat now." In the word right, the "eye" sound is really a close combination of two sounds, ah-ee. West African languages have no such long, two-part, changing vowel sounds; their vowels are generally shorter and more stable.

West African languages also have a tense which is called the habitual tense, used to express action that is always occurring, and it is formed with a verb that is translated as "be." "He be coming" means something like "He's always coming" or "He usually comes." Since Standard English has no regular construction for such a tense, black dialect uses the word "be" as an auxiliary —"My momma be workin"—and drops the "be" from the present tense—"My momma workin."

When anyone learns a new language, it's common to try to speak it with the sounds and structure of the old language. This tendency is further reinforced by social and geographical isolation, and by conflict of value systems. Many modern linguists are urging that we give black children (and white) the ability to use both standard and black English, so that they can communicate effectively with all their fellow citizens.

> 19. Can you summarize several reasons why schools fail as brokers of cultural migration (here and in Mexico?)
>
> 20. Specify several differences between standard and black dialects.

From this brief look at the viewpoints of Sociology and Anthropology, it should be clear that schools not only contribute to the socialization of society, but also are themselves changed in the process, and come to reflect significant changes in the culture. If we compare the dominant values and behavior patterns of today with those of a century ago, it is clear that significant aspects of our culture have changed. We are not only a pluralistic society, but also a rapidly changing one. This is especially true today, since the force of tradition is less potent and change by itself is more acceptable. Of course material changes (new curriculum materials, buildings, etc.) are more readily accepted than changes in ideas and ideals (nongraded individualization, year-round schooling, computer assisted instruction, etc.).

If a school admits to and attempts to reflect the culture of its community to some degree, it will also reflect the social changes and conflict of that community. There are a variety of approaches employed to handle this change and conflict, ranging from authoritarian dismissal of any variance from tradition and criticism of those who diverge or question, to invited scrutiny, clarification, and intelligent criticism looking toward mutual respect and compromise. The strategies adopted by the teacher and the school become part of each student's cultural experience. Now and for the foreseeable future, the ability to handle continual change and conflict comfortably is an indispensable skill for any satisfied adult in our culture.

> 21. Through socialization, most of us learn to rely to some extent on the approval of others for our satisfaction. Do you think this works to the benefit of the individual and his society, or not? Why?
>
> 22. Can you think of ways a school or other agent might help a student learn to handle change or conflict comfortably and productively?

Unit 4

SCHOOL AND COMMUNITY

School and community are closely interrelated social inventions, designed to satisfy the needs of individuals and the total society by preserving and teaching the culture and technology of that society. Traditionally the school has been inseparable from the community. It has existed as a community in microcosm, where children are taught the skills and ways of that community. Community has always denoted territory, a place where one lived and worked, was educated, went to church, and socialized.

In this unit, you will learn how and why these traditional conceptions are changing, the effects of these changes on various types of communities, subcultures, religions, and on the family, and several current strategies for dealing with school-community tension.

Then and Now

In our day, both schools and communities are changing. With technology and increasing population and mobility, the activities that formerly helped define a community are no longer localized. For most of us, the places where we eat, sleep, study, play, work, and socialize are all different. *Community* has come to mean a set of common interests shared by a group of people. A group of students who get together on weekends because they share recreational likes, or because they share a concern for a current problem, make up a temporary

51

community even if they "live" in different areas of the city. And people whose homes are near each other need not form a community, especially if their only shared concern is the local garbage collection procedure.

School and education are also being somewhat redefined. School is no longer the only educational agency; education is being seen as far more than schooling. In our past, the school has been a revolutionary agent for social change; now some view the school as a conservative institution whose future is uncertain. This change of attitude was not a sudden switch; it began at least seventy years ago when leaders of new intellectual and social movements appeared on the scene, took a look at the school and community, and gave both of them an "F."

The *social reform movement,* which occurred around the turn of the last century, took the form of a sudden, self-conscious, but energetic awareness of the squalor, poverty, and indignity of urban slums. The slums and their inhuman conditions were not new, nor were the reform movements to correct them. What was new was the intense willingness to look closely at these conditions, and the sudden conviction that they could be changed. A new generation of social critics described in vivid detail the hopelessness of the tenements and the sweatshops, and a new generation of literate and informed citizens read and reacted.

The concern might not have been sufficient except for a coincident *intellectual movement.* Based on a faith in science and on man's ability to determine his environment, the intellectual movement supplied a method and a motive to the social reformers. Several pioneers in the sciences laid the groundwork for the intellectual movement of the early twentieth century. Two Englishmen, Galton and Pearson, and an American, Cattell, developed mathematical constructs and methods for determining the relationships between factors, variables, or anything measurable. These and other developments in the techniques of observation, measurement, and statistical analysis, coupled with the rapid maturing of the science of psychology (which until this time was pure speculation without evidence) made possible the development of a scientific study of education.

Johann Herbart, a German whose influence reached the United States sixty years after his death, contributed greatly to the scientific study of teaching. He outlined five steps that comprise effective teaching: (1) preparation—introducing the topic and connecting it with anything that has already been learned; (2) presentation—making certain the students understand the new material; (3) association—showing how the new and the old ideas compare and contrast; (4) generalization—showing how many ideas can be related to these new concepts; (5) application—using the new material to interpret new experiences. The "Herbartian steps" were a vast improvement on anything available to teachers at the turn of the century, and it did not take long for their practicality to catch on in the United States.

Edward Thorndike, whose work was carefully scientific, impressed the educational world with his experimental studies on mental discipline and learning. Particularly radical was his conclusion that neither Latin nor mathematics was superior for disciplining the mind in general. Rather, he said, educational objectives should be stated in terms of specific skills or attitudes considered desirable for students to master, and then appropriate curricula and procedures should be devised to accomplish that learning. There is no evidence, Thorndike claimed, for any such power as a disciplined mind as such. What we do have, however, are human behaviors and skills, and these, he said, could be taught to any normal human.

Herbart's disciples and Thorndike were strongly attacked, not by a scientist, but by a philosopher, *John Dewey,* and the Progressive Movement of which he was the head. The Progressive philosophy was based on a point of logic in the psychology of William James. The meaning of an idea, James held, lay not in the rational operations performed on it by the mind but in its practical effects—the consequences that followed from acting on the idea. Ideas were only plans of action which had to be cashed in at the bank of experience before their meanings could be understood, or their truth known. Thought, therefore, was not contemplative, as the older philosophers had said, but instrumentally functional in the ordering of experience.

Dewey adopted this thinking and argued that man can make progress, in the Darwinian sense, if he uses his natural intelligence and his experience with the past in solving problems. In Dewey's functionalist version of the mind, the mind was triggered by the person's interest in his own goals and problems. Life was interacting with the environment, supplying the mind with cues and problems. The experiences, therefore, were the materials out of which men made meanings and upon which they based their plans and actions.

Dewey urged that education become the social agency for training the young to use this functional logic in dealing with the problems of human life. To Dewey, the school was the key to *social reform*—providing civic and social experiences, facilitating vocational and practical usefulness, and developing problem-solving skills. The school was to be agent and guide for planning social change, an embryonic community related to the world outside by reflecting the life of the larger society and its experiences. The curriculum of the school should be the experience of people, not mastered for its own sake but used to solve problems encountered in everyday life. Thus, subject matter becomes an instrument in the development of minds trained in the use of the new logic. Methodology becomes unstructured problem-solving in which the responsibility for learning shifts from the teacher to the student and is carried out in projects.

The contributions of Dewey and the progressive movement are numerous and significant; both school and society were altered drastically. Schools became less of a bore and more of an adventure, at least in the lower grades and for the less able students and teachers. But many students and teachers found much of the new curriculum trivial and mindless, a pooling of ignorance to solve insignificant problems. This wastefulness, which Dewey himself criticized, was based in part on tactical failures at the practical level; problem-solving by itself does not make for effective learning or growth.

Many progressive schools did indeed become revolutionary institutions in conservative communities. Offering health and counseling services, citizenship and moral development, vocational training, and adult education programs, such schools came to serve as the community center for all of the processes of self-development. But the progressive approach to education was also openly paternalistic—to "help these poor people become like us." Its goal was to educate all Americans to a predefined idea of democracy and the common good, to "Americanize" the post-1900 waves of European immigrants and all the culturally disadvantaged of the time. To be "American" meant to adhere to what was expected of every middle-class, native-born American, which is precisely what the ghetto dwellers of the time wanted. The progressive movement and its schools were greatly responsible for helping ghettoized European immigrants find the American dream.

> 1. Cite several ways in which the traditional roles of school and community have changed.
>
> 2. When did this change begin, and what started it?
>
> 3. Cite several elements of the intellectual movement of the early 20th century. Cite several leaders, and a contribution of each.
>
> 4. Summarize in your own words the basic purposes, curriculum, and methodology of education as advocated by John Dewey.
>
> 5. Summarize in your own words several merits and contrasting deficiencies of the Progressive Education movement.

Communities and their Schools

By 1950, there were new teeming masses of whites, blacks, Puerto Ricans, etc., in new slums (now called ghettoes). The escape of these people from their bondage seemed just as dependent on education as before, but for most of them, "Americanization" was not the solution. The barriers were, from the start, not only cultural but also physiological. And while the European immigrant was eager to adopt the American way, the new people of the ghetto were and are typically independent and suspicious of the paternalism of the educational and social establishment. The failure of "Americanization" in the new ghetto has deeply divided both the ghetto communities and the suburban middle class communities. A significant proportion of ghetto dwellers now refuse to let white power lead them out of deprivation, and they suspect any-one who becomes involved in that effort. A segment of Black America is say-ing that it will take, rather than ask for, the power to decide and have what is rightfully theirs.

The ghetto dweller of today, like his predecessors, still sees education as his principal route to freedom and security; but the school that his children attend seems like a massive white barrier to these goals. What the school teaches his child seems to have no relationship with the restricted world he lives in, the social contacts he has, the culture he has learned, and the real-world oppor-tunities he actually has. The only power many ghetto-dwellers have, even after schooling, is the power to survive in the urban jungle and, with others, begin to force some change. He and his ancestors have learned well, through decades of experience, that nobody else can or will give him freedom or even the power to free himself. He must join with his brothers to find and take it.

For reasons like these, the *community* has become the fundamental and critical agent of ghetto reform—reform of the school as well as of other ele-ments of culture and society. The revolutionary school of forty years ago no longer leads reform, but follows. Remember, though, that community is no longer defined purely in terms of location, but primarily in terms of com-monalities of conditions, experiences and aspirations. The community's bond and identity are basically cultural. Its demands are formulated from this cul-ture. One of its demands is that the school reflect the culture of this com-munity, including teachers and administrators who are part of that culture (with its experiences and aspirations), and who are therefore responsible to the community. Anything less is tokenism.

There are real changes taking place in our national society, not mere fluc-tuations. They are important changes for all citizens, because a change in one part of the social organization produces changes or adjustment problems in every other. National consensus on the need for consolidation of schools is now being challenged by the demand for decentralization of power so that the schools themselves will become more responsive to the needs of individual subcultures; and while all Americans agree (or say they agree) that every child should receive the best possible education, the demands of the ghetto com-munity have stirred violent disagreement nationally as to what "best" means for different children.

The above description of the ghetto community is both an incomplete and over-generalized picture of any given community. Most ghetto communities include several racial groups (blacks, whites, Puerto Ricans, Mexicans, In-dians, etc.) and each group is apt to include several *subcultures*. Furthermore, the values and goals of the members of the ghetto community are at least as divergent as those of a suburban community. Many ghetto-dwellers accept the conventional American system of schooling and of economic rewards, and they work within it for their satisfaction and improvement. Others resent any rocking of the boat which endangers what little they have already achieved. Some very poor families have adopted a life style which can be called a "culture of poverty." Such people are distinguished by their lack of concern for their future; they think only of day-to-day survival and whatever momentary pleasure is possible, and consider talk of reform foolish and irrelevant. And a ghetto school also usually includes children of descendents of immigrants or of minority groups, who remain in the inner city or its fringes and represent a different, middle class culture. The teacher or a school can make ludicrous and disastrous mistakes by being ignorant of the diverse cultural conditions and aspirations in the community, or by being paternalistic in applying generalizations.

Then there is the *suburban* community (another overgeneralization). Terms like wealthy suburb, suburb, and working class suburb indicate that suburban communities represent a variety of differing subcultures. Suburbs are subject to rapid change at least as much as inner-city communities. A suburb can come to be much like an inner-city community and can even be embraced by the city as the limits expand; empty lots can become towering apartments, and whole blocks can be transformed into industrial areas. Other suburban communities set up legal barbed wire to guarantee cultural uniformity in income levels, homes, taste, landscaping, aspirations, and collegiate careers for their children. There is also the *"exurb,"* a new kind of community smorgasbord located at the meeting place of urban and rural. Such a community includes trailer residents as well as isolates living on large estates, and the life styles of exurbanites are extensively mixed and varied.

Finally there is a general category called the *rural* community, comprising only about five percent of the 1970 population. Mechanization, mobility, and mass media have created several subcultures in the rural community. Some pockets of homespun independent farmers still exist (in the Midwest, for example), but most rural residents are businessmen, city commuters, etc. Students in rural schools come from wealthy families, poor tenant farm families, and a variety of other social, economic, and cultural backgrounds.

---

6. Describe several subcultures which may be found in a given ghetto; a suburb; a rural community.

7. Summarize several reasons why the "community" replaced the school as a primary agent of ghetto reform.

8. Can you describe several "communities" of which you are a member?

Religion and the School

The First Amendment, which says "Congress shall make no law respecting an establishment of religion, or prohibiting the free exercise thereof," was intended to guarantee the right of the states to regulate their religious affairs independent of federal control. The writers of the constitution saw themselves confronted with the growth of rival sects. The Presbyterians against the Anglicans in the South, and the Baptists, Methodists, Unitarians, Catholics, and other denominations against the Calvinists in the North. They wanted to keep the Constitution a political document, as free from the strife of religion as possible.

Early legislators had no intention of founding a "Christian nation," as we often hear. Religion was a private affair. And in fact there are data to indicate that in 1776 only about five percent of the population formally belonged to any church (though a greater percentage attended church on occasion, or professed allegience to a denomination). Nevertheless, religious faith and practices were an important aspect of the culture of the early communities. For that reason, there was no resistance to the teaching of religion in every school of colonial America. Even Horace Mann, who led the later Common School Crusade, wanted to save religion in school by reading the Bible without note and comment.

But it was difficult, if not impossible, for the teacher to use the Bible and other religious documents without introducing sectarian bias in some way, and usually there was no attempt at all to avoid such bias. At the same time, the growing number of immigrants of different faiths, the growth of relativistic philosophies and new scientific theories such as Darwinism created a widespread indifference, erosion, or hostility regarding many facets of the Christian tradition in this country. These conflicting ideas and traditions were the cause both of regulatory laws and religious schools.

Parochial schools existed in this country as early as 1606 (St. Augustine, Florida), but during the 1700s and early 1800s, most public schools simply reflected the dominant religious faith and attitudes of their respective communities. The wave of new immigration and the growth of new philosophies in the early 1800s changed this. Catholic immigrants, for example, found that they could not legally free the public schools from this Protestant domination, so they began to form their own school systems. By 1840 there were 200 Catholic schools in the country; today there are about 10,000.

The trend is changing, however. Many parochial schools closed or merged with others during the 1960s and early 1970s, and private school enrollment dropped 23 percent from 1965 to 1972. Private colleges and universities also began to decline in number and enrollment during the 1970s. Financial pressures on the schools, parents, and students, are primarily responsible for these declines, though in the case of parochial schools the decline may also be due to growing uncertainty about the need for this kind of formal religious education.

Recent court decisions have gradually established that public schools must truly be secular institutions, though the question of how far the state may go in aiding parochial schools and their students is still undecided. However, the law clearly says that (1) public schools may not give religious instruction, or pay teachers to do so, use Bible readings or prayers, or compose their own prayers, even if local religious groups agree to their use; (2) public schools may teach about religion, and may release students to attend religious instruction, provided students are not coerced into attendance; (3) states may not give parochaid for instructional programs, according to a 1972 Supreme Court decision, but they may extend aid for parochial school bus transportation and perhaps for secular textbooks, providing the particular state constitution allows it. In addition, the federal Elementary-Secondary Education Act (E.S.E.A.) of 1965 partially circumvents the religious issue by granting assistance to poverty-level students, regardless of the school they attend. According to this "child-benefit theory," aid is given to the student, not the school.

In addition, most school systems attempt to recognize the religious diversity of their students. They include in their curriculum a study of various religions and their customs, celebrations, and symbols. The school calendar is arranged in light of the religious holidays of the students and staff, and no one is penalized for religious observances. School observances that formerly were somewhat religious in nature (such as baccalaureate services) have generally been eliminated or transferred to churches and synagogues, and frequently an attempt is made to hire a staff that is at least as diverse in religious background as are the students and community.

In the 1963 Supreme Court decision in the *Murray* and *Schempp* cases (dealing primarily with devotional use of the Bible in public schools), Justice Brennan outlined the position of the Court on the relationship between religion and government:

> "The line we must draw between the permissible and the impermissible is one which accords with history and faithfully reflects the understanding of the Founding Fathers. It is a line which the Court has consistently sought to mark in its decisions expounding the religious guarantees of the First Amendment. What the Framers meant to foreclose, and what our decisions under the Establishment Clause have forbidden, are those involvements of religious with secular institutions which (a) serve the essentially religious activities of religious institutions; (b) employ the organs of government for essentially religious purposes; or (c) use essentially religious means to serve governmental ends, where secular means would suffice. When the secular and religious institutions become involved in such a manner, there inhere in the relationship precisely those dangers—as much to church as to state—which the Framers feared would subvert religious liberty and the strength of a system of secular government.

In contrast, there is a broad segment of the white Anglo-Saxon Christian community which is convinced that the truths of their religion are indeed truths, that these truths are an essential aspect of our cultural heritage, and as such should be transmitted by the culture's schools. Others, however, do not accept these truths and furthermore are not part of the consensus supporting the moral values in this cultural heritage.

Both arguments are appealing and contradictory. The intent of the constitution and the courts is to prevent America from becoming Middle America by force. The issue of religion and the schools is a serious one, involving basic questions about the purpose of human existence. We can expect uncertainty and contradiction to continue for some time as we attempt to redefine our orientation to human life and society.

> 9. Can you explain briefly why there were few parochial schools before 1800 and what changed that?
>
> 10. According to court decisions, can state schools use their own prayers, read a selection from the Bible over the public address system, bus students to parochial schools, give religious instruction, provide math texts for a parochial high school, let students leave school during the day to attend religious classes, or help a parochial school improve its reading program?

The Family and the School

As we have seen, the relationship between the culture of the school and the culture of the home has been a basic theme, particularly in pluralistic areas and in areas of rapid social change. In colonial times, most children received informal education from their parents or in an apprenticeship arranged by their parents. Those who received formal education did so from a live-in tutor hired by their parents or in a local school which reflected the faith and attitudes of the family. Tension arose whenever the consistence between these two socializing agencies was threatened. Immigrant families of the late 1800s came to see the school as a rival source of authority, dividing the child's world into two realms, each with its own rules and modes of behavior, and each with its own culture. The school was acculturating the child to the point where he became a mediator between the culture of the immigrant home and the culture of the wider society.

Today the same kind of tension exists. The teacher, as an agent of acculturation, has the dilemma of finding a balance between respecting the life-style of a family and attempting to change it. When the teacher's attitude is one of self-righteous imperialism, a power struggle is inevitable. At the same time, the family is largely responsible for the attitudes and abilities with which the child enters school, and the family supports or impedes the ongoing education of the child. The conflict between parents and the school that we have seen in recent years is in part the continuing struggle to define the role that the family and the school have in relation to each other.

Throughout our history there have been *two opposing trends* in this conflict. The first argues for removing more and more of the educational functions from the home (at least in cases where the family seems inept), while the second seeks to improve and increase the educational role of the parents. An extreme version of the first trend might be expressed this way: "the problem posed by the lower class can be solved fundamentally only if the children of that class are removed from their parents' culture at a very early age and brought up by people whose culture is normal, through the sale of infants and children to qualified bidders." However radical and unacceptable this might seem to Americans, it is not unheard of in American education. This strategy was used in an attempt to educate the Sioux Indians by virtually kidnapping them into government schools, cutting their hair, giving them different clothes, forbidding them to speak their own language, using military discipline to force a change of behavior patterns, and imprisoning children and parents who resisted.

Day-care centers, a less radical approach to removing educational functions from the home, have been advocated not only for children of working mothers, but also for those children whose parents cannot offer them a suitable home. Their purpose is to ready such children for a middle class way of life, and to provide them with the knowledge and skills they will need to lead it successfully and happily.

Additional proposals for extending nonfamilial education include extending the school day and year, and establishing homework centers, tutorial programs, and head-start schools. Preschool education is important in this process, since a child's early experiences seem to have a critical, and to some extent, irreversible effect on later achievement. The argument is that if deprivation starts to build up at an early age, it will progressively limit and may eventually block a child's potential for entering the mainstream of society. The danger is greatest for the lower class and minority child. All children have some difficulty bridging the discontinuity between the home and school experience, but it is minimal for the middle class child. Preschool education tries to familiarize the child with the standards of the school so as to narrow the cultural gap the student will face when he enters school.

In all of these methods, the purpose for removing more of the child's education from the home is to facilitate acculturation that will permit social mobility.

Recall that the second, alternative trend in the conflict between the two cultures is to improve and increase the educational role of parents. There are several ways in which this can—and is—being done. Educational television and programmed and self-teaching instructional materials are used by many parents to supplement or even replace the role of the school. Now, as in the past, parents have taken over major responsibility for education by establishing home tutoring systems, and parochial, private, or kin-group schools.

Another approach is to increase the involvement of the parents in the school. Typically this involves a communication system of letters, conferences, meetings, and workshops designed to inform the parents about the goals and methods of the school. Parents are also urged to take part by serving in a variety of supportive roles, such as aides or tutors, and occasionally in a decision-making or advisory role on a parent council or as a school-community coordinator.

These types of parental involvement are intended to reduce the gap between home and school, not only by keeping contact with and educating parents, but also by exposing the school to the scrutiny and the constructive criticism of the parent. Many school systems operate on the assumption that the cultural gap between home and school can best be reduced by making the home more like, or at least supportive of, the school. This is in line with the trend to reduce the impact of the parent on education. On the other hand, some types of community control, when seriously undertaken, presume that the best approach is to bring the cultural standards and experiences of parents into the school. This approach also presumes that parents either have or can readily acquire the knowledge, values, and attitudes necessary to make intelligent collective decisions about education.

The problem of maintaining a productive balance between the rights and responsibilities of the parent and of the professional educator is delicate. Most of the curriculum and methods of any school have at least an element of potential controversy in them. Censorship, then, is inevitable because no teacher or school can include everything and must therefore select. Parental reaction to such decisions can take the form of extreme pressure on the school board, the principal, or the teacher. In attempting to handle these problems, many communities establish broadly based committees of both parents and educators, in order to educate each other concerning their methods, goals, needs, and fears, and to guard the school both against vigilante attacks and against one-culture paternalism.

---

11. Summarize the cultural reasons for tension between schools and families today.

12. Specify the two opposing approaches to resolving this tension; describe several examples of each. Cite several possible advantages and disadvantages of each approach.

Current Views and Strategies

There are some promising new strategies and alternatives which focus directly on the school-community interface problem. The problem itself was described and highlighted for public debate by the *Coleman Report* on *Equality of Educational Opportunity* (1966). The report documented what most people knew or suspected: that youngsters from well-to-do families receive far better education than poor children; that most citizens and public agencies accept this fact as natural and inevitable; and that the traditional interelatedness of school and community is a major source of this inequality, since quality of school services correlates with socioeconomic status. But the *Coleman Report* stimulated controversy over the question of what, if anything, the school can do to overcome the disadvantages of poor communities. Is educational improvement to be achieved by improving the schools (class size, materials, quality of teachers, number of counselors, etc.) or by focusing on the communities (community rehabilitation, busing children to do away with the socioeconomic imbalances in the schools, etc.)? It is questionable whether we have the necessary resources and commitment to do both adequately.

Another recent report, known as the *Bundy Report,* sparked another old controversy by proposing that since New York's school system was too large to be manageable, it be redesigned to give control of small districts of schools back to local neighborhood-community areas. Arguments over this strategy usually pit the educational establishment against the community representatives. Will decentralization promote greater accountability, better school-community communication and relations, and better education, or will it result in lowered standards, inefficiency, and an uneven quality of education? The basic issue is one of redefining the school-community relationship.

Another proposed solution is referred to as the *"community school."* The definition of such a school is never quite clear, but in general it would include such features as community control, the cooperation of outside agencies (such as industry, the university, and community organizations), experimental and open-ended curricula, and the inclusion of amateur staff members (artists, writers, political and business men) and other talented but noncredentialed specialists. Such schools have operated in the past, but then it was a case of the school forming the community; in the case of community schools, the community is to be dominant in forming the school.

In a related strategy, some communities have set up *Community Resource Centers*—out-of-school settings in which remediation and parent education programs take place. In such centers, parents and children and teachers work to improve everyone's skills in dealing with educational questions and learning problems. In other localities, an attempt has been made to use the community itself as a laboratory for learning, in an attempt to make the learning more practical and more interesting. Such a *"school without walls"* looks to a gradual merger of school and community, with mutual improvement. A 1972 Gallup Poll indicated that a majority (56 percent to 35 percent) of the public approves this kind of approach, even though it reduces classroom instruction time.

Another current trend, compatible with some of the above strategies, is toward *commercialized* formal education. We see this in the reawakened interest in performance contracting, in which public schools subcontract out particular school functions, such as the teaching of reading or basic math, to private businesses that offer the services with stipulated guarantees. Businesses themselves, dissatisfied with the skills of university graduates, or having specialized needs, have for decades been offering their staff or prospective employees short-term training programs. In recent years, some of these programs have become very sophisticated, efficient and effective. This is due in part to the businesses' own economic constraints which forced them to find and adopt the most effective instructional procedures. Such trends, coupled with improved technology in both instruction and communication, make it possible to envision future education at all levels being offered in auto-instructional and automatically programmed cable TV "courses" in which the student or his parents select the goals, and each student's advancement is tailored to his own performance, needs, and desires.

In this sense, the basic question in the current school-community struggle is not which one will win, but rather what will happen to education in the broadest sense. Both the school and the community are social organizations which formalize patterns of behavior by people. Behavior patterns can and do change. It may be that the goals of education, of cultural integrity and diversity, and of human relationships will best be served by different social organizations reflecting these different behavior patterns. Perhaps both the school and the community will have to be redefined beyond recognition.

---

13. Briefly describe several new approaches to the school-community relationship. (Hint: decentralization, "community schools," resource centers, commercial education.)

14. Can you identify:
    Coleman Report
    Bundy Report
    Thorndike
    Dewey
    Herbart

TEACHING AS
A PROFESSION

Since the Middle Ages, society has recognized only three main "learned professions": theology, law, and medicine. Only in the last century or so has the list grown to include architecture, nursing, teaching, social work, and a number of other vocations which have raised their standards and requirements, and become recognized as public servants. Until about one hundred years ago, teaching in this country was regarded as a semi-skilled trade at best.

In this unit, you will learn about teaching as it relates to the criteria for a profession, about the responsibilities of a teacher, the need for teachers at various levels, teacher organizations, what it means to be a "good" teacher, and how good and satisfied you might be as a future teacher.

The Role

There are several current criteria by which an area of work is judged to be or not to be a profession:

1. The amount of formal education and the degree of skill required for membership;

2. The importance and the degree of dedication to society of the service;

3. The degree of personal responsibility required by each member for individual judgments and decisions based on his specialized knowledge.

By each of these criteria, teaching is a profession. First, nearly all states require a Bachelor of Arts degree and about thirty credits in education courses and supervised teaching for *certification* at the elementary and secondary levels, and many states now require a Masters' degree for permanent certification. In addition, many states are developing more explicit requirements by which continued certification will depend on a teacher's ability to demonstrate specific kinds of skills and knowledge deemed basic to effective teaching.

Second, there is no doubt that teachers perform an essential public service. The service is so vital to society's development that teaching has become a socialized profession, managed and supported by the state. Nor do teachers work strictly by the clock; the public knows that many teachers come early, stay late, and work at home in order to assist individual students, improve their teaching, and to develop schoolwide programs. The dedication of teachers has given their profession significant prestige. A recent Harris poll ranking professions according to the prestige accorded them by the public indicated that educators were accorded more prestige than corporate executives, psychiatrists, lawyers, clergymen, congressmen and artists.

Finally, all teachers assume personal responsibility for using their professional preparation to make daily decisions of great importance to their students. While elementary and secondary level teachers have less responsibility than college teachers for deciding the courses they will teach and the materials they will use, all teachers have considerable latitude in developing effective methods of instruction and evaluation in specific areas, and appropriate procedures for remedying specific learning deficiencies and behavior problems. They also assume the responsibility of working cooperatively with other teachers and administrators as professional co-members.

Throughout the course of a school year, a teacher must bring a variety of skills to a variety of tasks. The teacher must be an instructional planner and designer—breaking down a year's general objectives into a thoughtful sequence of daily unit objectives, arranging for the best means to teach the daily objectives, managing the implementation of this instructional unit, evaluating its effectiveness with each student, and remedying deficiencies whenever they occur. This implies that the teacher must also be able to make good use of a variety of materials and resources, must be able to motivate different kinds of students, and must be able to keep data records that make immediate and helpful decisions possible. The teacher must also be able to summarize and report on each student's progress, be a personal relations expert with other educators, parents and the community, a helpful counselor and confidant to some students, and a contributing member of a professional organization.

Not all of these tasks require the same amount of time and effort. Surveys indicate that elementary and secondary teachers spend about thirty hours a week in direct classroom work with students, seven to eight hours in other school duties, and another ten hours a week in outside, noncompensated activities related to education. The outside activities include not only homework and meetings, but also professional study activities designed to keep the teacher up to date.

Each of these tasks, however, requires talent and enthusiasm because each is important to the *focus* of education—the student. And each task also produces its own kind of short or long term satisfaction.

There are many other types of educational opportunities, in addition to regular classroom teaching. About 20 percent of public school employees are in roles such as those described in the following list:

> Preschool: supervisor, consultant, researcher, director.
>
> Elementary: exceptional child specialist, physically-handicapped specialist, supervisor of experimental school, principal, assistant principal, librarian, speech or hearing therapist, counselor, nurse, curriculum consultant.
>
> Secondary: disadvantaged child specialist, supervisor of experimental school, assistant principal, principal, supervisor of subject area or department, coach, counselor, librarian, curriculum consultant.
>
> Administrative: superintendent, assistant superintendent (of finance or instruction or personnel, etc.) business manager, secretary, research director, audio-visual director, community relations director, psychologist, psychometrist, vocational-placement director, statistician, cafeteria manager, dietitian, adult education director, nurse.

In addition, there are educational opportunities at the junior college, college, and university levels, with state and national professional organizations, with state departments of education, and with a variety of federal agencies.

We can't presume, however, that such a list of educational-role opportunities will remain essentially the same. Education is making a somewhat concerted effort not only to raise its standards but also to make its efforts more appropriate to the needs of a complex and changing society. Inevitably this will lead to discarding some role functions, creating others, and redefining most.

The Need

The teaching profession is a sizable one. Since 1970, there have been slightly over two million elementary and secondary teachers working in this country. Particularly since 1950, the increase in the number of teachers has been unusually large (averaging about a 4 to 5 percent increase each year), partly because of the post-war population increase, but also because of the great increase in school attendance during the last several decades. Though this trend

68   Introduction to Education in America

toward a larger percentage of school-age children enrolling in school and staying in school for longer periods of their lives is still rising, the decreased birth rate during the 1960s and 70s has already dampened the increase in the number of teaching positions available at all levels.

For example, during the 1972–73 school year, the number of working elementary school teachers decreased slightly, and the number of secondary school teachers increased only 1 percent. Population predictions are, of course, very risky, but Figure 5–1 pictures a government projection of school enrollment. Notice that a valley is predicted between 1970 and 1990 for elementary enrollment and between 1975 and 1995 for secondary. Whether the demand for teachers increases in the future will depend largely on how insistent American society is on quality staffing for quality education.

The teacher shortage ended in the late 1960s, and there are now enough certified bodies to fill the classrooms of the country. Schools are now in a position to require *excellent* teachers when filling new or old positions. Figure 5–2 shows the degree to which supply exceeds demand in most areas. It also identifies several exceptions (as of 1972) in the areas of secondary math, vocational-technical, sciences, and industrial arts.

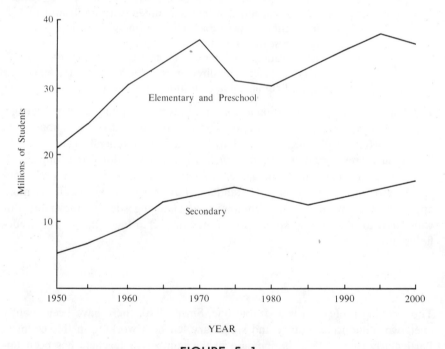

FIGURE 5–1.

PAST AND PROJECTED SCHOOL ENROLLMENT BY LEVEL.

(Source: U.S. Bureau of the Census, *Current Population Reports,* P-25, No. 473. U.S. Government Printing Office, 1972.)

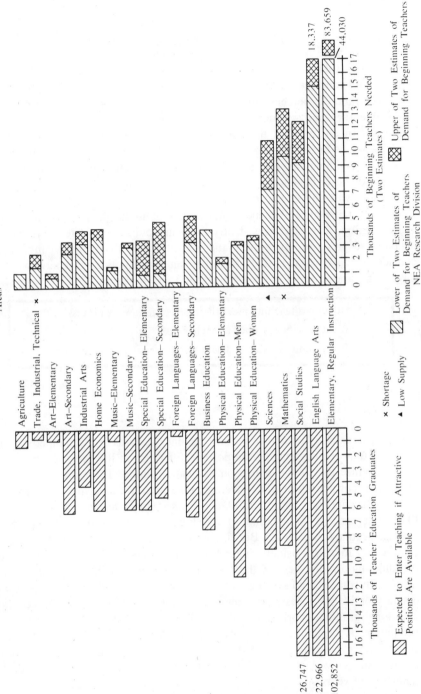

FIGURE 5–2.

SUPPLY AND DEMAND FOR BEGINNING TEACHERS, BY TYPE OF ASSIGNMENT, ADJUSTED TREND CRITERION ESTIMATE, 1972.

(Source: National Education Association, *Teacher Supply and Demand in Public Schools,* 1972, Research Report 1972-R8, p. 38. Reprinted by permission.)

However, counting certified bodies is a shortsighted way of looking at the situation; from another point of view there are actually not enough competent teachers available now to meet the actual needs of education in this country. Consider the following: 28 percent of the country's adults have had no high school (in Tennessee, Arkansas, West Virginia, and Kentucky it's 40 percent or more), and 52 percent have not completed high school; well over half of our elementary and secondary students either fail consistently, drop out, or barely get by for most of their school years; most children must wait six or seven years before beginning their formal education, and when it does begin it is only available for 180 days each year; and although we have recently recognized the critical need for a right-to-read program, we have yet to implement it with any degree of effectiveness and urgency. Each of these considerations represents an educational deficit of immense proportions.

In addition, there are at least fifty thousand public school teachers without a college degree, and perhaps many more whose effectiveness can only be considered marginal at best. Rather than an oversupply of teachers, what we have is an undersupply of competence and commitment.

---

1. How does teaching meet the three criteria of a profession?
2. What specifically does a teacher do?
3. Justify and criticize: "There is an oversupply of teachers."

Salary

While most teachers recognize that the primary rewards in teaching come from the signs that one has made an important difference in the lives of others, they also recognize that few can live on dedication alone. Therefore, salary is an important consideration. The average nine-month salary in 1973 for elementary teachers was about $9800, and for secondary teachers about $10,400. (The difference is largely due to the longer period of preparation by the average secondary teacher.) But like all averages, these figures indicate variation. Salary increases usually depend on years of accumulated service, amount of schooling and the degree, the teacher's specialty, and the particular school district. In some school systems, a teacher with a bachelor's degree begins with a salary of $6000 or less. As a teacher accumulates years of experience (and additional graduate work), the salary will increase, but this also varies across the nation. A beginning teacher with a bachelor's degree who starts at about $7000 can eventually reach $10,000 or more. A beginning teacher with a master's degree who starts at about $8000 would possibly reach $12,500 after a number of years.

There are significant geographic differences in salaries for teachers. Schools in the Mideast pay average salaries about $1400 higher than schools in the

Southeast, Southwest, and Rocky Mountain regions. The Great Lakes, Far West, and Far West, and Plains regions, in descending order, fall somewhere in-between. However, some states are exceptions to their regional averages, as Tables 5–3 and 5–4 indicate.

TABLE 5–1

SALARIES OF ELEMENTARY-SCHOOL TEACHERS, 1972–1973.

1.	Alaska	$14,549*
2.	New York	12,040§
3.	Michigan	11,600
4.	California	11,360
5.	New Jersey	11,050
6.	Maryland	10,910
7.	Nevada	10,721
8.	Illinois	10,700
9.	Hawaii	10,660†
10.	Massachusetts	10,440
11.	Delaware	10,430
12.	Pennsylvania	10,400
13.	Connecticut	10,300
14.	Washington	10,215
15.	Rhode Island	10,200
16.	Arizona	10,155
17.	Wisconsin	10,130
	UNITED STATES	9,823
18.	Minnesota	9,789
19.	Indiana	9,600
20.	Colorado	9,589
21.	Oregon	9,412
22.	Wyoming	9,300
23.	Virginia	9,268
24.	Iowa	9,101
25.	Florida	9,100†
	Ohio	9,100
27.	Louisiana	8,933
28.	Missouri	8,917
29.	New Hampshire	8,890
30.	North Carolina	8,877
31.	Texas	8,735
32.	Maine	8,699
33.	Utah	8,500

34.	Montana	8,461
35.	Vermont	8,380
36.	New Mexico	8,368
37.	Kansas	8,329
38.	Nebraska	8,200
39.	Tennessee	8,040
40.	Alabama	8,024
41.	West Virginia	7,968
42.	Georgia	7,916
43.	South Carolina	7,890†
44.	North Dakota	7,762
45.	Oklahoma	7,750
46.	Kentucky	7,660
47.	South Dakota	7,638
48.	Idaho	7,491
49.	Arkansas	7,209
50.	Mississippi	6,787

NEA, *Estimates of School Statistics, 1972–73,* p. 31. Reprinted by permission.

* Reduce 30% to make purchasing power comparable to figures for other areas of the United States.

† NEA Research estimate.

§ Median salary.

TABLE 5–2

SALARIES OF SECONDARY-SCHOOL TEACHERS, 1972–73.

1.	Alaska	$14,409*
2.	New York	12,700§
3.	California	12,350
4.	Michigan	12,200
5.	Illinois	11,865
6.	New Jersey	11,460
7.	Maryland	11,417
8.	Minnesota	11,231
9.	Arizona	11,160
10.	Nevada	11,030
11.	Connecticut	11,000
12.	Washington	10,988
13.	Pennsylvania	10,800
14.	Delaware	10,770
15.	Hawaii	10,750†

	UNITED STATES	10,460
16.	Wisconsin	10,737
17.	Massachusetts	10,600
18.	Rhode Island	10,498
19.	Iowa	10,213
20.	Indiana	10,120
21.	Virginia	10,033
22.	Colorado	9,963
23.	Oregon	9,720
24.	Wyoming	9,700
25.	Montana	9,696
26.	Ohio	9,650
27.	North Carolina	9,454
28.	Maine	9,424
29.	Florida	9,400†
30.	Nebraska	9,300
31.	Louisiana	9,297
32.	Missouri	9,271
33.	New Hampshire	9,238
34.	Vermont	8,890
35.	Texas	8,735
36.	Tennessee	8,700
37.	Kansas	8,669
38.	North Dakota	8,664
39.	Georgia	8,613
40.	Utah	8,610
41.	New Mexico	8,537
42.	West Virginia	8,430
43.	South Dakota	8,253
44.	Alabama	8,184
45.	South Carolina	8,175†
46.	Kentucky	8,075
47.	Oklahoma	8,000
48.	Idaho	7,803
49.	Arkansas	7,508
50.	Mississippi	7,100

NEA, *Estimates of School Statistics, 1972–73,* p. 31. Reprinted by permission.

* Reduce 30% to make purchasing power comparable to figures for other areas of the United States.

† NEA Research estimate.

§ Median salary.

> 4. What can a beginning teacher with a Bachelor's degree expect as a yearly salary in your state? Where would you earn more? Where less?
>
> 5. On what factors do salary increases usually depend?

NEA and AFT

The professional life of most teachers includes at least some involvement with an organization of fellow educators. Such an organization can be an effective agent in dealing collectively with teacher concerns. The two major national organizations are the American Federation of Teachers, a union affiliated with the AFL-CIO, and the National Educational Association, a non-union group.

The *National Educational Association* (NEA) is over one-hundred years old, and has over one million members. It resulted from an 1870 merger between associations representing teachers, school superintendents, and normal schools. Its two general purposes are "to elevate the character and advance the interests of the profession of teaching," and "to promote the cause of education in the United States." Its annual budget is over $11 million, with most of its revenue coming from membership dues. The NEA provides a wide variety of services for its members. It represents its members before the Federal Legislature and Agencies (as its local affiliates do at their levels of government), promotes the interests of education to the community at large, conducts a variety of workshops, and publishes journals, instructional materials and classroom aids. In addition, it assists local affiliates in collective bargaining and in improving working conditions.

The *American Federation of Teachers* (AFT) was organized in 1916. Though small in comparison with the NEA, it is the largest teachers' union in the United States and has close to seven-hundred local unions. As an affiliate of the AFL-CIO, it has the support of over fourteen-million other union members, and the AFT has frequently won better salaries and other benefits because of this support. AFT membership includes teachers, principals, and supervisors, but not superintendents, who are considered to represent the interests of the employer. The AFT carries on a strong economic welfare program and a variety of legislative activities, though its staff size and number of educational programs are considerably smaller than those of the NEA. A major portion of the AFT's membership is found in large cities, where it is the dominant teacher organization.

There are two major issues which divide the NEA and the AFT: (1) the fact that the NEA has no restrictions on administrator membership, and (2) the fact that AFT is affiliated with labor. The NEA has been criticized as a company union, a monolithic giant representing the educational establishment, and a racially conservative agency. The AFT has been called a tool of Big Labor, a violator of state laws regarding strikes, and a haven for leftist malcontents and clock-watchers.

Both the NEA and the AFT are in a state of transition, and both are heading in similar directions. Though a 1968 offer by the AFT to begin merger discussions was rejected by the NEA, several substantial pairs of locals (e.g., Flint and Los Angeles) have since voted to merge on their own, and other state locals have begun merger discussions.

> 6. Can you briefly describe and differentiate between the NEA and the AFT on the basis of size, major concerns, membership location, and issues separating the two?

Accountability

The strikes (AFT) and the sanctions (NEA) of the 1960s and 70s achieved some important gains in salary and working conditions for teachers, and they also focused the public's attention on the rights and responsibilities of teachers as professionals. But they also produced new and increasing demands for what some call "accountability" from the teaching profession. Though these demands are still vague, it is becoming apparent that the critical new goal of teacher organizations will be to develop convincing programs which guarantee quality education.

Accountability means that specific and measurable public goals or objectives are defined as part of a job, and the person who accepts the job accepts the responsibility of meeting those objectives, knowing that part or all of his payment depends on how well he actually achieves those objectives. Salesmen who work on commission are on a kind of accountability contract. Politicians are supposedly accountable to their constituents regarding their management of resources to fulfill their platform.

In the past, education has been noted for its lack of accountability. The state built schools and certified teachers, parents sent their children, and the teachers presented material and graded the students. The net result was that less than half of the students mastered what the schools attempted to teach. Now schools, administrators, and teachers and their associations are being asked "why only half?" The new call for accountability in education is a call for:

1. A very specific set of objectives: a very precise statement of what the school intends each student to be able to do after, say, nine months of instruction (partly determined by the skill-level of the student at the beginning of the period).

2. Precise measurement of the results: not just a general IQ or achievement test, but a specific measure of the skills detailed in the instructional objectives.

3. Public reports of the results of the measurement of each student's mastery of each objective, so that all concerned about the results are informed.

4. Compensation proportionate to the results awarded to those responsible in one way or another for the results (teacher, principals, and other participating school personnel, or a contracting company); such compensation might, for example, be in the form of a graduated bonus added to a minimum salary.

The City of New York and the city's teachers, in their 1969 agreement, pledged themselves to "develop objective criteria of professional accountability." Virginia has authorized funds for guaranteed results through performance contracts. Several cities have contracted with private companies to eliminate specific educational deficiencies in target groups through competitive bids and performance contracts.

The "Good Teacher"

Still unanswered is the basic question: "What is effective teaching?" The last forty years have produced an enormous, almost unmanageable amount of research aimed at defining the specific ingredients in the "art of teaching." Typically, each study produces insignificant findings, or significant results that are contradicted by the next study. We have learned much about what the effective teacher is *not,* and what variables lead us nowhere.

For example, attempts to connect teacher effectiveness with personality factors, such as the teacher's adjustment, needs, attitudes, and intelligence, have produced no significant results. The same is true for the teacher's cultural background, socioeconomic status, sex, marital status, etc. In short, after forty years of research we still do not know how to define, prepare for, or measure teacher competence.

Perhaps you yourself can identify one basic reason for this failure by asking yourself when was the last time you saw a need, or an attitude, or an IQ. At worst, these personality factors are simply hypothetical constructs; at best they can be measured only indirectly and with great difficulty. In any case, the conventional approach to defining teacher effectiveness (studying the personality of the teachers) has proved futile.

There are, however, new approaches which appear to be much more promising and powerful. They involve looking at specific measurable behaviors of the teacher and of each student and at the interaction of these behaviors, primarily their temporal relationship. Instead of a teacher simply being a subject matter specialist who dispenses pearls of wisdom in an order and method unrelated to a student's needs, a teacher can be a *learning manager;* he can arrange a series of brief and specific tasks which elicit the desired responses from the student (or a response that comes close to the desired response), and he can arrange for each student to be given feedback and positive support for each such improvement (or immediate remediation if the desired response is not learned). With this method, each student proceeds at his own pace, mastering each small step before proceeding; there are no academic dropouts, only faster and slower progress, and every student sooner or later masters the objectives of the school. Thus, personality factors become less relevant. For this teacher, and for this kind of instruction, accountability becomes a useful and precise process, working to the advantage of the teacher, the profession, and each student.

The current thrust toward accountability will probably produce changes in several areas of the teaching profession. The emphasis will first switch from teaching to learning. (It is not rare to find one without the other.) Quality of schooling will no longer be equated with quality of resources—including teachers—but with the degree of student learning. To achieve this, educators will have to develop very specific and measurable performance objectives, so that any results of instruction can be measured and justified against these objectives. This implies that the teacher will no longer be the dispenser of information, of normative grades, and of lables for students who learn and don't learn; instead the teacher will take on the role of a designer and manager of instruction for each student, evaluator of progress and deficiencies, and inventor of responsible and effective procedures.

In this sense, accountability can be the catalyst for the development of a strong and capable teaching profession. A teacher (and also a would-be teacher) must remember that when he accepts employment, he pledges to every family sending a child to school, to every community paying his salary, and to each student receiving his services, that every student will receive clear and significant benefit from his services. Accountability can be both the measure and the guarantee of teaching's expertise and integrity. But good teaching is more than a responsibility; it is also a critical necessity. H. G. Wells wrote that "human history becomes more and more a race between education and catastrophe"—and it is not yet clear which will win.

Think of the appropriateness to our times of this description of another revolutionary period: "It was the best of times, it was the worst of times, it was the age of wisdom, it was the age of foolishness . . . it was the spring of hope, it was the winter of despair, we had everything before us, we had nothing before us, we were all going direct to Heaven, we were all going direct the other way" (Dickens 1775). Ours is an age that is dangerous, difficult, and explosive, yet simultaneously exciting, rewarding, and hopeful. Many human lives are being needlessly destroyed today, yet this same period holds for more people than ever the promise of achieving their potential.

Teaching offers a fighting chance to make a difference. Teaching is where the worthwhile action is—the action against ignorance and the stifling of human potential, the action of facing and forming today's social realities, meeting the needs of individual learners, and developing humane values and human potentials. Through teaching, a skilled and conscientious person can make his life count by giving to hundreds of others the skills and confidence they need to be free and fully human.

---

7. In general, what does "accountability" mean? What are the four components of educational accountability?

8. Give one reason why personality research has failed to identify factors in effective teaching.

9. Describe the teacher as a "learning manager." What are several advantages to this approach?

10. Explain in your own words several ways in which accountability may change the teaching profession.

You—A Teacher! (?)

Becoming a teacher today presents a greater challenge than ever before. More personal, intellectual and professional skills are being required and expected of the teacher by students and parents, by school and government officials, and by one's fellow teachers. In the past, (and occasionally, even today), a person was considered qualified to teach if he could do the things he was expected to teach the students to do and if he could maintain discipline. Contrast that with the following statements about the current and future role of education:

1. Modern life has been drastically reshaped by technological processes. Our work requires more brain power than physical power. We travel around, live close together, have access to many material things, and have an increasing amount of free time. We are highly dependent on the skills of other individuals whom we will never meet. As part of the preparation for such a life, schools must do much more than simply teach a child to read, write and obey.

2. The vast differences between students can no longer be ignored. Students come to school from different cultural backgrounds, with different needs and expectations, and with widely differing degrees of readiness. They learn at different rates and by different methods. Many learn very little and drop out. Schools can no longer teach classes of students gathered together by chance; they must now

receive students as they are and tailor each one's instruction and motivation to his own needs and possibilities.

3. Leading a satisfying life now requires a high degree of subtle mental skills. Students must learn to make very fine discriminations in what they see, say, read, and hear in order to make appropriate and productive decisions in the face of highly skillful efforts to deceive them by advertisers, neighbors, salesmen, government officials, and propaganda experts representing a variety of pressure groups.

4. The educational influence of the family is decreasing, due in part to increased mobility, working mothers, increased years of schooling, etc. Yet it is possible that a large part of schooling will return to the family via computerized cable television, whereby each student will have access at the touch of a button to whatever learning package is appropriate for him. This implies that students will need to learn well how to manage their own learning and that of their future children.

5. Leisure is replacing work as the major part of many people's lives; it is losing its stigma as an unvirtuous shirking of obligations. Students must be taught the personal and intellectual skills they need to make this free time an opportunity for growth and satisfaction in a variety of areas. History tells us that no nation yet has been able to survive the acquisition of a large leisure class.

6. The range of career opportunities for women is approaching that for men. But a girl with only a home economics background has not really been given a free choice about her future.

7. The interrelationships between skills is becoming as important as the skills themselves. The need now is for the application of disciplines to other areas—chemistry to air pollution, architecture and psychology to urban planning, social skills to the problems of aging and poverty. The teacher of today and tomorrow can no longer be simply a subject matter specialist. He will have to be able to relate disciplines to each other, to transcend local attachments and demands, to be cosmopolitan, knowledgeable and enthusiastic over a broad range of interests and areas.

8. Knowledge, both basic and applied, is accelerating at an unmanageable rate. It is said that man's knowledge has doubled itself five times in the last 2000 years; three of those times occurred since 1900, and twice man's knowledge has doubled in about the last decade. It is estimated that 90 percent of all the scientists who have ever lived since the dawn of history are alive and working today. Yesterday's education becomes obsolete about as fast as an automobile. This implies that learning and the management of learning must be a lifelong process for all of us.

9. The skills of brainpower management and social engineering are becoming as basic as the skills of writing and math. Instead of the past need to pool muscle power, the need now is for meshing a vari-

ety of intellectual skills, each contributing productively and at the proper moment to the solution of an overall problem. And the complexity of modern life, together with the computer's ability to analyze large numbers of variables and to simulate complex models of human behavior, all indicate the increased need and opportunity for society to control and be controlled. Careful and effective control must be adopted or we will drown in our complexity. Schools must train people to be able to handle the ethical problems of who and what is to be controlled, by whom, and for what ends.

10. The technology of teaching is developing rapidly, implying an ethical problem of control. In the past, society has not had to worry excessively about what, in addition to the three R's, was being taught in the schools because it was seldom taught well to all students. Now that a technology for effective individualized teaching is becoming available, a decision by schools to teach well implies the need for decisions about what to teach, particularly in the area of attitudes, values and behavior patterns.

> 11. Which of these ten statements about the current and future role of education do you consider most important—and why?

Many states are considering—and some are moving rapidly towards—performance-based certification standards, by which teachers will be certified on the basis of how well they actually can arrange for learning to occur in live settings, rather than on the basis of a college grade point average and course requirements. Implied in this approach is a variable time requirement for each student to meet certification standards, and also periodic reexamination of a teacher's abilities to teach as the instructional demands on the schools increase.

From this it is clear that when you consider the possibility of becoming a teacher, you must do much more than simply match yourself up with teachers you have had in the past. During the next several decades teachers will be expected to have diverse, flexible, high-level intellectual skills, to be eager to work with individuals of varying ages, abilities, interests, and cultural backgrounds, to choose to teach what is most relevant both to the individual student's needs and to the needs and aspirations of society as a whole, to keep pace with the knowledge explosion and with refinements in the technology of teaching, and to help define and preserve basic individual rights and freedoms in a changing, complex culture. It is difficult to imagine a profession that could be more demanding and challenging, or more potentially satisfying.

Recent attitude research studies (e.g., by the National Center for Information on Careers in Education, as reported in the American Association of Colleges for Teacher Education Bulletin, January, 1972) have produced some interesting findings regarding student attitudes toward education as a career. While a large number of students express an interest in a career in education, a much smaller number of them actually expect to enter the profession, viewing it as a compromise or "second choice" career. There seem to be three general reasons for this hesitancy: (1) Many students are uncertain that education has the potential for being an effective means for constructive social change. (2) Many students say they are unenthusiastic about education careers because of the negative images they received as students; while these students generally speak favorably of their instructors, criticizing them mostly for being out of step with the times, their chief criticisms are directed toward the educational system itself, which they see as cold, impersonal, unchangeable and stifling. (3) Some students are turned off by education because they view the elementary or secondary teaching job as suffering from low pay, low support, and low prestige.

Like most attitudes toward careers, these contain a good deal of myth. The above stereotypes are what are sometimes called half-truths; they apply in some respects to some job situations in some education careers, and they probably apply in the same way to all other careers. The potential for achievement and satisfaction in a teaching career, as in any career, usually depends largely on the skills and interests the individual brings to a specific job.

It used to be true that if a college student couldn't make it in the sciences, he could always make it as a teacher. In the past, many students have majored in education not because they really wanted to teach but because a teaching certificate was easy to get and offered a modest but reliable income and an easily marketable skill—something to fall back on until marriage and again after the kids were in school. Today a student with this motivation is probably wasting his time and setting himself up for frustrations and hard times. Such a student may still be able to get the certificate (though with increasing difficulty), but he will have great difficulty competing with others for the available positions, and will find it nearly impossible to gain satisfaction in the responsibilities of teaching in the schools of tomorrow. Whether or not you feel you are ready, you have to make decisions now that are critical to your future career satisfaction and fulfillment. Your only choice is to make them as wisely and honestly as you can.

Following is a checklist which might be of help to you in making a personal assessment of your possibilities as a teacher. The list is not complete, and some items probably deserve more weight than others. Furthermore, nobody can be (or should be) perfectly fitted to any professional model. But spend some time going through the checklist—honestly and thoughtfully. If you rate yourself "usually" on most items, then perhaps the teaching profession is worth your serious consideration, though you should reexamine the "sometimes" and "rarely" checks to see how serious and reparable your needs in those areas are. If, however, you find yourself with a lot of "rarely" and "sometimes" checks, you should probably look elsewhere for satisfaction—and be grateful you were able to make that decision at this stage of your life.

Self-Rating Checklist For Prospective Teachers	*Infre-quently*	*Some-times*	*Usually*
Are you in good health?			
Would you be proud to be a teacher?			
Are you able to remain cheerful and cool even when tired, ill or irritated?			
Are you able to criticize yourself objectively?			
Are you known to be reliable and punctual?			
Are you able to work long and hard for a goal you consider worthy?			
Are you thought of as emotionally stable and sound?			
Are you able to stay flexible regarding your goals and responsibilities?			
Are you able to earn an A or B in any general or education college course?			
Do educational subjects turn you on?			
Do you find it easy to study and concentrate?			
Do you express yourself clearly and succinctly?			
Do people find your explanations easy to understand?			
Do you read books and articles on current events?			
Do you find yourself getting concerned about current educational and social problems?			
Do you like to work out ideas in practice?			
Do you manage your time well?			
Do you organize your materials well?			
Do you organize routines so people share responsibilities?			
Do you do extra study of interesting topics?			
Do you like to talk about "intellectual" topics relating to the sciences, the arts, history, etc.?			
Are you known as a cheerful, happy sort of person?			
Do people think of you as a patient, tolerant person?			
Do your acquaintances find it easy to get along with you?			
Do you enjoy working with people—especially children and adolescents?			

Self-Rating Checklist For Prospective Teachers	Infre-quently	Some-times	Usually
Do people know you like them?			
Do people think of you as cooperative?			
Do your acquaintainces feel confident you will accept different life styles and ways of doing things?			
Are you known as a tactful person?			
Do you operate effectively in new situations without direction?			
Do people think of you as an enthusiastic person?			
Do people think of you as consistent in your dealings with them?			
Do you accept and try to use criticism from others?			
Are you honest and free in expressing your feelings and ideas?			
Do people think of you as persuasive?			
In making decisions with others, do you find it easy to compromise on nonessentials?			
Do you have a pleasant speaking voice?			
Do you have a pleasant and broad vocabulary?			
Do people think of you as a good listener, who is able to hear others with sympathy and understanding?			
Are you able to sense correctly how others feel about you, other people or events?			
Do you remain friendly with someone who disagrees with you and proves you wrong?			
Are you able to make something enjoyable out of routine and unimaginative tasks?			
Can you imagine yourself as a teacher?			

REVIEW AND
APPLICATION I

As a part of this review unit, you may be asked to participate in a group discussion with three to six other students. Use the attached Review Discussion Sheet for Unit 6 to record your discussion. Be sure to complete your own private review beforehand, so that the discussion can be as profitable as possible for everyone.

In addition to reviewing all the study-guide questions for each of the previous units, you should attempt to relate their ideas to each other and apply them, when possible, to practical situations. The following items are *examples* of questions you might practice asking yourself as you review the units.

1. Construct an original example of an accident to a child in which the teacher is liable, and one in which the teacher is not liable.

2. Summarize the major changes in governmental attitudes and policies toward education, from the Northwest Ordinances to the close of the Universal Education Movement.

3. Summarize in your own words the stages in the development of our elementary, secondary, and teacher education systems.

4. If you and other teachers wanted to change some conditions of your work, what are some methods you could use?

5. Construct an original example of a situation in which a student's rights are being violated.

6. Describe several ways in which you, as a teacher, might handle the topic of religion.

7. Be able to argue for joining the AFT, for joining the NEA, for merging the two, and for keeping them separate. Which organization might you really consider joining, and why?

8. Cite an example, from your own experience, of cultural tension between family and school, and describe its causes.

9. Cite several sources (persons, issues, philosophies, etc.) for the constitutional idea of separating church and state.

10. Cite a nonracial example of the "American Dilemma."

11. Choose one word that you feel best describes Dewey's philosophy of education; defend your choice. (Remember that he was highly critical of some practices of "Progressive Education.")

12. Defend and criticize the position that the school's role in society should be expanded.

13. Outline a system which you think would fairly and helpfully evaluate a teacher's effectiveness. Defend your system.

14. Trace the history of federal involvement in education, citing examples of laws and court cases that show its continuing concern.

15. Cite several ways in which your understanding of the "American Dilemma" might help you as a teacher.

16. As a child increases in age and experience, the relative importance of his socializing agents changes. Identify the socializing agents which typically have the most influence on a preschooler, an elementary student, and a secondary student, and describe how the socialization occurs at each level.

17. Compare the expectations and methods of a Mexican teacher of Mestizos and Indians with those of an American teacher of mixed-race students.

18. Cite several reasons why your ability to identify cultural symbols might be helpful to you as a teacher.

19. Be able to argue for and against keeping education as a state function.

20. Be able to argue for and against increasing federal aid to education.

21. Cite several conflicts about values that you might encounter as a teacher, and outline how you might deal with them.

22. Be able to argue for and against the advisability of a student deciding to be a teacher, in terms of teaching as a profession, its pay scales, its educational requirements, the job market, accountability, and personal abilities and interests.

23. What specific skills will being a teacher require of you?

24. Describe how you would feel and act toward a teacher or school that was teaching your child the culture of an ethnic or social class different from your own.

25. Assume you are a principal. Develop a set of guidelines for your teachers to help in avoiding negligence suits.

26. Cite several specific weaknesses beginning teachers are apt to have. What steps can be taken to avoid these?

27. Which of the checklist qualities (Unit 5) do you consider most important for teachers?

28. Cite several specific skills which you as a teacher would teach but which your own pre-college teachers did not consider important.

29. Are there any conditions under which you as a teacher would join in a strike?

30. Financially, to what comparative degree is your state committed to quality education?

31. Defend or criticize: Teacher unionism and militancy will hinder progress toward teacher professionalism.

DATE: TIME:

STUDENTS (identify chairman, recorder):

Summary of Topics, Questions, and Situations Discussed (identify contributors):

Part II

INTRODUCTION TO TEACHING

Unit 7

ANALYSIS OF TEACHING AND LEARNING: AN INTRODUCTION

Experimental Analysis of Learning

The art of teaching is becoming a science.

In the past, widely publicized efforts to improve education have rarely been directed toward analysis and improvement of teaching and learning as such. Instead, large sums of money were spent for more and better schools, more and better teachers, more and better students going to school and to college, and more and better curriculum and audio-visual materials. Rarely has it been asked *how* those better teachers are to teach those better students in those better schools, and how the new materials are to be made effective.

There are, of course, truly artful teachers and brilliant students. Perhaps some day we will understand their skills and talents and how they acquired them, so that we can systematically produce more of them. At present, however, they are true exceptions that defy specification. We simply do not know what makes an artful teacher. So most teachers must make do with information, routines, and rules of thumb passed on to them by other teachers, or rely primarily on their own experience. Unfortunately it is very difficult for teachers to learn from their experience; they rarely see any of their long-term successes or failures, and they have neither the time nor the skills to trace any short-term effects to their specific causes. And most students spend most of their school days doing or trying to avoid things they don't want to do. Though

91

we've abandoned the cane, education is still based largely on punishment (scolding, ridicule, loss of privileges, embarrassment, extra work, fines, expulsion).

This intuitive and compulsory approach to teaching is no longer necessary. A more effective technology of teaching is becoming available. Based on laws and principles derived from an experimental analysis of human behavior, teaching can be viewed not simply as the dispensing of information in entertaining ways, but as the careful arrangement of relationships between a student's behavior and the events that precede and follow it so that he learns. The resulting methods are especially useful for the 90 percent or so of the teachers who are not artful and of the students who are not already brilliant.[1]

Careful observation is the basis of any science. Of course, people are always observing things, but scientific observation is different from everyday observation because it includes observations of behaviors or events in great detail, accompanied by the precise recording and measurement of these details. When many such observations have been made of the same event in the same situation, the scientist can use this precise information to define relationships between this event and others, as well as to predict new occurrences of this event.

An example: Hilary Rottenkid is a student in a school near you. Everyday observation of Hilary has been done by teachers, parents, social workers, probation officers, etc. They describe Hilary as hyperactive, unpopular, fat, emotionally disturbed, and mentally retarded. Notice that none of these terms describe Hilary's behavior (what he *does*). If you sat in on his class in order to observe and record hyperactive events, or unpopular behavior, or the details of his learning disability, you would have trouble being specific. And if a friend of yours did the same thing during the same class period, chances are your two records wouldn't agree at all. Of course you could observe and measure his fatness by putting him on a scale. But how do you

---

1. Why can't we train teachers to be artful teachers?

2. How does the experimental analysis of behavior define teaching?

3. Can you identify the basic elements of any science (observe, record, measure, relate, predict)? What's the difference between everyday observation and scientific observation?

4. How would you define "emotionally disturbed?" Is your definition precise—based on observable behaviors—so that other people could use only your definition to agree on exactly which students are or are not "emotionally disturbed?" Try it; if you have difficulty—join the club!

---

[1] See B. F. Skinner's *The Technology of Teaching* (Appleton-Century-Crofts, 1968), especially chapters 2, 4 and 5.

measure hyperactivity? When Hilary trips another student in the aisle, or gets out of his seat, are these always instances of hyperactivity?

Science requires that objects of study be events or behaviors that are clearly observable and measurable, and that the descriptions of these events be in *behavioral terms*—terms that identify behaviors clearly enough for several people to agree on the occurrence or nonoccurrence of the behavior. In the case of Hilary Rottenkid, this means observing and measuring what Hilary does, and when, how often, after what other events, and before what other events. We might find for example, that Hilary got out of his seat twenty times during the period, and each time the teacher yelled "sit down" or "get back in your seat, kid" (kid was one of his nicknames). On five of these occasions the teacher didn't notice Hilary out of his seat for about a minute, until he had bumped, punched, or thrown something at another student. The other student responded with "get lost, kid," or a counterblow, which of course attracted the teacher's attention and another "sit down." After each such command, Hilary sat down.

These behavioral records are useful because they represent real behaviors. We can begin to predict some behaviors of Hilary (when he will sit down) and of the teacher and other students (when they will say "get lost" or "sit down"). And we begin to see some relationships between behavioral events. Whenever the teacher says "sit down," Hilary sits down (which is probably why the teacher keeps saying it). Why does Hilary keep getting up and disturbing others? One possibility is that whenever he does, he gets attention—the teacher looks at him and talks to him (even if it is critically), and at times other students do too. But this is not an empirical statement, it is just a guess. Hilary might also have a nervous system that won't allow him to sit still for more than a few minutes at a time. An empirical statement about these behavioral relationships must, by definition, be *based on data* carefully collected and precisely measured.

If there is a relationship between Hilary's getting-out-of-seat behavior and the teacher's yelling at him, then one behavior should change when the other does. We could investigate this by changing the variable we guess is controlling the behavior. In this example, we could make sure that the teacher yelled at Hilary within five seconds *every time* he got out of his seat (perhaps his seat could be wired so that when he got out, a small light went on behind some books on the teacher's desk). If after several days of this, we counted Hilary's getting-out-of-seat behavior and found that it had increased from twenty to thirty-five times, we would have some empirical evidence for stating that there was a *functional* or controlling relationship between these two behaviors.

It's still possible, however, that some other event "caused" the increase. So we might try another change. Say we arranged it so that the teacher *never* paid attention to Hilary when he was *out* of his seat, but *always* gave him some kind of attention whenever he had been *in* his seat for more than 2 minutes. If after several days we counted only 5 out-of-seat behaviors by Hilary during a class period, we would have convincing evidence that these forms of teacher attention were controlling out-of-seat behavior. Furthermore we would know that teacher-attention also could control the opposite behavior (in-seat) and probably several other behaviors besides.

This was a hypothetical example. Hilary's behavior might just as well have been controlled by the attention of other students, his math workbook, or a hemorrhoid. The point is, we can't be sure until we observe and record specific behaviors, describe them in measurable terms, and look for empirical relationships between them.

> 5. Construct your own hypothetical behavior-problem example. Specify the precise behaviors, frequency records, "guess" relationships to other events, and empirical procedures for defining the real controlling relationship.

Notice in the example that once we had decided on *specific behaviors* to observe, we were able to obtain some useful information. In practice we might refer to Hilary's behaviors as "hyperactive" behaviors; and as long as that name refers to those observable and measurable behaviors, it is simply a shorthand label for those behaviors. But frequently these labels become implied explanations. The label "hyperactive" is often used not only to describe a class of physical activity behaviors by a student, but also to explain why the student does all these things; emotional immaturity might be used to describe a student who does not study by himself for more than a few minutes at a time, who throws temper tantrums, who demands his way with other students, etc., but the label frequently implies that the reason why he does these things is because there is some part of his body or mind which has not developed beyond the infant stage. The same is true for such labels as slow learner, intelligent, popular, aggressive, good attitude, paranoia, learning disability, bright, etc. Rarely do we have any empirical justification for claiming a causal connection between the behaviors we observe and their implied internal cause, because nowhere do we make contact with anything except the behaviors themselves.

It is easy to fall into this *pseudoexplanation trap*. If you observe one of your students reading books at every opportunity, taking them home with him, working hard to finish other assignments so that he can read a few minutes extra, and talking a lot about the books he has read, you would report to his parents that this student has a good attitude towards reading, or that he likes to read. If they ask you how you know that, you can describe the set of behaviors that you referred to when you said he likes to read. If they ask you why he reads so much, you might say it's because he likes to read or because he loves reading for its own sake. This answer is not really an answer at all: it doesn't explain the behaviors nor add any new information. To say that he likes to read means that he reads a lot; "he reads a lot because he likes to read" is the same as "he reads a lot because he reads a lot."

A *pseudoexplanation* (pseudo is a Greek word meaning false or deceiving) is born when we take an everyday label that we use to summarize a class of behaviors and begin to imply that the label actually is a cause of these behaviors. Of course, this is circular; we start with several behaviors, put them together with a shorthand label (rather than describing each behavior every time we want to refer to it), then presume that because these behaviors all have the same label, they are therefore caused by the same thing, and finally we imply that this cause for these behaviors is in fact the label, which originally was no more than a communications convenience.

But this circularity is usually subtle. We don't usually come right out and say that Johnny is unable to read because he has a disability; we frequently leave it as an unspoken implication. The danger, of course, is that when we have a pseudoexplanation for a problem, we stop looking for the real explanation, and choose ineffective methods for changing the behaviors. As if that's not bad enough, pseudoexplanations often lead to *expectancy effects,* sometimes called the Pygmalion effect (recall the plot in Shaw's play or in *My Fair Lady*). Labels, as well as many other aspects of the educational environment, can and do establish expectations of what a student will achieve in school, and these expectations often come true—a sort of self-fulfilling prophesy. However, although a teacher may wish or hope that a student will do well, her realistic expectations for him can be affected by the student's past IQ score, notes and labels given him by past teachers, his race and social class. Thus, the teacher's expectations alter the teaching behaviors and ultimately the achievement results of the student. This effect is predictable in certain settings, particularly urban, where the overall expectations are low.[2]

A science of learning must go beyond pseudoexplanations. *Empirical explanations* begin with careful and systematic observation of specific behaviors that are really observable and measurable. Then by careful and controlled manipulation of one factor or variable in the situation, and then another and another, relationships between the behavior and other (preceding or following) events can be measured and defined. The general procedure is:

1. Specify the behavior precisely enough so that independent observers would all agree when it occurs and when it does not occur.

2. Record the repeated occurrence of this behavior, its frequency during a set period of time, its duration each occurrence, and its intensity; record events that are antecedent to or consequent to the behavior; record also any changes in the situation or time or place in which the behavior occurs.

---

[2] For an interesting review of related studies, see Finn, J. D., Expectations and the Educational Environment, *Review of Educational Research,* 1972, *42,* 387–410.

3. When the data show that a certain event reliably precedes or follows the behavior whenever it occurs, then test the relationship between these two events. For example, see what happens to the behavior when the preceding or consequent event is arranged so as not to occur with the behavior.

4. If the behavior ceases or drops dramatically in frequency, then you can say empirically that these two events are actually related.

Such relationships are also called *functional relationships*. As in math, one thing is a function of another when its occurrence is in some way or to some degree dependent on the occurrence of the other. Two behavioral events are functionally related when one's frequency or duration is dependent on the other's frequency or duration, as in the case of Hilary Rottenkid's out-of-seat behavior and his teacher's attention to it.

---

6. What is pseudoexplanation? Give an original example, and show how it might develop.

7. Explain how a pseudoexplanation can lead to a harmful expectancy effect.

8. What does "empirical" mean? What is a "functional relationship?" What are the specific steps in developing an empirical explanation of a functional relationship?

Once a teacher has identified a functional relationship between some behavioral events in the learning situation, he has acquired scientific knowledge about that learning, which can be put to use in two powerful ways. First of all, if the occurrence and characteristics of Event B depend on the occurrence and characteristics of Event A, then your knowledge of Event A gives you the ability to *predict* the occurrence and characteristics of Event B. In Hilary's case, we can use the identified functional relationship between Hilary's out-of-seat behavior and the teacher's yelling at him to predict several things: about how many times Hilary will get out of his seat tomorrow, how often the teacher will yell at him tomorrow, what would happen if the teacher stopped yelling at him, etc.

In addition, functional relationships give you the ability to *control* Event B, by arranging that Event A does or does not occur, by changing some characteristics (such as the frequency or duration) of Event A, or by inserting another controlling event between A and B. In Hilary's case, we can use the identified functional relationship to control either Hilary's behavior or the teacher's behavior. Hilary is already controlling the teacher's behavior, whether she knows it or not. Hilary can get the teacher to yell or to stop yelling, just by varying his out-of-seat behavior. And the teacher can control Hilary's out-of-seat behavior by varying her response to him. This hypothetical case is symptomatic of most social-interaction situations. What we do depends largely on how people have in the past reacted (and can be expected to react) to similar behaviors of ours; but their responses are also controlled in turn by our reactions. Control of human behavior is always a two-way process.

Behaviors or events such as these, when under scientific observation, are often called variables. The term *dependent variable* refers to the specific behavior whose occurrence or frequency or value is dependent on the occurrence (or frequency or value) of another behavior or event. This other event is then called the *independent variable,* since its occurrence or characteristics are independent—not dependent on the occurrence of the first behavior. In the above description, the antecedent event (Event A) is the independent variable, and Event B is the dependent variable. In Hilary's case, his out-of-seat behavior is the dependent variable, since its occurrence and frequency varied with (was dependent on) the teacher's attention behavior (the independent variable). Notice that in Hilary's case and in many other cases the dependent variable might just as well have been the independent variable. If our immediate focus of interest had been on the teacher's yelling behavior, we would have observed and measured its occurrences and its antecedent and consequent events. We would have found, of course, that the teacher's yelling behavior (which we have now made our dependent variable) was indeed functionally dependent on the antecedent event of Hilary's getting out of his seat (our new independent variable). This interchangeableness is to be expected, however, when we realize that every behavior is controlled by some other event or events, and every behavior, in turn, controls some other event or events, in some way or to some degree. In practice, then, the dependent variable is the behavior we want to be able to predict and control, and the independent variable is the behavior we hope will provide the tools to do so.

---

9. Construct original examples of the two main uses of identified functional relationships.

10. Can you distinguish between independent and dependent variables? Construct original examples.

THE MAKING OF
A BEHAVIOR

Let's consider now some of the general terms, principles and procedures of the analysis of human learning. In general, the probability that a specific kind of behavior will occur (or will not occur) depends on three kinds of variables: (1) the antecedent events and conditions which precede and accompany the behavior; (2) the contingencies which functionally relate the behavior to its immediate and historical consequences; and (3) the consequent events themselves. We'll look at these three sets of variables in some detail, though not in the above order.

Consequent Events

Most behavior is functionally related to its *consequences*. Such behavior is called operant behavior. When we flick a light switch, we get light; when we work we get a paycheck; when Hilary got out of his seat, he got a response from his teacher. The probability of just about every kind of behavior depends on its consequences. If you didn't get light after flicking the switch, you'd soon stop flicking the switch; if the paycheck stopped coming, you'd stop working (unless there were some other favorable consequences for working); when Hilary no longer got the teacher's attention, his disruptive behavior decreased; and when Hilary started getting attention when he was in his seat, he stayed in his seat more.

Naturally, a behavior which is already completed can't then be changed. What changes is the probability that *that kind of behavior* will occur again. So when we speak of "behavior" being affected by its consequences, we mean behavior of a certain kind.

This is a basic law of behavior: *A behavior's probability depends on its consequences.* And like the law of gravity and other laws of nature, this law of behavior applies to all humans, twenty-four hours a day, at home, work, and in the classroom, and to elementary, secondary and college students as well as to their teachers. Furthermore, this functional relationship between behavior and its consequences is true whether this relationship is purely accidental or deliberately arranged. The art of teaching starts to become a science when the teacher starts to arrange these relationships carefully in order to facilitate each student's learning.

Contingency

The usual name for behavior-consequence relations is "contingency." A contingency is a specific relationship between a certain behavior and a certain consequence; the relationship specifies that *if and only if* the behavior occurs will this consequence occur. Contingencies can be purely natural (if a person steps out of a thirteenth floor window, he will be mopped up off the street), or carefully arranged ("if you practice your piano lesson for thirty minutes, you can watch the next TV show"), or completely unintended (a child hates to see his father come home from work, because he frequently punishes the boy for the day's misbehaviors identified by the mother).

---

1. Identify the three kinds of variables which together determine the probability of a behavior occurring.
2. The consequences of a specific behavioral event don't change that event. What do they change?
3. Give an example of a behavior of your own and show how it is controlled by its consequences. Identify the contingency and the reinforcing or punishing event.
4. Give an example of another person's behavior that is controlled by the consequences that *you* give or don't give. Identify the contingency and the reinforcing or punishing event.
5. Can you define "contingency?" Construct original examples of natural, accidental, and arranged contingencies.

Since there are innumerable kinds of events that occur as a consequence of behavior, the best way to talk about consequent events is in terms of their *effect* on the behavior they follow. If a consequent event maintains or increases the frequency of a behavior it is called a *reinforcer*. If a consequent event decreases the frequency of a behavior it is called a *punisher*. If a consequent event has no effect, it is called a neutral event. For example, if you criticize a friend whenever he brags to you about his accomplishments, your criticism is a reinforcing consequence if his bragging to you continues or increases; your criticism is a punisher if his bragging to you decreases; and your criticism is neutral if his bragging continues whether you criticize it or not.

Notice that there is no such thing as a reinforcer or punisher *un*related to an actual behavior. We can't say that food is always a reinforcer; people who are very sick to their stomach do not come to the dinner table because the consequences (smell, sight, and eating of food) are punishing to them. As we have seen, criticism can reinforce some behavior, and punish other behavior. Before we decide whether a certain consequent event will act as a punisher or a reinforcer for a given behavior, we have to look at its *actual effect* on the behavior. In other words, reinforcers and punishers must be defined behaviorally.

The temptation is to decide beforehand what is reinforcing and what is not. The problem with this is that the *real effects* of consequent events are not at all influenced by the names we give them. This is the danger in thinking of a reinforcement as "the giving of a reward." Some consequences that we call "rewards" will strengthen some behaviors; some don't. Some "punishers" also strengthen behavior. Remember in grade school when the teacher loudly and publicly ridiculed Tommy Largemouth for being the only bad boy in her class? Remember seeing Tommy grinning from ear to ear after receiving this individual attention? What was the effect on his behavior? Often a child will figure that any attention is better than none. Furthermore, the same "thing" can act as both a punisher and a reinforcer, depending on whether it is presented or withdrawn. Giving someone a kiss can reinforce a lot of preceding behaviors; withholding a kiss can punish the same behaviors. If you find the loud, constant talking of your friend punishing, then any behaviors that remove you from that noise (or the noise from you) will likely be strengthened. For this reason, the total consequent *event* is more important than the "thing." A consequent event can be the presentation of a thing, the occurrence of a behavior by someone else, an opportunity to do something, the withdrawal of a thing, the nonoccurrence of a usual behavioral response, the elimination of an opportunity to do something, etc. For example, money is a *thing,* but it cannot be a reinforcing *event* for you unless you are given the opportunity to receive it; *receiving* money or spending it is a reinforcing event. Whatever the event is, if it follows a behavior and strengthens it, then it is a reinforcer and the process of following the behavior with this event is called reinforcement. If the event follows a behavior and weakens it, then that event is a punisher, and the process of following the behavior with that event is called punishment. To test your understanding of these definitions, try these questions:

(a) You tell your date, "Sorry, no necking tonight because you got angry with several other drivers. You know I think that's dangerous and childish. Goodnight!" Is this an example of reinforcement? Punishment? If so, what is the reinforcer or punisher?

(b) During the next several dates, your friend restrains himself from reacting dangerously to other drivers. Now can you say what has happened?

(c) After these dates, you thank him for his improved driving and give him a kiss, etc. The improved driving continues. What is the reinforcer?

(d) Whenever the child whines or cries to get her way, her mother calmly puts her in a chair (or empty playpen or crib) and says "When you are done, you can get down and play again." After several days of this contingency, the whining has almost disappeared. Is this reinforcement? Punishment? If so, what is the reinforcer or punisher?

(e) The coach says "five extra laps for anyone missing a signal." The players are more attentive to the signals. Is this reinforcement or punishment? Careful!

Answers:

(a) Reinforcement and punishment are defined behaviorally, that is, in terms of the actual effect on subsequent behavior. In this example, you don't know the effect so you can't tell.

(b) Now the change in driving behavior appears to indicate that you have punished the behavior of getting back at other drivers.

(c) You (presumably) are reinforcing his restraint with your acts of affection. Notice that the reinforcer is an event, or at least the expected opportunity for that event.

(d) The whining behavior is being punished by requiring the child to stay in his chair, and perhaps also by withdrawing his opportunity to play.

(e) This is reinforcement because the attentive behavior increases. The reinforcing event is the absence of a punisher.

Notice that we can reinforce and punish by not giving something as well as by giving something. We can reinforce by delivering a reinforcer (e.g., a kiss) or by withdrawing a punisher (less running). We can punish by delivering a punisher (sit in your chair) or by withdrawing a reinforcer (not tonight, Henry). The critical question is: What is the effect on behavior?

Sometimes you will hear people using the term "negative reinforcement" to refer to punishment. This, of course, is a contradiction in terms and makes for confusing communication. By definition, reinforcement strengthens behavior, so it can't weaken behavior, even if it is "negative." Negative reinforcement refers to the process of strengthening a behavior by withdrawing a consequent punishing event.

> 6. Be able to define reinforcer, punisher, and neutral consequence, with original examples involving *you* as the person who is either behaving or administering the consequences. Identify the contingency in each example.
> 7. Is praise a reinforcer? Is spanking or scolding a punisher?
> 8. Why is a reinforcer an event rather than a thing?

If some events act as reinforcers for some people and as punishers for others, and in some situations but not in others, we have a real problem in identifying how an event will function without having to try it out first. There are several ways to be fairly certain beforehand.

Some events are reinforcers or punishers because of their dependence on our biological makeup. We all seem to come equipped from birth with the capacity to be reinforced by food when we are food-deprived (and the more deprived we are, the less difference it makes what kind of food it is), by water when we have been deprived of water, by many kinds of sensory stimulation (visual, tactile, auditory, movement in space, etc.), and by a variety of other bodily conditions which are related to the survival of the individual or the species. Similarly, there are biologically-dependent events which are punishers for us all, such as blows and cuts to the body, organic malfunctions, extremes of heat and cold, loud noise, etc. We can usually rely on such events having pretty much the same effect on most humans. Such events which are biologically-related are called *unconditioned,* or unlearned, or primary reinforcers and punishers. They make up only a small proportion of the important consequent events that influence human behavior.

A far larger proportion of reinforcing and punishing events is related to the specific culture and the individual experiences of each of us. These events are called *conditioned,* or learned, or secondary reinforcers and punishers. At birth these events were neutral events for each of us. But as we began growing and experiencing, some of these neutral consequent events were frequently *paired* (presented at the same time) with unconditioned reinforcing (punishing) events. The gradual effect of this frequent pairing was to give the neutral event the effect of a reinforcing event. In our culture, such events as approving or disapproving, smiling or frowning, and giving money, become conditioned reinforcers because of their frequent relation, often right from birth, to other unconditioned consequent events.

Pairing

Consider the following example from a study of smiling behavior in infants. Every time the four-month infant smiled, the mother picked him up, smiled in return, spoke softly to the child, jostled, patted, and stroked him for half a minute. After a series of such events, the smiling behavior of the infant increased from two to over five times per five minutes. Some of these consequent events, such as the jostling, were functioning as unconditional reinforcers (reinforcing the infant's smiling), but other events, such as the return smile and the talking, were probably neutral events that were being paired with the unconditioned reinforcers. Later these events will come to act as conditioned reinforcers for this child because of this pairing. However, the effect of this type of pairing is not permanent; the pairing of a conditioned reinforcer with some unconditioned reinforcer must be repeated at least occasionally or the conditioned reinforcer will lose its reinforcing properties.

As another example, consider praise. At birth, praise was not a reinforcer, but now it is for most of us because very early in life praise accompanied a variety of other consequences that were already reinforcing. And if a student is not turned on by a teacher's praise, she can usually change that by giving him a lot of actual reinforcers for small tasks done well and pairing them each time with praise for the work.

In pairing, the neutral consequent event does not have to be paired with an unconditional event: it can be paired with an event that was itself previously conditioned. In general, to make a neutral consequent event into a reinforcing or punishing consequence, arrange so that when the reinforcing event is given, the neutral event also occurs at the same time or just before it.

Conditioned reinforcers can develop in another way, by being made means to a reinforcing end. If a chain of successive responses and consequent events is related in such a way that each member of the chain is a necessary condition for obtaining the next member, but only the final event was a reinforcer before the chain began, then the intermediate events become conditioned reinforcers because they are conditions to the final reinforcing condition. This process is called *chaining*. Money becomes a conditioned reinforcer by chaining; we work, then we get money, then we pay money and get other learned reinforcers, or unlearned reinforcers like food. For a hungry man, food is an unlearned reinforcer, but a city map which helps him locate a restaurant, the

Pairing:

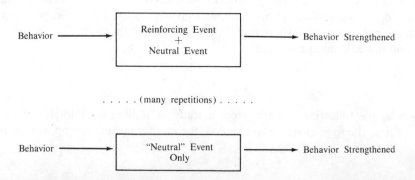

starting of the car after he gets in and turns the key, the appearance of certain street signs after he drives along the road, the appearance of the restaurant after he turns the corner, the arrival of the waitress after he sits down at a table, the descriptions on the menu after he opens it, etc., are all conditioned reinforcers for him, presuming he has had previous experience with these events.

By following a behavior with both a reinforcer (which by itself would strengthen the behavior) and at the same time a neutral event (which by itself would have no effect), the neutral event will gradually take on the reinforcing properties of the reinforcing event and will no longer be "neutral."

Chaining:

$$\text{Behavior}_1 \rightarrow \text{Neutral}_1 \rightarrow \text{Behavior}_2 \rightarrow \text{Neutral}_2 \rightarrow \text{Behavior}_3 \rightarrow \text{Rfer}$$

$$\ldots \ldots \text{(repetitions)}$$

$$\text{Behavior}_1 \rightarrow \text{"Neutral}_1\text{"} \rightarrow \text{Behavior}_2 \rightarrow \text{"Neutral}_2\text{"} \rightarrow \text{Behavior}_3 \rightarrow \text{Rfer}$$

$$\text{or Behavior}_1 \rightarrow \text{"Neutral}_1\text{"} \rightarrow \text{Behavior}_1 \text{Strengthened}$$

In this situation, the formerly neutral events become conditioned reinforcers (Rfer) by being frequent links to an event that is already reinforcing. Then, like money, such "neutral" consequences can stand by themselves as reinforcing events.

One difference between pairing and chaining that may help you is the time lag between the neutral event and the reinforcing event: in pairing, there is no time lag, but in chaining, the neutral event leads to, and occurs some time before the terminal reinforcing event.

9. Be able to define unconditioned (unlearned) and conditioned (learned) reinforcers and punishers, with original examples of each as they affect you.

10. How do neutral events become reinforcers or punishers? (Hint: pair, chain.) Construct an original example of each and describe how the event came to be reinforcing (or punishing) for you.

HOW TO TEACH
A STUDENT TO LIKE
(OR HATE) SCHOOL

Premack Principle

While unconditioned (unlearned) events affect most humans in generally the same way, we can't be as certain about the effectiveness of conditioned (learned) events before we actually see their effect on behavior, because we often cannot know enough about the history of an individual to be sure the event is actually a reinforcing event for him, at the particular time, and in the specific situation. There is, however, a quick way to assess the relative effectiveness of a great many such events and it doesn't require detailed knowledge of the individual's conditioning history. It is based on a general rule called the Premack Principle (first analyzed and stated by psychologist David Premack, in 1959) which states that of any two events or behaviors, the more probable one will function as a reinforcer for the less probable one. A very loose way of saying this is "Do what I want you to do, then you can do what you want to do." But "want" is hard to specify behaviorally. A more precise and helpful statement of the principle is this: *If any higher frequency behavior is made contingent on a lower frequency behavior, the lower frequency behavior will be strengthened* (that is, it will increase in frequency).

The use of this principle makes it much easier to identify beforehand some effective reinforcing events for a given individual, especially in the classroom. Consider this situation: In a classroom, we arrange materials for a variety of activities, including some reading material, some math workbooks and games, some materials for physics and electricity experiments, a phonograph with records and a headset, etc. We allow the students *free access* to any of these activities for one-half hour and we record the amount of time each student spends in each activity. We find that Wenda Whoopy spends fifteen minutes grooming herself, five minutes talking with Gladys and ten minutes promenading among the boys. The Premack principle tells us that if we restrict Wenda's access to the comb and mirror, and make such access contingent on a specified period of time talking to Gladys (that is, talk to Gladys in order to groom), we can increase the amount of time she spends talking to Gladys. Of course, we could make any of the other activities in which she didn't spend any time contingent on the opportunity to groom and strut (for example, a small math or reading assignment), and any of those would increase also. Say we also observe that Timothy Titmouse spends all his time reading and seldom talks to anyone. If we observe that these preferences remain fairly stable over several observation periods, we might decide to make Tim's opportunity to read contingent on a little social activity, such as five minutes of talking with a classmate, or playing a game with several others. In this way we would be reinforcing a less preferred activity with a more preferred activity.

The educational importance of this principle is that it gives the teacher an easy to use motivational system. All she has to do is observe her students, measure their preferences among the available activities, and make access to one activity dependent on prior engagement in a less preferred activity. She can use the activities already available, without needing to bring in a lot of elaborate activities from elsewhere. And she can be pretty sure, in advance, that her choice of reinforcing events is accurate, because it is based on student preferences in a free-access situation.

Relativity

The Premack Principle illustrates another important fact about reinforcement: the actual effectiveness of reinforcing or punishing events is *relative*—relative to other possible consequent events, and relative to other circumstances or situational variables. In Wenda's case, for example, promenading could be used as a reinforcer (that is, a high probability event) for talking with Gladys, and for math, reading, etc., but not for grooming. So promenading is a reinforcer for Wenda, depending on what other options are available to her. Watching a football game regularly on Saturday may be a reinforcing event for you, unless on a given Saturday you are given tickets to a game; the chance to actually go to the game might decrease the reinforcing effectiveness of watching TV. So reinforcement is relative to the *other options* that are available, and the effectiveness of a specific consequent event depends on whether it is a higher or lower probability event than these other options.

In addition, reinforcement is relative to other *situational* factors, present or past. There are a variety of ways in which this relativity takes effect. For example, the relative probabilities of several consequent events can easily change over time. If a student prefers reading to math, and if reading is made contingent on math for a period of time, doing math correctly might eventually become the preferred activity of the two, especially if the contingencies are carefully arranged. Current situational factors can also modify the reinforcing effectiveness of a consequent event. Watching a certain weekly TV show may be a regular reinforcing event for you, but if on a given day the show is a rerun, the event might lose some of its reinforcing value.

As we have seen, food is a reinforcer in one situation (hunger) and a punisher in another situation (nausea) for the same person, and it is probably a neutral event just after a satisfying meal. To move to a room that has a temperature of thirty degrees is a reinforcing or a punishing event, depending on whether the room you left was zero degrees or sixty degrees. If someone smiles at you and says "good work," this consequent event is reinforcing or punishing, depending on whether you had just completed a good piece of work or just tripped over your feet and landed in the mud.

These examples of the various ways in which reinforcement is relative illustrate the need for careful and continuing consideration of the past and present circumstances surrounding the consequent events and their relationships to behaviors.

> 1. Can you define the Premack principle *precisely*, with an original illustration of how you have used or experienced it?
>
> 2. Think of several specific ways you could use the Premack principle to improve your teaching.
>
> 3. Construct original examples illustrating several ways in which consequent events are relative in their effect for you.

Extinction

As we saw before, the effects of most reinforcing and punishing events are somewhat temporary. When a reinforcing event no longer follows a certain kind of behavior, and when the behavior is not otherwise reinforced, the frequency of that behavior will eventually decrease. This process of withholding all reinforcing consequences for a certain behavior is called *extinction*. We saw an example of extinction when the teacher ignored Hilary's out-of-seat behavior.

Extinction works if the reinforcer for the behavior is completely withdrawn. But the "if" is critical and sometimes difficult to pull off, for two reasons: First, withdrawing one reinforcing consequence for the behavior may not be enough; there may be *other reinforcing events* which we overlook or over which we have no control, and these may continue to operate to maintain the behavior. In Hilary's case, the attention from other students for his antics might maintain (reinforce) his behavior, even though his teacher was attempting to extinguish that behavior by withholding her attention to it. (Notice that extinction, like reinforcement and punishment, is defined by its effect on behavior, not simply by the procedure that is used.) A second reason why extinction is sometimes difficult is because its effectiveness requires complete *consistency*. It's tough to consistently withhold attention from someone who keeps whapping you on the back. When a child puts up a fuss at not being able to have or do something, you might be able to ignore his fussing consistently for a while; but it becomes increasingly difficult as his fussing becomes louder and more disruptive. Then, when you give in with attention, one of the things you have reinforced is the increased intensity of his fussing and, by definition, the chances are greater that he will yell louder the next time he wants his way. Once you decide to ignore a bit of behavior, you can't allow any exception to occur.

TIME-OUT

A stronger type of the extinction procedure, called "time-out," sometimes helps to overcome both these difficulties. Time-out means the loss of *all* reinforcers for *all* responses for a certain period of time following a certain kind of behavior. A child who throws a tantrum can be put in a room until a minute or two after he stops fussing. If the procedure is carried out calmly, quickly, and with as little attention as possible, if the room is devoid of potential reinforcing activities, and if subsequent good behavior is immediately reinforced, the tantrum behavior will quickly decrease in frequency after several such experiences.

Children and adolescents sometimes use a form of time-out with their peers by excluding one member from all activities of the group because of some behavior. The exclusion is not usually permanent unless the behavior reoccurs. Adults are reported to do the same thing on occasion. Teachers used to combine time out and ridicule (punishment) by using a dunce cap and a chair facing the wall for misbehaving students. Many teachers today think of ways to use time-out (but without ridicule) for an especially disruptive student, but it generally is not necessary for very long. Remember that in using time-out it is important to reinforce desired behavior immediately and frequently.

Preceding Events

So far we've looked at behaviors, consequences, and the contingencies relating one to the other. There is a third variable that influences the probability of human behavior—the preceding stimulus conditions which set the occasion for the response or behavior to occur. A preceding stimulus is an event that precedes a kind of behavior, and influences when or how the behavior will occur. The clock has a great deal of this kind of "stimulus control" over our daily behaviors, because our past experience has taught us that at such-and-such a time, we had better get moving or we will miss the bus or ride to school, that another time is the period for eating, etc. When a teacher says "Look at this" or when he starts writing on the board, this is a preceding stimulus for the student's response of looking. The consequence is the information conveyed. In most cases the degree of control that a preceding stimulus event has will depend on the *consequences* for responding to that event. If the information the teacher offers is seen as worthless and of no personal consequence to the student, the student is apt to stop looking in response to future stimulus events of this kind.

Preceding stimuli are important in education in various ways. A great deal of school work, such as reading printed symbols, adding numbers on a page, following printed diagrams, interpreting formulas, etc., are tasks which require certain kinds of responses to certain kinds of preceding stimuli. We can get such responses going in the first place by using heavy prompts, which are one kind of preceding stimulus. We might say to a student: "What is this letter" (a preceding stimulus), to which he replies: "I don't know." (his response to the question and to the written letter "M"). We could then introduce another kind of preceding stimulus, a prompt, by saying "Say Mmmmmmm," while also showing him the letter "M". Since the child already can produce imitative responses, he says "mmmmmm," and we can consequate that response by saying "good."

By itself this bit of chaining is not enough to teach the child to say "Mmmmmmm" whenever he sees the letter "M". But by *pairing* one preceding stimulus (the prompt) that already gets the desired response with the preceding stimulus that we want to control the response (the letter "M"), and by reinforcing the response in the presence of both stimuli, we have increased the probability of that stimulus-response relationship.

In this method of pairing preceding stimuli, several elements are necessary: (a) a preceding stimulus which elicits the desired response, (b) a preceding stimulus which does not elicit the desired response (but which you wish to do so eventually), (c) pairing these two preceding stimuli, and (d) reinforcing the correct response when it occurs in the presence of these preceding events. The result of this pairing will be that eventually the response will occur to the desired preceding stimulus when presented by itself.

In sports and music, we learn by making responses to several types of preceding stimuli. Some of these preceding events strongly affect the response (e.g., instructions, sample response by another for our imitation), while others have little or no effect at first (e.g., what we are thinking or saying to ourselves, the kinesthetic feedback or "feel" of the previous response, the sound of the previous chord, the notes on a page). But these "neutral" preceding stimuli soon gain more and more control because of their regular pairing with the stimulus that has already elicited the response. When a checkout person, for example, first learns to punch the cash register keys, the controlling preceding stimulus is the symbol on each key; but gradually the control shifts to kinesthetic feedback cues (the *feel* of where the fingers are in relation to parts of the machine), and the checkout person no longer needs to look at the keys. These feedback cues were there all along, but only by consistent pairing with the controlling preceding stimulus (sight of the key symbols) did they gain effectiveness as controlling preceding stimuli.

In addition, we want to make sure the student attends to and responds only to those characteristics of the preceding stimulus that are *essential*. We do this by varying the nonessential characteristics of the stimulus (the size of the letter "M", its position on a page, its shape, etc.), and by presenting stimuli that have none of the essential characteristics of our target stimulus) such as the letter n, or e, or p), and consequating each response accordingly.

When a person consistently responds one way to one stimulus and another way to a different stimulus (e.g., to the letters "M" and "N"), we say he has learned a *discrimination*. In Chemistry, a student learns to discriminate between (respond differently to) the symbols NaCl and HCl or he's in big trouble. Notice that the learning of a discrimination is defined by the discrimination *performance* of the learner, not by what he or his teacher says he has been taught or by what lesson he has been submitted to.

There is another, perhaps competitive, process called *generalization,* which means that a person responds the same way to two different stimuli which have much in common. A student may respond the same way to the letters "M" and "N" or to "b" and "d", because each member of the pair has several characteristics in common with the other. We usually don't discriminate between such comments as "good work," "beautiful job," "well done," "fine job," or "right on;" they are all seen as social reinforcers for something we have just said or done. If we teach a child that the color of a fire-engine is called "red," then he is likely (but less so) to call burgundy or light-red "red."

---

4. Can you illustrate two problems to be careful about in using extinction?

5. In what kind of situation would you use time-out rather than extinction?

6. Can you think of an original example in which one kind of preceding stimulus is used to get a response under the control of another preceding stimulus? Explain how it developed.

7. Check to see if you can define preceding stimulus, discrimination, and generalization, with original examples.

And there is the story of a college student who regularly slept from the beginning of a certain class straight through to the bell. During one class, he abruptly sat up, closed his notebook and headed for the door, because an alarm clock had been set off beneath his chair. He generalized when he should have discriminated.

Later units will analyze more thoroughly these and other aspects of the preceding stimulus variable in human learning and teaching.

Rules for Managing Consequences

By way of both review and application, let's look at some rules for using the above principles effectively in the classroom. Keep in mind, however, that although we use labels like "teacher" and "student," the rules apply also to other relationships such as parent-child, friend-friend, husband-wife, and counselor-counselee. And even in the classroom, the roles of teacher and student are often reversed in the dynamic interplay, especially since the good teacher learns something everytime he interacts with a student.*

Rule 1: Consequence Identification. Describe consequent events (reinforcers or punishers) *only* in terms of their effect on the student. To put it negatively, don't call a consequent event a reinforcer for a certain student because you think it will maintain or increase his behavior or because it has worked that way for other students. It's perfectly reasonable for you to use these reasons for making your initial choice of consequent events for a student. But you can't be sure they will work that way for this student until you try them or until you assess his preferences in a free-access situation. Most students will work for praise and attention, but some will not; other students will work for the attention of their peers, but not for yours. Even though having students compete for a set number of A's and B's seems to be reinforcing to many teachers and administrators, it may not be so for some students, particularly those who rarely got such a mark in the past. Nor is what a student says about his own motivation the critical factor; students who say they are trying as hard as they can and really want to learn a particular subject can still show considerable improvement when contingencies for academic improvement are carefully arranged.

This rule applies also to punishers. A teacher frequently uses "punishing consequences" such as scolding, criticizing, or embarrassing a student because she is immediately reinforced for doing so—the student stops his misbehavior,

---

* The following section is partly based on *Management of Behavioral Consequences in Education,* an excellent monograph by Jack Michael, published by the Southwest Regional Laboratory for Educational Research and Development, Inglewood, California, 1967. Material is used with permission.

or freezes in his tracks, or blushes, or stares in rapt attention. But is her consequence a punisher for the student? Careful observation frequently shows that the behavior the teacher criticizes continues to occur at least as often, even though it stopped momentarily when she scolded. If a behavior is being maintained or increased, it is being reinforced. In this case the teacher's attention to the student is a reinforcing event for his misbehavior.

Rule 2: Relevant Criteria. "What you reinforce is what you get." In establishing your contingencies for reinforcement, be sure your *criteria are precisely related to your goals.* If you reinforce spending time on a task ("work on your math for twenty minutes and then you can . . ."), all you may get is time spent. Or if your criteria is speed ("as soon as you can finish ten problems, you can . . ."), you may not get the accuracy you want.

What a teacher really wants is academic *improvement* in each of her students. So you must make your criteria for each contingency conform precisely to the goals of each particular task. Violation of this rule is responsible for much of the failure in our schools, since it is possible for students to participate in public education without learning. We punish a student for being disruptive, truant, or uncooperative; but if he is generally cooperative he can avoid much of the punishment, interact considerably with the teacher and other students (which is probably reinforcing), and still learn very little.

Rule 3: Consistency. Pay close attention to the consequences of a student's behavior *at all times and in all situations.* If you are sure that your criteria are reasonable and fairly easy to achieve for this student, then be consistent—don't make exceptions, don't relax your attention or forget about it during some periods. Of course perfect consistency is impossible. But the principles of behavior and its consequences are still working when the teacher is tired, angry, preoccupied, or otherwise unobservant. Consequences affect behavior, whether the contingencies are in the lesson plan or not.

Rule 4: Immediacy. Consequences should come *as close in time after the behavior* as possible. If you delay the reinforcer or punisher, the effect will be weaker and the consequences might very well affect some other completely irrelevant behavior. If a student comes to you for help on his math and you scold him for something he did earlier during recess, you may decrease the likelihood that he will again ask for help from you or that he will work as hard on his math or that he will like math as much. If you want a student to pay attention to his work, or to hang in there when he has some trouble with a task, then reinforce him at the time he is doing that; waiting till later will weaken the effect.

Of course there are ways to mediate reinforcement or punishment, and these ways often seem to be violations of this rule. Verbal promises and threats, grades, points, and tokens are frequently used to delay the backup consequences. But when they work it is because these mediators have become conditioned reinforcers or punishers themselves. When we carefully examine such long-range activities as getting a grade or a degree or doing research, we can usually find many consequent events along the way that maintain the behavior.

Rule 5: Frequency.   Don't underestimate how often you should reinforce for optimal behavior change. Most teachers do. They want to get the most educational activity with the least reinforcement. The problem is that the longer the period of educational activity without reinforcement, the more likely it is that the appropriate response will extinguish and some interfering behavior will occur, such as daydreaming, doodling, or other irrelevant activity. Notice the difference between this rule about frequency and the rule regarding immediacy. If a student's response (or task) is to "do this assignment," you may be requiring dozens of individual responses before reinforcement. Even though you reinforce him immediately after this total "response," this may not be frequent enough, depending on his past experience with consequences for this type of work. Even a task of working one simple addition problem involves a series of responses (sitting down, gathering materials, looking at the problem, adding mentally, writing, etc.). This may require too many responses before reinforcement and may violate the rule of frequency if the student has not been reinforced for any of these behaviors. Optimum frequency depends on the student and how he responds.

Furthermore, long periods of responding without reinforcement usually imply long periods without feedback about the accuracy of the student's work, and this can make large amounts of his current and future work worthless, or even a hindrance. In general, if you want a certain kind of behavior to dominate over all others, give as much reinforcement *as often as possible* for this kind of behavior.

Sometimes this is difficult. Some reinforcers are in limited supply, others are subject to rapid satiation, and some (like certain activities) take a lot of time. In such cases, give the reinforcers frequently but in *small amounts*—just large enough to still function as reinforcers; allow frequent periods of preferred activity, but keep each period as short as possible without losing their reinforcing value. In general, however, whenever an error is made in this regard, it is usually in the direction of stinginess.

Rule 6: Small Steps.   Sequence your student's work so that *the steps you reinforce are small and frequent.* This rule is related to the previous rule in that large steps do not allow for frequent reinforcement, evaluation and feedback. To avoid this, most units (chapters, assignments, sets of problems, etc.) must be broken down into a series of small steps.

Again, the usual error in determining step size is overestimation; teachers who already know the material tend to underestimate the difficulty students will have in learning it. Think of some courses you have taken in which most of the material was new to you and you got little opportunity for feedback until after the midsemester exam. A few students do very well in these (and all) courses. But if you were unfortunate enough to have made a few key misinterpretations early in the semester, they may have snowballed into massive problems by midsemester time; or perhaps you became discouraged by the "difficulty" of the course. Small steps with frequent feedback and reinforcement make this problem unnecessary. Now think of primary students just beginning to learn to read and handle numbers. Here the snowballing effect is much more likely because the skills being taught are almost always prerequisites for the next skills—that is, unless you master the first (addition and subtraction, or letter sounds), there's no way you can hope to master the next (multiplication, or word sounds). The size of each step should be determined on the basis of the difficulty of the responses for a given student. This will of course vary from student to student. A useful rule of thumb is this: If a given student can be expected to get at least 75 percent of his responses correct following the step, then the step is probably small enough. When in doubt, however, choose the smaller size.

Rule 7: Be Careful with Punishment.   Punishment works, and it's simple and efficient—which is why it is the favorite and even the dominant technique of many teachers. But punishment is painful, and schools should offer as little pain as possible. In some cases, punishment is a reasonable choice, because a few brief painful experiences are preferable to the unending pain of a lifetime maladjustment. But *punishment should only be used when it will eliminate a behavior that produces even greater punishment.*

Furthermore, there is the problem of conditioning. Any stimulus event that is frequently associated with punishment tends to take on a punishing effect itself. Even threats of removing a privilege must occasionally be backed up by punishment to be effective. When a large proportion of a student's contacts with his teacher are followed by punishment or threat, you can expect all the typical reactions of avoidance, escape, aggression, etc. Even if the student doesn't break windows, attack the teacher, or become a truancy problem, he is apt to initiate fewer contacts with the teacher, show less interest in school and in school activities, and badmouth the teacher and educational affairs in general.

Any teacher, whether or not she has a native gift for the art of teaching, can teach effectively by carefully arranging and managing the events surrounding behaviors of each student. In this sense, *teaching is the careful arrangement of contingencies of reinforcement under which a student's behavior changes.*

8. Be able to describe each rule, when given its title, and for each rule describe a typical classroom situation in which a teacher might be tempted to violate the rule.

9. Describe a real-life situation in which an event intended to be punishing is really reinforcing.

10. Explain why a mediating consequent event need not violate the rule regarding immediacy.

11. How can you give reinforcement frequently and avoid satiation or excessive time off task.

12. State the rule-of-thumb regarding step size. Give an example from your own experience in which this rule was followed or violated.

13. Give an example from your own experience of where a frequent punishing event affected more than just the behavior being punished.

14. We often hear people saying things like "I never did like math" or "I never was very good in music—I guess music-lovers are born, not made." Cite three or more of the rules which, if followed, might have made things different for such a person, and explain how.

15. State and defend or criticize the concluding definition of "teaching."

OBSERVING AND RECORDING BEHAVIOR

Why Measure?

You already have rather well-developed skills in observing the behaviors of others. You have already learned how to be sensitive to important cues and how to respond appropriately to these cues. But these skills of selection and interpretation may be a hindrance as well as a help. Since you have learned to select or pay attention to certain aspects of another's behavior and not other aspects, and since no one can attend to every detail, you run the risk of over-looking some details which may be functionally related to future events. Fur-thermore, your perception and your interpretation of behavior can easily be swayed by your expectations: perceptive selection habits you have developed, details you have frequently noticed before in similar situations, what others expect you to see and report, and what would be most advantageous for you to see and report.

The reports of witnesses to accidents, criminal acts, and ordinary conversa-tions supply many examples of the human observer's tendency to observe selectively and to insert subjective interpretation as if it were really observed. The same kind of tendency occurs daily in classrooms. In her end-of-the-year report on students, a teacher might describe one student as hyperactive. What the teacher observed was something like this: the student sat in his seat for three minutes and drew with his crayons, then got up and went to another student's seat and took a different colored crayon, went back to his seat and drew for thirty seconds, got up and returned the crayon, went to another student's seat and took another crayon, punched him in the arm when the other student objected and so on. Many rapid series of behavior units like this might disturb the teacher, and as a result the teacher would be more apt to pay attention to and even exaggerate all of this student's behaviors, though she might not notice similar behaviors of another student who was less disturbing to her. The student's teacher next year, after reading the report, will tend to expect the "hyperactivity" to continue in the next grade. At the end of the next year, the student's report might contain words like "maybe some brain damage or a learning disability." Such labels may not represent careful observational data and they surely represent subjective interpretation.

The teacher who wants to be an objective observer must stick as closely as possible to the actual data of behavior and be careful of interpretive remarks that are based on inferences. It is not easy to do this, partly because pure behavioral data sounds so dull and unnatural. To observe and record only the behavior that occurs demands a great degree of self-discipline, both in continued concentration on a series of behavioral details and in recording only what was observed, without subjective interpretations.

Once you have observed and recorded a stream of behavioral events, you can then begin to analyze this data by looking for *patterns* between similar behaviors and their consequences or their preceding events, patterns of interaction between the student and peers or teacher, and the particular *effects* of certain procedures (new and old) on specific behaviors. You will probably not find what you are looking for with certainty, but you will probably find suggestive evidence that certain events usually followed certain behaviors, that other events usually preceded other behaviors, and that the frequency of certain behaviors changed or did not change when new procedures were introduced. On the basis of these suggestive data, you may have a hunch that a certain consequent event, if made contingent on a certain kind of behavior, might increase that behavior. But this would have to be tested out by implementing the contingency and then carefully observing the specific behavior, the consequence, and their frequency. Of course, analysis of behavioral sequences must be tailored to fit the kind of problem one is investigating.

When you are doing purely exploratory observation, you want to keep a running account of as many behaviors as you can, as well as when they occurred, how long they lasted, and what behaviors by others preceded, concurred, or followed them. From this running narrative, you can find evidence to suggest one or a few specific behaviors to look at closely. Then you gather more detailed information on these behaviors and analyze this data very carefully.

"I can just picture myself as a teacher trying to record all the behaviors and their times for thirty students for seven hours a day." The picture is ridiculous, of course. Seldom does a teacher need to be concerned about all the behaviors of all the students all the time. But whenever there is some question of concern, there is need for precise and accurate data. To make the task of data recording less overwhelming, a beginning teacher might choose to focus at first on just one problem student for a sample period of time each day. Later on, several behaviors of several students can be recorded without much trouble.

The academic progress of each student is of prime importance, so here the need for continuous measurement is critical. The good teacher cannot risk guessing in this area. She must have at least daily records of what each student did: what tasks each attempted, where each had trouble, how long it took each, the reinforcing event preferences of each, and so on. Without these accurate records, the teacher has no reliable basis for making daily decisions about the best next step for each student.

Furthermore, as we will see in later units, if the teacher has a truly individualized academic program for the students, and manages the consequences well, there is seldom any cause to worry about disciplining the students. The consequences for good work can be made strong enough to override rather quickly the temptation of students to engage in counterproductive activities. But it's impossible to manage instruction and its consequent events well without precise data.

It is also helpful and convincing to have solid evidence when you try to enlist the cooperation of parents ("Johnny always finishes his work at home") or explain results to other teachers ("It can't work"), or convince the principal ("The students don't need that"); so extensive data recording has many important values for a teacher who wants to teach well. Precise descriptions of behavior allow the teacher to: (1) verify whether or not preconceptions about a student are true; (2) discover behavior patterns which might suggest a solution to a problem; (3) make instructional decisions which increase each student's achievement and satisfaction; (4) evaluate the effectiveness of each part of each student's program; and (5) document a situation, a result, or a need in communicating with other educators and interested parties.

---

1. List several kinds of errors a teacher could make in observing students.
2. What do you look for in a recorded stream of behavioral events? And if you find it, what do you do with it?
3. Describe several values in data recording for a teacher.

Baseline

Let's say you wanted to increase the amount of time Johnny actually spends working on his assignment, because your impression is that he wastes a lot of time daydreaming. Before you try to change it, however, you should first verify your impressions; just how much time does Johnny spend working? First you *define* what you will accept as "working" behavior. Since you can't get inside his head and discover whether he is actually reading or thinking, you might decide that whenever he is using the appropriate materials and has his eyes directed towards them, you will count that as "working." Then you begin to *record* how much time he spends working. You might choose a fifteen-minute independent work period to use as a sample period. A stop watch would make the job much easier; simply start the watch whenever he is working, stop it when he stops working, start it up again when he starts, etc. At the end you have the total number of minutes he spent working out of the total possible fifteen minutes. And you would want to repeat this data recording for at least several days, because his behavior during a short period on a given day may not be typical of what he usually does.

This kind of preliminary data, collected before you make any change in your procedures, is called baseline data. One reason you need this baseline data is so that after you have introduced some modification you can compare the results empirically with the behavior rate before the change, and tell whether or not what you did made any difference.

How long the baseline period should run depends on the behavior, the observation sessions, and the data you get. What you want is reasonable assurance that if you continued collecting baseline data it would look very much like what you already have. You can't have this assurance if the behavior you are concerned with occurs throughout the day and you have observed and recorded it only five minutes each day for three days, and always at the same time and in the same environment. Furthermore, if the data shows a possible downward or upward tendency, you will have to continue collecting baseline data until the tendency is confirmed or until the data levels off within a predictable range.

In most cases, you should probably observe and record unobtrusively—that is, in such a way that the person does not know you are closely observing his behavior. If a person knows he is being observed, he may change his behavior from what it typically is, because based on his past experience, he expects you to deliver some good or bad consequences contingent on what he does. But in certain situations you may judge, for example, that the person might lose confidence in you if he discovered your recording activities. If the person does know you are observing him, his change in behavior might be just temporary, and he might soon revert back to his usual behavior when he learns that there is in fact no new consequence contingent on his behavior. Prolonging the baseline phase of data recording will show you when and to what degree this happens. But you can't rely on this temporary change; sometimes the behavior never reverts back, especially when the observer is an important reinforcing agent to the person being observed. In self-management, for example, there are many reported studies in which finger-nail biting, hair-pulling, and even cigarette smoking, decreased steadily to a zero rate when the person began simply to record the baseline frequency of his own behaviors. In these cases the new procedure of carefully recording the frequency of such behaviors was enough to accomplish the objective, perhaps simply by helping the person discriminate his own behavior.

Graphing

Now back to our example of Johnny's working behavior. Say your record for one week looked like this:

Day	Minutes
Monday	8
Tuesday	6
Wednesday	12
Thursday	7
Friday	8

A column of numbers is not a good way to display measures, especially as the column gets longer (as yours will). But you can easily transform it into a graph that will give you a quick and easy picture of the information:

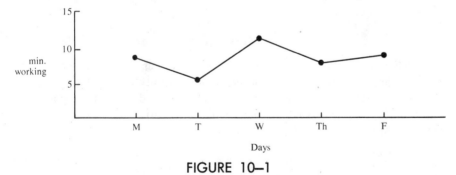

FIGURE 10–1

As you can see, the units of time are plotted along the x (horizontal) axis, and the behavior frequency (in this case minutes of working) is plotted along the y (vertical) axis. Each data point is plotted by lining up the point with the scales on both the vertical and the horizontal axes.

Instead of recording the rate of behavior (that is, its frequency per unit of time) as was done above, you might sometimes want to record the ratio of behavior to opportunity. This is an especially useful method when the time period for observing does not stay the same from day to day. For example, say that when you were observing Johnny's working behavior, Wednesday's independent study period lasted twenty-five minutes instead of the usual fifteen minutes, for some unforeseen reason. Looking at the above rate graph you might think that Johnny did much better on Wednesday than on the other days. But the longer period on Wednesday simply means that he had more opportunity on Wednesday to add up the minutes of working time. You can correct for this misleading impression by graphing the ratio of behavior to opportunity. Change each data point into a percentage by solving a fraction whose numerator is the actual behavior frequency and whose denominator is the total possible behavior frequency. For example, on Wednesday Johnny worked twelve minutes out of a possible twenty-five minutes, so the ratio is twelve to twenty-five or close to 50 percent, which means that about half the time he was working. A ratio graph for this baseline period would look like this:

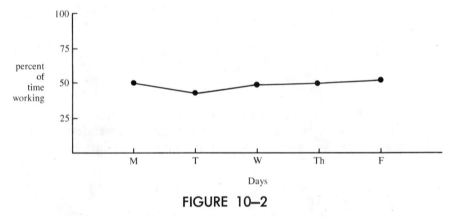

FIGURE 10–2

Now it is clear that Johnny's rate of working behavior stays pretty constantly at about 50 percent. Whenever the opportunity for exhibiting the behavior varies significantly from one observation period to another, you must make some adjustment such as the ratio method to make your behavioral picture accurate.

Experimental Phase

Once you have a baseline of data that seems stable and reliable, you can proceed to implement the change in contingencies that you suspect will change the behavior in some way. This change marks a new phase in your graph and in your observational study which is called the *experimental phase*. But you continue to record data on the same behavior and in the same way as you did before, so that you can justifiably compare the data in the baseline and new phase.

Now you need a way to tell whether what you are doing is having any effect, or enough effect to make your efforts worthwhile. There are statistical calculations you could make with your data, and in some cases they may be the most appropriate way to tell. But statistics are not always necessary to make quick on-line judgments about the effectiveness of your changes. Wells Hively has suggested a very useful way to eyeball a graph to make these judgments. He calls it the "envelope method."[1] Suppose you want to see whether giving a student time to read comic books in math class will increase the number of problems he answers correctly. For your baseline you give him a thirty-minute period each day to work problems, without saying anything about comic books, and count the number of problems he answers correctly each day. Notice that with this behavior there's no need for a stop watch; you can simply make slashes or mark numbers on a piece of paper. Your graph at the end of two weeks looks like this:

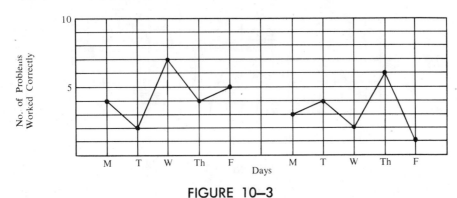

FIGURE 10–3

You can see from this that he's doing a little work every day, but not a lot; and as time goes on he doesn't seem to be getting any faster or slower. You might be willing to predict what the third week's data would look like. You

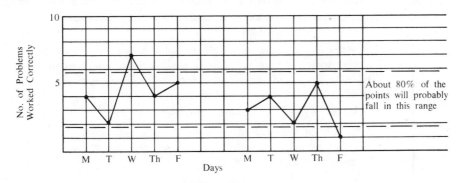

FIGURE 10–4

---

[1] Wells Hively, unpublished notes. University of Minnesota, 1970.

can do this by eye: imagine you are fitting an envelope over the record so that the envelope covers about 80% of the points, and extend it into the next week.

It is very important that you make this prediction before you make a change in the conditions or procedures. If you make an arrangement for the student to work for comic books and then try to look back and see whether it makes a difference, your prediction will be so cluttered up by what you know really happened that you'd never be able to trust it.

But after you've made a prediction, you can do something different and compare the results to that prediction. Suppose you arrange to let the student spend five minutes reading a comic book for each ten problems that he completes correctly. If the results looked like the following, you could be fairly certain that the comic-book contingency was effective.

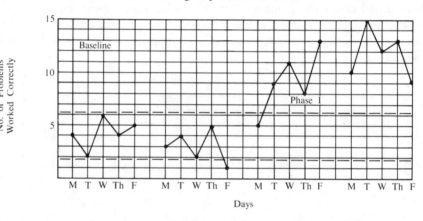

FIGURE 10–5

Any method of prediction is very risky if you only have a few data points in the baseline. For that reason you will usually need at least a week of baseline data. If the baseline is not as stable as Johnny's, then prediction is more risky. But again this risk can be reduced by extending the baseline period. In general, the more variable the baseline record is, the longer the baseline should

4. Why is a graph useful?

5. Try drawing a graph of imaginary data. Be sure each axis is clearly identified, the behavior is an observable one, and the baseline phase and at least one experimental phase are clearly marked.

6. What is a baseline? Why is it necessary?

7. Why is it important to make a prediction based on your baseline before introducing a change? Describe the "envelope" method.

8. How long should the baseline phase last? Describe how baseline observation can, by itself, produce behavioral change.

be continued. There are no hard rules telling you how long to collect baseline data before introducing a change. In general, before you make a change, you should be convinced that if you continued baseline, 80 percent of the data points would continue to fall within the 80 percent envelope range.

Evaluating the Change

But what if the baseline record looked like this:

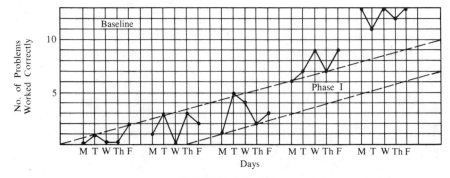

FIGURE 10–6

Even before you've made any change (baseline), you can see that his baseline rate is increasing. You can still make a prediction, but since the baseline is not "stable" the prediction is much chancier. A "straight-line" prediction as illustrated in this graph may or may not make sense. Some sort of curve line might be just as reasonable. In the graph above, it looks like there was a clear effect because of the contingency. But how can we be sure? There is also the danger, no matter how stable the baseline appears, that the effect is real, but due to some other change, not the one you made. You might have inadvertently been giving the student more attention and praise at the same time that you offered him the comic-book contingency; or his parents might have imposed some contingency on the student at the same time. It is often difficult to separate and pinpoint the cause-effect relationships.

There are procedures you can use to convince yourself that the change you make is critical and has important effects of its own. You could get some other students, keep the same records on them, and introduce the comic-book contingency at different times. If most of their records showed a rather sudden change shortly after this arrangement, you may begin to feel confident that the effect is "real". This idea of exposing several behaviors to systematically different conditions and comparing their performance has in it the basic statistical notion of *"control group."*

Or you might use *reversal* procedure. Remove the comic book contingency in a second experimental phase and return to baseline conditions to see if the

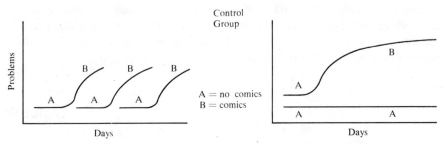

FIGURE 10–7

behavior rate returns eventually to baseline rate. In this method, the one person is serving as his own control. Many teachers don't like to use the reversal method because they don't want to lose the good results they have achieved, even for a few days.

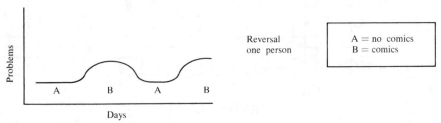

FIGURE 10–8

The trick in making up your plan of procedures is to arrange a sequence of conditions for one or more persons and behaviors in such a way that you will learn as much as possible as quickly as possible.

9. Be able to describe two ways to be sure that the experimental change you made really made the observed difference in the data.

Unit 11

SELF-CONTROL

Most behavior is a function of its preceding and consequent events. A person is likely to do a certain thing in a certain situation because in the past that kind of behavior in that kind of situation frequently was followed by desirable consequences. He is likely not to do a certain thing in a certain situation because in the past that kind of behavior was frequently followed by neutral or undesirable consequent events. The probability of a certain behavior can be changed (increased or decreased) if the frequency or kind of consequent events is changed, and also if the preceding events (situations) which signal the usual contingency between the behavior and its consequence are altered.

Frequently behavior change of this type occurs because *someone other than the behaver* changes the preceding or consequent events, or causes them to change. The other person or persons may do this deliberately or accidentally, or the cause of change in these surrounding conditions may be nonhuman agents or events. But whatever the source for the change in preceding or consequent events, that source is frequently not the person whose behavior changes as a result.

We usually think of such preceding and consequent events as being external to the person whose behavior is influenced by them. Not necessarily so. We know that many influential things happen "inside our skin" or "in the head." These events can and often do control what we do and say. The sight of a book can act as the preceding stimulus for your thinking of an exam tomorrow and you are then reminded of the consequences you can expect if you do or do not study for it. Whether you actually do study or do something else instead, this external behavior is not only the result of your past experience with similar exams and grading contingencies, it is also the result of this internal thinking and imagining chain of events.

In fact, most of our behaviors are controlled by both external and internal events and contingencies. Furthermore, just as many external events become reinforcers, punishers, or signals, by conditioning—that is, by frequent close association with events that already function that way—so many internal events also become effective by a process of conditioning. Just as the sight of a friend can become reinforcing in itself because in the past that event has frequently led to pleasant times, so the internal thought of that same friend can become reinforcing in itself, because thinking of him has frequently been followed by pleasant events (internal or external).

Self-control is a special case of behavior control, in which the person whose behavior is changed or maintained and the person who changes the antecedent and/or consequent events is the same person. In self-control, the same person is both object and subject, but he influences his behavior precisely the same as he would the behavior of anyone else: by changing the *variables* of which that behavior is a function. Technically, the person does not change his own behaviors; what he does is change or arrange the events which in turn change his behavior.

1. Choose a behavior that you do regularly, describe it behaviorally, and list several probable reasons why you do it.
2. What do we mean by "self-control?" Why is it not true, technically, that we can change our own behavior?

Changing Your Behavior

If you want to change one of your behaviors without the direct aid of someone else, your probability of success will depend on how well you *rearrange the contingencies* between that behavior and its consequences and/or how well you control the opportunities for doing it. If you want to eliminate over-eating, you must change the discriminative stimulus and contingent reinforcement conditions in such a way as to make the probability of saying No to yourself greater than the probability of eating at certain times, or else make food unavailable at certain times. Or, if you want to be more cheerful in the morning, you have to arrange some discriminative stimuli which will get you to think cheerful thoughts, smile and say cheerful things to others, and then arrange for reinforcing consequences to follow. Of course if you succeed in this effort to control your environment, you are more apt to try to do so again because your success will probably reinforce this general kind of self-control behavior.

A major practical problem lies in the *initial strength* of reinforcement for another behavior incompatible to the one you want. Even if you get your new set of stimuli and contingencies started, they are in immediate competition with contingencies which are well established by other strong reinforcers. Instead of studying at night, you usually watch TV or go out somewhere; though you want to diet, there are a variety of preceding stimuli inviting you to eat, and the immediate consequences are very rewarding. Resisting these temptations is a behavior which is likely to have fewer effective preceding stimuli, and weaker and less immediate consequences than does the incompatible behavior.

If you choose to watch TV after supper instead of hitting the books, that's simply a way of saying that TV watching at that time was a higher-probability event than studying. The next morning as you head for classes, your choice might be the opposite, except that the opportunity for either is no longer available. The trick is to be able to arrange conditions that *overcome a dominant probable response* at a specific time or in a specific situation.

There is experimental evidence to indicate that the *probability of a choice* between two behaviors at a given time depends on both the *strength* of the reinforcing consequence for either choice and also on the *delay* of that consequence. In terms of a math formula, it would be:

$$\frac{\text{Choice}_A}{\text{Choice}_B} = \frac{\text{Reinforcer Strength}_A}{\text{Reinforcer Strength}_B} \times \frac{\text{Delay of Reinforcer}_A}{\text{Delay of Reinforcer}_B}$$

The reinforcer for watching TV is more immediate than the reinforcer for studying, so that one will choose to watch TV unless the strength of the consequence for studying is much stronger than the enjoyment from watching TV—for you. Similarly, the reinforcer for eating is more immediate than the reinforcer for not eating (losing weight, looking better, etc.). The same analysis presumes, of course, that the discriminative stimulus functions are held constant.

If a reinforcing effect is weak, it could be either that the reinforcer itself is weak or that there is too much of a time delay between the behavior and the reinforcing event. To change the immediate probabilities of two opposing behaviors, a person must introduce conditioned reinforcers that are strong and *immediate*. There are several ways to do this. One way is to *arrange external conditions* ahead of time to make sure the undesired response is very unlikely to occur, or that the probability of one response will be much greater than the other. There are numerous examples of this in everyday life: We set the alarm clock out of arm's reach or sign up for automatic payroll savings deductions or put a time-lock on the refrigerator. A student who had three papers to write in three weeks gave thirty dollars to her friend with instructions to mail ten dollars each week to her most detested political candidate unless the friend received a completed paper before the weekly deadline. The first paper was a day late, but the student got all three papers done and twenty dollars back. Homer suggested this technique also, when Circe urged Odysseus to plug his boatsmen's ears and have himself tied to the mast in order to avoid turning his boat toward the bewitching songs of the Sirens and crashing on the rocks.

This technique has the drawback that you must either rely on someone else to enforce the contingency or, if you do it yourself, you are liable to cheat. It's easy to say, for example, "if I finish this chapter I'll give myself a ten-minute break and go get a drink, but until I do I won't let myself have a break"; it's not as easy to stick with that contingency. How can that be made easier—that is, more probable?

A second general way is to *arrange internal events and contingencies* with enough strength and immediacy to control the probabilities of opposite behaviors. The potential power of this strategy comes from the fact that you will be able to carry around with you your own source of reinforcement or punishment. Instead of being dependent on certain persons or certain external conditions which are not always available when you need them, your internal events and contingencies can always be called up for service.

This general strategy makes use of the Premack principle which says that a low probability event can be reinforced (strengthened) if it is followed frequently by any high probability event. These are the steps in using the *internal* procedure:[1]

1. Decide what specific behavior you want to strengthen or weaken. Call it your target behavior.

2. Make a list of many aversive consequences of not achieving your target behavior. Be sure the reasons or images are really aversive to you, not someone else.

3. Make a list of many good consequences for doing your target behavior; list as many as you can think of, but only those that move you.

4. Select a preceding stimulus to which you always respond in the same way. For example, reaching for the phone to make a call, lifting a cup of coffee or soda to take a drink, reaching for the faucet to wash your hands, reaching for your keys to open the car or house door. Each of these preceding events occurs regularly during the day but not constantly, each situation is easy to discriminate, and each is always followed by a specific response which is therefore a high probability response.

5. In the presence of the preceding stimulus situation, complete the chain of responses:

---

[1] Suggested in part by Lloyd Homme and Don Tosti in their excellent autoinstructional text, *Behavior Technology*, Unit 4, published by Individual Learning Systems, San Rafael, California, 1971.

(a)   imagine the list of aversive consequences, as vividly as you can;
(b)   imagine the list of good consequences, as vividly as you can;
(c)   engage in the high probability event, that is the event that the preceding stimulus always leads to (drink, or wash, or turn the key, etc.).

6.   When the thought of doing or not doing your target behavior occurs, use this too as the preceding stimulus for going through the imagination chain. Then reinforce this by engaging immediately in either an activity that is highly probable at the moment or some other event that is reinforcing to you—taking a quick break, or a sip or nibble (unless dieting is your objective), or simply complimenting yourself on your progress in "mastering your own fate."

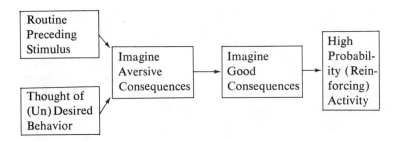

After a day or two of practice, the whole chain should only take you several seconds.

7.   Keep a continuous record of the frequency per day of your target behavior. This is necessary because achieving your target behavior is the ultimate reinforcer, and without clear and regular feedback, your efforts to change through self-control will extinguish.

You usually can't rely simply on step 6 to successfully change your behavior. If you decide that whenever you think of doing (or start to do) the undesired behavior you will remind yourself of the aversive and good consequences, your decision will probably have no effect (since it has never worked in the past, why should it now). One of the reasons why we do things we later wish we hadn't is because we remind ourselves of the good and bad consequences only after the behavior is done. Thinking of doing it, or starting to do it, is usually not enough to remind ourselves of the consequences. The trick is to get us to talk to ourselves *before* we act, not after.

By inserting the internal chain of thoughts and imaginings between a strong preceding stimulus and a high probability event, you are not only increasing the likelihood of the internal chain's occurrence *at that time* but you are also reinforcing its occurrence and thereby increasing the likelihood of its occurring again *in the future*. And this increase in the thoughts and imaginings makes the target behavior more probable because its reinforcers, though vicarious and conditioned, are immediate. For example, even though the ultimate reinforcer for not eating is loss of weight, fitting into a bikini, etc., the thought of achieving these things can also be a strong conditioned reinforcer and a very immediate one. Either or both of these general procedures for arranging preceding and consequent events and contingencies are effective and specific ways to change your own behavior. They are different from the usual methods of exhortation, moral persuasion, and appeal to your will-power, because they help you to analyze your own behavior and its relationship to controlling events. They also give you specific techniques for achieving the results suggested by good advice.

Exhortation

Notice the difference between changing one's own behavior by changing internal or external consequences, and the usual method of arranging for someone to exhort us to change. Throughout history men have relied on exhortations to "Think positively!" "Have confidence!" "Don't eat so much!" "Have faith!" "Repent!" and so on. This method seems to have worked occasionally, at least temporarily, but we can never rely on it. The reason is that moral persuasion and appeals to "will power" do not specify ways of accomplishing the desired change. The two procedures for arranging preceding and consequent events and contingencies, however, are effective because they help us analyze our own behavior and its relationship to controlling events. They also give us specific techniques for achieving the results suggested by good advice.

Exhortation may be of some value, however, especially with the internal chain procedure, since the persuasion may lead you to decide to change by getting you to think of very powerful reasons for deciding to change.[2] Unless you decide—rather firmly and emotionally that a behavior change is desirable, you won't follow through with either external or internal procedures. Unless the initial emotional intent to change is stronger than the reinforcers maintaining the present behavior, you won't begin the procedures which will allow you to change.

But it is not true that once you really decide, you've won. Most smokers, for example, have quit dozens of times. By itself a decision, even with its emotional charge, can't overcome the control that years of learning have established. Because the emotional charge is very *fragile,* if it does not lead to initial success, it will evaporate rather quickly. Each such failure makes the next failure more likely, because through overuse (habituation) the emotional

---

[2] Suggested by David Premack in his 1971 article "Mechanisms of Self Control," found in W. Hunt (Ed.), *Learning Mechanisms and the Control of Smoking* (Chicago: Aldine Publishing Co.).

charge dissipates into clinical dispassion, like a joke that has lost its humor at the tenth telling.

Self-control is not magical or supernatural. Self-control is a form of behavior change based on the arrangement of preceding and consequent events. By disrupting and rearranging such events, especially internally so that we can mentally instruct ourselves about the consequences of our behavior, we ourselves can arrange the contingencies which control our own behavior. Perhaps this is the most useful way to think of terms like conscience, ideals, attitudes, values and will power.

Self-Management of Studying

These self-control methods can be applied successfully to a wide variety of behaviors. Students have used them to stop smoking, lose weight, be more cheerful in the morning, be more prompt, be less obnoxious to a specific person, stop pulling one's hair, etc. The choice is wide open, and the success depends on the decision and the methods.

Self-management of study behavior is an especially important area of self-control for students. If you could use some improvement in this area, the following illustrations might help to get you started. If your study habits are already working to your satisfaction, the following will serve as an illustrated application of the internal and external methods of self-control. In either case, remember that the specific details of the procedures may not be as appropriate in your case as they were for the students who adopted them, but the general procedures are applicable to all.

One college student was just barely getting by in his courses, and was regarded as lazy by his professors, indifferent or slightly slow by some fellow students, and forgetful by his girl friend. He chose to do something about it, and decided to use a combination of internal and external change methods.

For the *internal* chain, he had his girl friend make him some stiff-cloth bookmarks of bright colors, on each of which was written "A" and "F" and "Weekend." He put one in each of the books he used for classes, including notebooks. Their color, and the fact that they protruded from the books, made them easily noticeable. Each time he noticed one (starting in the morning when he assembled his books for the trip to school), he would mentally go through the chain of thoughts about the good consequences of regular, persistent study and the bad consequences of sloughing off (marks, panic and long hours at exam time, time for weekend flings with his girl friend or with the boys, embarrassment at his reputation as a student, pride in being thought of as a good student). Each time he would stop what he was doing (heading for the car, starting to leave a class, putting his books down after school, etc.) and run through the chain before completing the action he had interrupted. Soon he no longer had to read the bookmarks, and the internal chain took only a few seconds.

Externally, he made arrangements with his girl friend whereby some reinforcers that she had under her control were to be made available to him contingent on weekly persistence and accomplishment in studying for his courses. He had divided his semester's work up into small units for each course, and assigned a certain number of units for each week of the semester. At the end of each week, when and if the week's allotment of reading, paper writing, etc. was finished, they could use the weekend time for activities together. Also, on weekdays when the day's allotment of units was finished early, a phone call or even a brief get-together was allowed.

He did not always meet the contingencies, and the girl friend was unselfish enough to impose the consequences. But he met all the contingencies after the fourth week, and he ended up with a 3.6 grade point average for the semester, which improved his overall average considerably. He still maintains that one professor dropped his grade to a B solely because of his past reputation; the professor says he was afraid to give him an A for fear it would be the only one on his transcript. However, that's no longer a problem.

To get the most out of your study time and effort, there are other kinds of procedures and devices you can use that usually help considerably. The environment in which you study can be very important. The student in the above example posted his daily and weekly schedule at his study desk, and he used the bookmarks as reminders. The same kind of prompting mechanism can operate if you choose for your study area an environment that is as free of outside distractors as possible, and has many study prompts. One way to secure this is to arrange things so that the *only* thing you do in that specific place is study. In that way, the normal stimuli in that place will become associated only with study behavior, and will be more likely to prompt you only to study.

Another important procedure is to *schedule* your time and work in some detail. Students who always get A's usually do this to some extent anyway, but even they can be helped by scheduling, in that they will be more apt to avoid the occasional need for late hours spent finishing a paper or preparing for an exam.

To schedule your time, you must first get the detailed *requirements* for the semester for each course: how many pages you must study, how many papers or projects you must complete, and exactly what each requires. If the requirements are not clear, or if you've heard that the professor doesn't really insist on some of them, the best procedure is usually to ask the professor directly for the details. Then break this work up into *small units* of perhaps one to three hours each, unless the professor has already done this for you, and schedule these units out over the semester. A paper, for example, is really a series of such units; you have to define the topic, do a literature search, outline, a rough draft, and a final writeup. A midsemester test over 250 pages of text

Class:_____

Project Due Dates:

Small Tasks

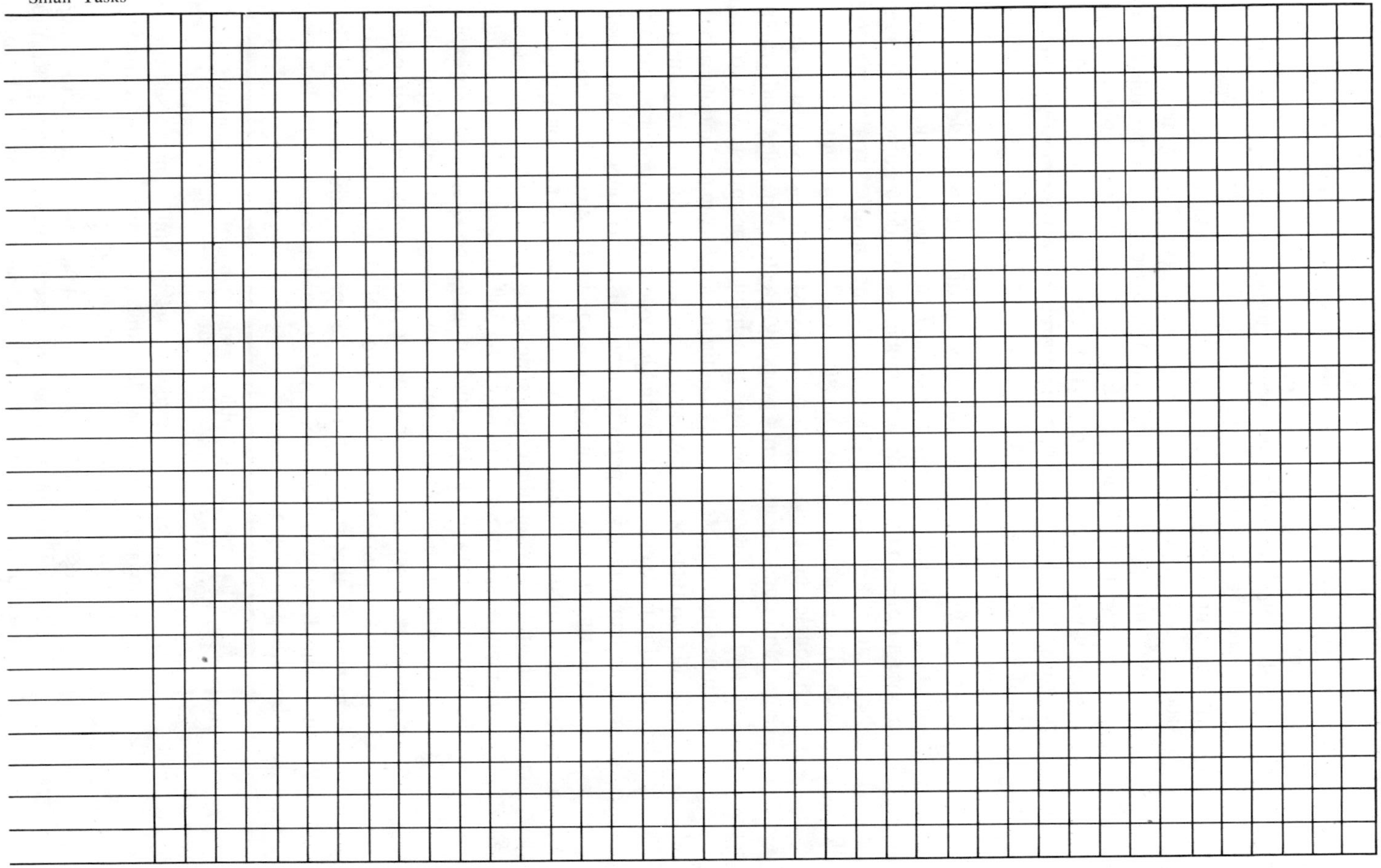

Days

FIGURE 11–1

comes out to about thirty-six pages per week, or about six pages per day (giving yourself one day a week off).

It also helps to *graph* your progress through these units. Set up a cumulative graph (see Figure 11-1, and the graphs at the back of this text) for each course, with the units of work on the vertical axis (from bottom to top), and the actual study days, or class days, on the horizontal axis. Then you can plot your daily progress through the requirements of each course, and be able at any time to know how you are doing relative to your goals for the course. If you fall behind, you will be reminded of this in plenty of time to recover. Graphing your progress also has a very helpful reinforcing effect for most students. And helping yourself in these ways will probably cost you no more than thirty minutes per semester.

You should also try, as much as possible, to schedule your daily use of time. If you want to use a couple of free periods during the day for study, choose an on-campus study area much as you do a home study area (e.g., in the library), and commit yourself to going there every day during those periods. The same applies to your use of after-school hours.

Of course, none of these procedures will help unless you arrange the preceding and consequent events properly. Posted schedules and graphs, time of day, and even other people can be helpful in prompting you to begin and to continue studying. Reinforcing contingencies, arranged and enforced by yourself and/or others, will increase the ease and satisfaction in your study efforts. If you don't have access to a buddy system for reinforcing your efforts, you yourself can arrange to put off phone calls, work on your car or bike, TV or other recreation, or even money for a special purchase, until you have finished the day's scheduled units. Of course in this case you are on your own as far as consistently enforcing the contingencies.

In many cases (perhaps most, at the college level), these methods can make the difference between a poor student and a good student. To explain a poor student's grades in terms of laziness, indifference, or forgetfulness is a pseudo-explanation. They have simply not learned to manage their own study behavior, and it's unlikely at the level of college that anyone will actually teach them how. At that stage, self-teaching is probably the only recourse. But with the technology of self-control, that no longer needs to be left to chance or exhortation or magic.

> 3. What are two possible reasons why one consequent event is chosen over another?
>
> 4. How does the "internal chain" technique make self-control more probable? How does this differ from the "exhortation" technique? How might exhortation help?
>
> 5. Choose a behavior of your own that you might like to change (strengthen or weaken) and describe in some detail *two* procedures (external, internal) you might use with this behavior.

Unit 12

BEHAVIORAL OBJECTIVES

Objectives, as used in education, are statements which describe what students will be able to do after completing a specific unit of instruction. For example, this unit has several objectives. After working through it, you should be able to: (a) construct an original cognitive objective which specifies the conditions, the behavior, and the criterion precisely enough that another person knowledgeable in the field could construct a fair test of how well your students mastered that objective; (b) identify major defects in one or more of the three components of sample objectives; and (c) rewrite deficient objectives according to the three criteria.

The Need

The skill of constructing clear and precise objectives is an important one for the teacher, for several reasons. Without clear objectives, choosing materials and activities for instruction is largely a random effort. It's a difficult job to choose and arrange a set of curricular materials and activities, and to design teaching procedures that actually produce the kinds of student behaviors you want; it is impossible to do this if you are not clear and precise about what those desired end-result behaviors are, *before* you begin to choose and design.

Secondly, without clear objectives, it is difficult for a teacher to give himself and a student day-to-day feedback on how he is progressing, where he needs additional help or practice, and so forth. That is, if you don't know ahead of time precisely where you are heading, it is difficult to tell where you are along the way. As a student, you have probably experienced this frustration; you are assigned ten chapters of the course text, you put off reading them (partly because you are not quite sure what "read" really means) until a few days before the test; then you cram (knowing you can't memorize or become an expert on all ten chapters and hoping you have emphasized the same points the prof will when he makes out the exam the night before). You take the quiz and find out you hit on some points and missed on others, and then you find out a week later that many other students had medium luck too.

Thirdly, since without clear objectives a teacher can't get reliable feedback on the effectiveness of the instruction, he also can't identify problems as they occur, or design effective remedial activities when they are identified. Waiting until the end, or even the middle of a course or a school year to identify those students who are "behind," means that a lot of time and instruction has been largely wasted for those students.

Finally, without precise objectives, there is no valid way to measure the *effectiveness* of the instruction. A final test might tell you who did better than whom, but without measurable objectives there is no way to measure how well each student performed in terms of the goals for the instruction. This is because the test-maker will not be able to select test items which clearly measure the student's mastery of the goals of the instruction. Behaviorally-stated objectives help solve this problem.

The Components of a Behavioral Objective

If the course objective or criterion is stated in terms of measurable behaviors and situations (e.g., "when presented with a written list of ten randomly-chosen, single-digit multiplication problems, the student will write the correct answers to at least nine of them within ten minutes"), the teacher and the student both know what the desired behavior is, appropriate materials and activities can be selected, and the change in student behavior can be measured, remedied if necessary, and communicated to all concerned. A precise behavioral objective has three parts:

1. *The Condition*—the situation, in all important detail, in which the student is expected to perform the desired behavior. For example: "when presented with a written list of ten randomly-chosen single-digit multiplication problems . . ."

2. *The Action*—the response or behavior we want the student to be able to do, always in terms of an action we can observe and measure. For example: ". . . the student will write the correct answers . . ."

3. *The Criterion*—the precise quantity, quality and rate of responses which you will accept as mastery of the desired skill. For example: ". . . to at least nine problems within ten minutes."

CONDITION

The condition or situation in which the criterion behavior will be measured should be complete and clear enough to indicate the kind of test items and prompts which are appropriate for measuring the behavior you want. For example, you may have actually taught a student very well how to identify the various stages of cellular mitosis, but he might very well bomb your test if he learned from illustrations in the text and you test him on slides under a microscope; the response is basically the same (identifying stages), but the preceding stimulus situation (illustrations versus slides) is different. This difference can be critical.

The fact that you have taught your students to add and subtract any sets of numbers does not mean that they will be able to solve word problems calling for addition and subtraction; word problems involve other skills in translating words into numbers before adding or subtracting, and your students may not have learned these translation skills. It's poor teaching to "presume" that some skills don't need deliberate specification and teaching. Elementary students (the author, for one) have been known to become confused when given addition problems with the numbers arranged in a horizontal list, instead of the usual vertical list. And if mastery of a given skill is to be demonstrated in an oral situation, the student may fail if all his learning activities have been written. From your own experience you know that a multiple-choice exam, for example, does not test exactly the same skills as a short-answer or essay exam.

Notice that this component does *not* deal with the conditions under which the student will be *taught* (e.g., "after studying the unit on . . ."). It only deals with the conditions under which he will demonstrate his mastery, usually after instruction is given. The conditions, then, should clearly state what resources and prompts you will supply the student, the conditions under which you will test his mastery, and only those skills which you have deliberately attempted to teach him.

ACTION

The action identifies the observable behavior of the student that you will accept as evidence of his mastery. Such words as "know," or "understand," or "appreciate" are not useful in specifying an objective so that it can be measured or communicated. Since the teacher can't get into a student's mind (or "heart") to measure knowledge, understanding or appreciation, the teacher must observe some form of overt behavior, such as what the student writes, says, defines, differentiates, solves, lists, compares, or constructs.

This is not to say that understanding or appreciation are worthless goals. The problem is that these words do not help the teacher or the student to *arrange* appropriate instruction or *decide* when the goal has been reached. For example, it may be important for a student to understand the theory of evolution. But what does this mean? How can we tell when a student has achieved this? Which of the following does it include: defining such terms as genetic equilibrium, diagraming the Hardy-Weinberg law, identifying the causes of mutation, comparing Lamarckism to Darwinism? Perhaps all of these, and many other discrete behaviors.

How can you tell whether a student appreciates music: do you simply ask him, or count how much money he spends on Bach or Stones records, or ask him to hum three themes from Beethoven's Ninth, or ask him who Mel Torme's drummer is? Any *one* of these behaviors might not be enough to convince you that the student has developed an appreciation for some form of music, but a *set* of them together might.

The point is, in defining precisely what it is you intend to teach, be sure that the words you use, especially in describing the action, are clearly *measurable and observable behaviors*. Then it is much easier to decide whether those are really the behaviors you want and whether you can actually teach them.

CRITERION

The criterion specifies how well you want the student to perform the action, and what measure you will use. It specifies the standard of success clearly enough for any knowledgeable person to decide whether the objective has been achieved, and it specifies what kind of measure will be used.

For example, you might specify a *time limit*. Sometimes this is unstated, presuming a reasonable time limit is understood (one addition problem in one hour is usually considered unreasonable). But sometimes it is important to specify a time limit, and if part of your goal is *rate,* then include it in the criterion. Or you may want a certain amount of work (*quantity* of behavior) or a specific degree of *quality* (a certain percentage, or a certain order, or other qualitative aspect).

Frequently, the criterion must also specify other characteristics of performance *accuracy* that you deem important. If you ask a TV repairman to adjust your set, you may be interested not only in how long it takes him, but whether your set still has any distortion when he finishes. The quality of the picture is an important measure of his performance. In the sciences, objectives frequently specify the criterion with such phrases as ". . . rounded off to the nearest whole number" or ". . . to the nearest milliliter."

Remember that the best test for a useful and clear behavioral objective is to ask: If this was someone else's objective and he had already attempted to bring the students to mastery of this objective, could I (presuming I knew the subject matter) devise a fair test for these students, using only the information in the objective itself? If you can, then it's a good objective; if you can't, then the objective is unclear—not only to you but probably also to the teacher and his students.

---

1. Describe four ways in which behavioral objectives can contribute to instructional effectiveness.

2. Describe the three components of a cognitive behavioral objective.

3. What test is suggested to determine the clarity and usefulness of a behavioral objective?

Educational Objectives

Let's examine some sample objectives to see whether the conditions, the action, and the measure and criterion are stated in sufficient detail. Consider this objective, and try to pinpoint its deficiencies, if any, before reading on:

> The student will develop the rational thinking powers which underlie scientific modes of inquiry."

Of course there is no way this could be considered a clear behavioral objective; neither the conditions, the action, nor the criterion are stated measurably, and it would be impossible to test students fairly on their achievement of this objective. (If you have any doubts about this, be sure to review the previous pages.) This objective is a good example of what is called an *educational objective*—a very broad and nonspecific statement of general goals. Educational objectives are typically used by institutions or groups to indicate their overall direction and purpose.

We could rewrite the above objective into a behavioral form in a variety of ways: "When given a microscope and yeast culture, and asked to give empirical support to the theory that yeast is alive, the student will establish an observation schedule and record the time and frequency of observed growth and reproduction events, 90 percent of which agree with those of another observer, and describe the series of events in writing." Or: "After having demonstrated his ability to explain the bending of a bimetallic strip under heat, the student will cite the same principles to explain how a thermostat works, when given a diagram of a thermostat." Notice that in this last example the criterion is more implied than stated, since there is no time limit or percentage-correct criterion stated. The implied criterion is 100 percent, since there are a set number of facts and sequences which must be identified to "explain" the thermostat's workings. Someone who already knows the principles involved would have no trouble in developing a test for this objective.

Instructional Objectives

Consider this objective: "The student will be able to list the steps a bill follows through the state legislature, specifying the requirements for passage in each step."

This kind of objective is usually called an *Instructional Objective* because it omits the conditions and the criterion. An instructional objective has many uses in communicating one's instructional intentions to others in an abbreviated form. They are usually written after the behavioral objectives have been completely specified. For example, the above objective might be an abbreviation of the following behavioral objective: "After studying the unit on the legislature and participating in a field trip to the capital, the student will, in a half-hour test, be able to list, in correct order, the steps a bill follows through the state legislature, specifying the requirements for passage (matching those in the text) in each step."

When evaluating or writing behavioral objectives, you might find it helpful to use the following prompts: *Condition:* resources or restrictions; testing situation; skills which have actually been taught. *Action:* what the student will do to demonstrate mastery; measurable words. *Measure-Criterion:* how to evaluate; lower limit of acceptable performance.

Self-Test Problems

Work the following self-test problems to pinpoint for yourself any details you may have missed. Don't look back or forward in the text while you are working these problems, since your purpose is to find out how well you can do without extra resources. Remember the test: you must be able to construct and grade a test fairly, just from the information given. Rewrite the following objectives into acceptable form, *if* they have serious faults; otherwise mark them acceptable.

1. The student will state in sequence the six basic steps in typing a business letter.

2. The student will play the C major scale through two octaves on the violin, in third position.

3. Given all necessary equipment, the student will determine experimentally the density of an unknown solid.

4. On a written test, the student will demonstrate his thorough understanding of Newton's three laws.

5. The student will correctly identify 80 percent of the chords as dominant, subdominant, seventh, or tonic, when played singly on a piano.

6. When given any paragraph from the class text, the student will identify the tense and mood of the main verb in every sentence or main clause.

7. When shown any unknown organism, the student will correctly name its genus and species.

8. The student will know the eight rules for managing consequences.

9. The student will be able to define reinforcement.

10. After studying the unit on organic compounds, the student will correctly identify the structural formula of 80 percent of the compounds, when given the name.

Answers to Self-Test Problems

1. Conditionally acceptable; depends on whether or not we can assume the condition (oral or written, no prompts) and criterion (100 percent).

2. Needs further criteria details, e.g., regarding speed, accuracy, and perhaps even tone quality.

3. In this case, the criterion probably can't be assumed. Perhaps you would want to allow, say, a 3 percent margin of error.

4. Understanding, by itself, is not measurable (even when the words "demonstrate" and "thorough" are added); therefore the action is faulty; and the criterion is also faulty, since you can't specify a measure for an unmeasurable.

5. Probably acceptable, although you might want to indicate that the chord will be played only once, with a ten second pause between chords.

6. Acceptable. The criterion is presumed to be 100 percent.

7. While the criterion is presumed to be 100 percent (which may not be reasonable in many classes), the condition is not clear enough. In cases like this, it can make quite a difference whether the organism is shown live, via picture, or in a slide.

8. "Know" is not an action word. And because we don't know what action is really intended, we can't tell if the condition can be assumed or not.

9. Oral or written, literal or paraphrase, examples?

10. Unacceptable, though it appears to have all the components. Study the objective again, before reading the discussion below.

Superficial Objectives

Consider the following objective and try to analyze it before reading on.

> After completing a unit on behavioral objectives, the student will dem-
> onstrate his knowledge of the topic by correctly answering 75 percent of
> the questions on a post-test designed by the instructor.

This objective seems to state a condition ("After completing . . ."), an action (". . . answering . . ."), and a criterion (". . . 75 percent correct . . ."). We can presume that the action implies writing. But apply the basic test to this objective: Could you write a fair test for it? What specific questions would you include in the post-test? Would you ask the student to write behavioral objectives which clearly specify the three components, or would you ask him to identify the components of sample objectives? Would you require him to distinguish good from poor objectives? Would you require psychomotor and affective as well as cognitive objectives? Would you require cognitive objectives at various levels? Or would you require all of these skills to be demonstrated? Even though this objective seems to include all the right things, it ends up telling you very little about precisely what the student will be taught to do, and you would be hard pressed to develop a fair test just on the basis of the information in this objective. The basic problem with this objective is that the specified action (answering questions), has no useful meaning for the purposes of instruction or evaluation. You still need to know what *kinds* of questions, that is, a *specific* statement of what the student is expected to be able to do after studying the unit. Notice the difference between this objective and the kinds of objectives included in the unit you are now studying (i.e., the study-guide questions). Which test would you rather take?

The fault with the objective in question ten, and with many objectives, is their lack of specificity in what the student is expected to do. The student's action is *superficially clear* (say, write, choose, etc.), but it is not clear *what* he will say or write. For example, "answer eight out of ten questions correctly" doesn't specify the expected behavior very well; "answer" may imply writing (and that's acceptable unless the student is very young), but the action doesn't identify anything about the ten questions—we still have the question "*which* ten questions?" It's no better than saying "after reading Chapter five, the student will pass a multiple-choice exam over the material in the chapter." Superficially, this objective meets all the criteria for a good objective, but it doesn't pass the test for a good objective—being able to create and grade a fair exam just from the objective.

An objective must clearly state *exactly* what the student is expected to be able to do after the instruction, even if the student will be tested over only a sample of these desired behaviors. The action component of an objective must state (or clearly refer to) not only the physical action (write or say) but the *content* and the precise *preceding stimulus* event for the desired behavior.

Another way of looking at it is this: your objective must narrow down the field of possible behaviors to a reasonable and clear limit. Some place (in the objective or in the text or in a handout, etc.) the student should be able to pinpoint *all* the behaviors he is expected to master and might be required to demonstrate—all the behaviors from which you take a sample for your test.

For example, "After reading the unit on the contemporary novel, the student will correctly match eight authors with titles, when given a scrambled list of ten authors and ten titles." In this objective the action is too vague because it doesn't specify *which* matches or *how many* the teacher expects the student to be able to make. Someone creating and/or grading a test from this objective might ask: Can I conclude any twentieth-century novelist, or just those in the chapter? can I include any novelist mentioned in the chapter or should I exclude some? If the teacher has decided on only ten, which ten are they? And why not tell the students beforehand (in the objective) which they are?

A better objective would indicate precisely which novelists and novels are thought to be important to learn and might be included in the quiz.

Remember that however and wherever you specify the action, you must clearly *communicate* to others (especially the students) exactly what you expect as a minimum. Study-guide questions or handouts must themselves be specific and measurable to qualify as usable components of an objective.

Few, if any objectives do this perfectly for a large class of students. But imperfect objectives are better than no objectives; that is, a teacher who uses objectives that are not perfect will be a more effective instructor than a teacher who uses no objectives at all.

---

4. Cite several examples of objectives that contain defective elements (condition, action, measure and criterion) and include a *corrected* version of each example.

5. Be able to identify and correct defects in a new sample of cognitive behavioral objectives, when you see them on a quiz.

6. Differentiate educational, instructional, and behavioral objectives on the bases of characteristics and uses, with an original example of each.

Practice Problems

Now try your hand at writing some behavioral objectives of your own. Below are some broad educational objectives related to a variety of subject matter areas and levels. To reach each general objective would of course require achieving many specific objectives. Just pick one or two of these specific objectives and write it up, remembering the test for a useful objective. Afterwards you should also practice writing some objectives that are appropriate for the specific tasks you will be teaching.

1. Familiarity with the styles of the five major romantic poets.
2. Understanding of the simple proofs in Euclidean geometry.
3. Familiarity with the basic theory of classical harmony.
4. Understanding of cubism and dadaism.
5. Development of proficiency in sports.
6. Development of a more creative ability through art.

Answers To Practice Problems

For these problems, there are many possible correct answers. You will have to evaluate the acceptability of your examples, using the criteria explained in the unit. Below are some suggested objectives and some hints on specific problems.

1. With this objective, your first task is to define precisely what you want to include by "familiarity." Perhaps you want the students to be able to identify passages as to their authors. A matching test would be appropriate, so your objective might be: "When given ten passages of four to ten lines each, written by Wordsworth, Shelley, Keats, Byron, or Colderidge, and included in the students' text, the student will correctly identify the author of nine of them." If you want your students to "compare and contrast" these styles, then you have to specify on what bases they should make these comparisons (structure, symbolism, etc.), and how many comparisons you expect as a minimum.

2. Again, you must decide what you mean by "understand simple proofs." If you want your students to be able to reconstruct the proof for a given theorem, then state that; or if you just want them to identify a proof as being for a specific theorem, or perhaps simply to be able to find the circumference of a circle, then just state that. State the specific tasks you want them to be able to do, and also, whether or not you want to allow them to use some resources (tables, slide rules, etc.).

3. "Basic" might include harmonic recognition (e.g., identify major, minor, augmented chords when played on the piano singly, with a 10-second pause between each), or it might extend to actual composition (e.g., in an overnight take-home exam, the student will compose an original four-part piece of eight lines in the style of Palestrina, J. S. Bach, Handel, and Mozart, according to the style criteria sheets handed out). If you want to include quality norms, be sure to specify them.

4. Some possibilities: When shown twenty prints of 20th century paintings, the student will identify at least 90 percent of the works

representing cubism. Or, identify at least one feature of each work which characterizes it as cubist. Or produce an original work that has at least three characteristics of cubism. The "characteristics" referred to in these examples must, of course, be specified in a text or handout.

5. Given three tries on the athletic field, the student will throw a softball at least seventy feet, with no more than a ten-foot deviation on either side of a straight-line marker. Or, the student will mount the trampoline from either side, using the jump-sit-swing method, in three tries or ten minutes. Perhaps this later objective should include criteria regarding style and smoothness, if these can be specified.

6. See the discussion on creativity which follows.

Objectives For Creativity

To teach creativity in any area, you must first ask yourself what creativity *is* and whether or not it is observable. "When I say that someone or something shows creativity, on what bases do I say that—what signs prompt me to say it?"

One sign we usually rely on is *unusualness*. A student displays creativity when his art product is *different* in some important aspect—perhaps he used a new color or new color combination, a style that was different in some respect, a new medium or media combination he hadn't used before. So your objective would be that the student will produce one or more art products of his own that successively show features that are new and different for that student. You should also specify the classes of features in which you want originality to be shown. For example: "Each student will produce ten drawings during the semester (the noncreativity criteria should be specified also), dealing with ten different subject matters, and each drawing will show a noticeable difference from his previous works in terms of color, style, or medium." For more advanced art students, your objectives for creativity might be more demanding and detailed.

Of course, there are other aspects of creativity that are important. For example, the degree of unusualness must to a certain extent be tempered by *acceptability standards* of the culture. Perverts can be highly creative, but the main stream of society does not reinforce such creativity. On the other hand, there are many examples of creativity in the history of music, art, and science, which were initially rejected by professionals as being bizarre, which eventually helped reshape society's views about the acceptable limits of creativity. This is one respect in which the criteria for creativity cannot easily be specified until long after the fact.

But a great deal of creativity can systematically be developed in students before the issue of public acceptability becomes crucial. The school can provide a supportive environment for creative experimentation so that the skills and the preferences associated with creative effort can become reliable.

To Use or Not To Use

From this brief introduction to behavioral objectives, you can see that the specification of objectives for a unit of instruction is not an easy task; it requires a lot of work and attention to detail *before* the instruction even starts. For this reason, teachers are tempted to use published collections of objectives. These can be of help, but they usually do not relieve you of all the work, because many (perhaps most) of the sets of objectives currently available are nonbehavioral and nonmeasurable. After you eliminate the "knows" and "familiar withs," and "appreciation ofs" and the "awareness ofs," very few useful objectives are left.

Some educators argue that behavioral objectives are useful only for teaching trivial or very basic skills, because the other more important goals of education (like teaching creativity, attitudes, etc.) are "intangible" and can't be specified measurably. The argument is frequently voiced by those who have just recently become acquainted with behavioral objectives.

Of course, it's not easy to specify objectives for basic skills, either. But that's no excuse for escaping the responsibility of measuring what is taught. English teachers often claim that it is next to impossible to identify acceptable essays—yet they do it every time they grade an essay. An English teacher must have criteria in order to make judgments. What behavioral objectives force him to do is put his criteria on the line, out in the open for examination. He won't do this if he is defensive and insecure about his teaching. But if he can relax with the fact that even teachers can learn and improve, then stating his objectives and criteria will help him to make them more precise and valid. Only when we begin the task of specifying the conditions, action, and the measure and criterion for such "intangible" skills can we design more effective procedures to teach them in a systematic and organized way.

For another example, consider the social studies teacher who says that his objective is to develop in his students a commitment to the democratic way. Who could criticize such a profound and worthwhile objective? Yet his measure of success might be simply how well his students do on a multiple-choice exam concerning what the "loyal American citizen" does. A large amount of trivia is hidden very nicely beneath noble statements. Precise specification of behavioral objectives (cognitive and affective) allows us to choose only important goals.

The basic instructional requirement cannot be avoided: *what you attempt to teach you must attempt to measure*. Whether your instructional goals are cognitive or affective, concerned with basic skills or aesthetic refinements, you as a teacher have the responsibility of designing some way to detect the effect of your teaching on the student's behavior; the burden of proof is on you. (That's basically what accountability is all about, by the way.) You need to know this effect in order to know where you and the student are going, whether and when you've arrived at mastery of each objective, and whether remediation is called for at a given time.

The critical nature of measuring what is taught has led some experts to advise teachers to focus on the *post-test* items rather than on behavioral objectives. They argue that current objectives are too vague and unmeasurable, and that educators spend too much time arguing about the theory of objectives and neglect the actual improvement of instruction. Instead, they suggest that the teacher devise a complete list of post-test items that he feels are clear, fair, and comprehensive. When the teacher can say: "If a student can handle all these items, then I've achieved all my goals," the post-test items become a true statement of the teacher's objectives. In this sense, post-test items are the best way to express what is really being taught; they clearly state what you the teacher expect the students to be able to do as a result of your teaching, and a student's performance on each item tells you and the student about the quality of that instruction.

---

7. Construct ten *original* behavioral objectives concerning different goals in your field of concentration, some of which require the student to do more than just memorize. Have your instructor evaluate them before you complete this unit.

8. What's the basic rule relating teaching and measurement? How do behavioral objectives help in meeting this requirement?

9. State the argument against the claim that "Behavioral objectives apply only to trivia."

10. Explain the usefulness of a post-test as a statement of instructional objectives.

QUESTIONING

Questions are one type of preceding stimulus event. They function in the same general way as do words and instructions in a workbook, announcements or directions on the blackboard, sounds that are heard, and pictures or diagrams that are seen. Each kind of preceding event tends to elicit a certain kind of response from the student, such as working a problem in the workbook, starting the spelling assignment after finishing the math assignment as indicated on the blackboard, looking around to see who just screamed, attending to the details of a picture, and so on.

But the effectiveness of these preceding events in eliciting a response depends primarily on the consequent events that follow the behavior. A person who lives near the airport may eventually "adapt" to the intermittent roar of the jets and never "hear" or attend to the noise; the response to that preceding event extinguishes. In the same way, a student can cease responding, outwardly and inwardly, to verbal directions or questions, because he has learned that such responding gets him nothing that he finds worthwhile.

The question is a frequently used preceding stimulus event in the classroom. Some teachers spend up to 80 percent of their time asking questions. When used well, questions can elicit a variety of kinds of responses, especially mental responses, and at all levels: from memory recitation to thinking of new ways to combine rules for solving problems. In this unit, you will learn how to construct different kinds of questions to get your students to think or act in different ways. But remember that even the best question will not achieve its purpose unless the teacher also pays close attention to the consequences he provides for responding to questions.

The questions you direct to your students can greatly influence the cognitive level at which they think. Many research studies report a high correlation between the level of student thought displayed in student answers, and the type of question asked. When you think about this, it's an obvious point; a student is very likely to think only at the knowledge level when he is asked a purely recall question, because there's no payoff for doing otherwise. But it is equally obvious that if your objective is at the application or problem-solving level, then you should choose a question that requires responding at that level.

The next few pages outline a system for classifying questions on the basis of the level of thought required to answer them.[1] Your knowledge of this system will help you to identify different kinds of questions and to choose the type that best fits your instructional purpose.

Classifying and Choosing Questions

In very general terms, questions fall into two classes: narrow and broad. *Narrow* questions call for answers that are very predictable, because there is only *one* specific answer that is appropriate. Narrow questions typically require more memory than original thought, and more discrimination and comprehension skills than application or principle learning skills. Here are some examples of narrow questions:

> What time is it?
> What is the area contained in this circle?
> What is the definition of energy?
> What is a cell?
> What is the name of Hamlet's sister?

Narrow questions are useful for collecting information, and for testing knowledge and comprehension of basic facts and skills. The teacher needs this kind of information to manage the instruction and to make decisions about whether each student is ready for more complex learning. If they are overused, however, higher-level cognitive skills may receive less deliberate training than they should.

---

[1] This classification system is adapted from the following sources, which you might wish to consult for elaboration: *Improving Teaching: The Analysis of Classroom Verbal Interaction,* by Edmund Amidon and Elizabeth Hunter, 1967; *Productive Thinking in Gifted Children,* by James Gallagher, 1965; and *Developing Teacher Competencies,* edited by James Weigand, 1971.

Broad questions, on the other hand, permit a variety of answers, any of which might be appropriate. Broad questions require the student to do more than simply recall; the student must put facts together to form concepts, put concepts together to form principles, or put principles together to form higher-order rules. Frequently there are several ways in which this kind of putting-together can be accomplished, and so there may be several "right" answers to the question. Here are some examples of broad questions:

> How could you communicate in the classroom if you could not ask questions?
> How might education be different if all teachers were men?
> Why do you want to be a teacher?
> How could you determine the volume of this box without using a ruler?
> If Jesus was alive today, what might he say and do?

Broad questions can be used to stimulate a student to exhibit independence in using information, to become more creative in analyzing and synthesizing facts and rules, and to become more precise in evaluating his own cognitive principles.

Practice constructing some examples of your own of narrow and broad questions, and compare them with the above descriptions and criteria before continuing.

---

1. How do the questions you ask affect the cognitive level at which students answering them might think?

2. Differentiate between narrow and broad questions on the basis of (a) the type of answer each elicits or the kind of skill required of the respondent, and (b) the uses of each.

Within these two general classes of questions, there are further useful distinctions which can be made. Narrow questions can be subdivided into *memory* and *convergent* questions; broad questions can be subdivided into *divergent* and *evaluative* questions. Notice, as you study these subclasses, that

they are not exhaustive; there are other types of questions that could elicit other kinds of responses (e.g., questions concerned with analyzing and synthesizing, or with developing new rules and applying them to new problems).

NARROW-QUESTION CATEGORIES

Memory questions are a type of narrow question, requiring no more than recall of memorized information. Memory questions ask for naming, identifying, or defining something and frequently call for a one-word or yes-no answer.

Convergent questions are also narrow, but not as narrow as memory questions. Convergent questions still "converge" on one right answer, but they require the student to put together some facts, compare and contrast several concepts, or paraphrase in his own words in order to get the correct response.

Examine each of the following questions and decide whether they are memory or convergent questions. If you have trouble, review the above descriptions.

1. What is identical about the angles of a square and any triangle?
2. What is a square?
3. What did you observe in this demonstration?
4. Why does the sun appear to rise and set?

Questions one and four are convergent questions since they converge on one answer, and the student must put several facts or concepts together (squareness, triangleness, angles and degrees, earth's rotation, relationship of sun and earth). Questions two and three call for naming and defining and are therefore memory questions.

Notice that convergent questions can become pure memory questions after some instruction. Question one, for example, is convergent for a student who is being asked to find these common characteristics for the first time. But if he is asked the same question later, he may be able simply to recall the answer he gave the first time. In this unit, we will presume this has not happened.

BROAD-QUESTION CATEGORIES

Divergent questions comprise one class of broad questions, since they admit more than one acceptable response; that is, they "diverge" into more than one acceptable answer. They might require the student to infer, hypothesize, or in some way predict an event on the basis of facts or concepts that he already knows. Not only do they require the putting together of such information (as do convergent questions) but once he has done this, they allow him to repeat the process with different combinations of facts or concepts to arrive at a different answer.

Evaluative questions are the broadest type of question; they not only permit more than one acceptable response, but they require the student to judge the merit of several possible answers. Not only must the student put together information in several ways, he must then make a judgment about the relative merits of each possible answer, and perhaps justify his choice or defend his judgment.

Examine the following questions and classify each one as memory, convergent, divergent, or evaluative. If you have trouble, review the descriptions of each.

1. How could you communicate to someone from a foreign country that you wanted his friendship?
2. Explain why the brick did not float.
3. Why is this novel better than the other one?
4. Why would you like to live in Canada?
5. Is syphillis contagious?
6. How is a cell like a person?
7. What might your life be like if you were a Neanderthal?
8. Who is your favorite musician and why?

Question five is a memory question requiring a recall answer. Questions two and six are convergent questions requiring explanation and comparison. Questions one and seven require the student to infer, hypothesize, or predict, and thus are divergent.

Questions three, four, and eight are evaluative, requiring not only a combination of information, but the evaluation of these facts, and an evaluative judgment.

There are some cues that are often helpful in identifying one kind of question or another. Memory questions often begin with words like who, what, where, which, when, and sometimes how and why. Convergent questions more often begin with words like how or why or compare. Divergent questions might begin with if, or what if, or what would happen. And evaluative questions might include phrases like "do you think," "in your opinion," or superlatives like best or most. But you can't rely on these clues; the rest of the sentence can change the nature of the question completely.

To further illustrate the similarities and differences between these four types of questions, let's see what it might be like to move from memory to evaluative questions with a specific topic of study.

Let's say you and your music class are studying Beethoven's Ninth Symphony. After some introductory listening and study, you might then play excerpts of themes on the piano and ask your students what movement each belongs to. This is a memory question and it is important because this knowledge is prerequisite to other things you want to teach them about the symphony.

Later in the study you might ask them to identify the first time a variant of the Choral Movement's main theme is introduced in the symphony. This is a convergent question because it requires the student to put together several facts in arriving at the correct answer.

At a more advanced stage of study, you might ask the students to identify several devices Beethoven used to build up to the last movement. This is a divergent question because it requires the student not only to remember facts and put them together, but also to repeat these processes in coming up with several correct answers.

And finally you can prompt the students to evaluate different aspects of the work as a whole, in comparison with other symphonies. You might ask them, "What is your favorite movement?" or "What do you think has made the Choral Movement so famous?"

> 3. Be able to write an original example of each of the four general kinds of questions.
>
> 4. Be able to classify a new sample of sentences as one of the four kinds of questions, and justify your choice.

Phrasing Questions

It is important for you to know not only what type of question to use for specific types of responding but also how to phrase the question so as to make it as effective as possible. A properly chosen question can still cause confusion or prompt an undesired type of response if it is poorly phrased.

Confusing questions violate the basic need for clarity. If you want your question to prompt a certain kind of thinking, then you must be sure that your intent is clearly communicated. Questions like "tell me about evolution" or "are you sure?" are often so vague and ambiguous that the student doesn't have any useful criteria to guide the direction of his thinking and responding. Even when such questions are placed in the context of a topic and an ongoing dialogue, they unfairly require more of the student than what he has been taught. When a student has to guess at the point of the question, he can easily be wrong for irrelevant reasons; he will of course find this punishing and may learn ways to avoid answering questions.

Simple *yes-no* questions are poor for a somewhat different reason. Questions like "is there another way to solve this problem?" require the student to respond only with a yes or a no. Without thinking at all, he will be right about half the time. Furthermore, when the teacher gets a yes or a no, he will have to come back with another question, like how or what is it, and that requires an uneconomical use of time. Such questions can easily be rephrased by using an interrogatory term to start with, such as who, what, or why. For example, "What is another way to solve this problem, without using a ruler?"

Too-obvious questions are poorly phrased questions because they include so much information that the student is not required to contribute anything. For an example, a question like "is this block white or black?" or "so this weighs more than this, is that right?" simply force an answer on the student without requiring much independent responding at any level. Such questions can be rephrased by asking "What color is this?" or "How can you tell which weighs more?"

Presenting Questions

The best measure of an effective question is the answer it elicits. Effective questioning depends not only on proper choices and clear phrasing, but also on your presentation strategies. Here are four general rules that will make your question-asking more effective:

1. *Mix your types of questions.* If you rely solely on a multitude of narrow questions, your students won't have the opportunity they need to develop skill in analysis, application and evaluation. At first you need some narrow questions to prompt the student to clarify his knowledge and understanding of basic facts. Once this stage has been set, however, broad questions are necessary to prompt thinking and responding at higher levels.

2. *Mix your rate of questioning.* A rapid-fire pattern (question-answer-question-answer) is an economical and attention-producing method for many types of narrow questions. However, quantity does not ensure quality. With many types of broad questions, a rapid-fire pattern can be counterproductive. That is, in answering a broad question the student must do more than simply recall; he must compare ideas, put them together, evaluate, and then phrase a clear response. This takes some time to be done well, and the student can't be expected to do it well if the questions are fired rapidly at him. The teacher must learn to be comfortable with a few seconds of silence.

3. *Encourage everyone's participation.* If you must work with large groups in your questioning process, you have to find methods that tend to keep *all* your students thinking *all* the time. This means that you must avoid directing most of your questions to the "bright volunteers" (a sort of mutual reinforcement clique); mix it up between volunteers and nonvolunteers, and attempt to tailor the type of question to the individual student's current

abilities. It is best not to identify the respondent until after you have stated the question; otherwise the other students might tend to tune you out until their name is called. Instead, state the question and then call on someone to answer it. Best of all, whenever possible, phrase your broad questions so that they can be answered by several students, each with an answer that contributes something to the general point. For example: "There are several ways we could solve this problem; who can think of one?"

4. *Reinforce individual improvement.* Be sure that every student is reinforced for the slightest improvement in the quality of his response, even though his current skill may not be developed nearly as well as another student's. This requires, first of all, that you set the stage for reinforcement by asking individual students the kinds of questions they can probably handle. Levels of learning are interdependent. A student who does not yet understand some basic facts will surely not be able to formulate new principles. The purpose of questioning (and of teaching in general) is not to categorize students into "dumbs" and "brights" but to bring each student from the level he is at, to the highest level possible. When a student's response is wrong or incomplete, it is often wise to supply some prompts or rephrase the question into a narrower type so as to encourage his eventual correct response. An incomplete answer can also be handled with prompts that elicit the rest of the answer; and in all cases, appropriate and desirable aspects of a student's response should be reinforced, even if all the student produced was a good try.

---

5. Be able to correctly rephrase confusing, yes-no, and too-obvious questions.

6. Be able to summarize and illustrate each of the four suggested presentation strategies, when given its title.

Unit 14

REVIEW AND
APPLICATION II

As a part of this review unit, you may be asked to participate in a group discussion with three to six other students. See the attached Review Discussion Sheet for Unit 14 to record your discussion. Be sure to complete your own private review beforehand, so that the discussion can be as profitable as possible for everyone.

In addition to reviewing all the study-guide questions for each of the previous units (one through fourteen), you should attempt to relate their ideas to each other and apply them, when possible, to practical situations. The following items are examples of questions you might practice answering as you review the units.

1. Which types of questions do you think you will be using at the grade level you plan to teach? Which type do you think you will use most often? Why? What type of question is the above?

2. Devise a rule relating behavioral objectives to accountability.

3. Construct an original example of a pseudoexplanation dealing with socialization.

4. How is socialization an example of reinforcement in practice? Cite several examples.

5. Give a functional and behavioral explanation of some of your behaviors related to this class (e.g., when you study, how often you take a quiz, the answers you give, etc.).

6. From the procedures for this course, identify several contingencies and several consequences (reinforcing, neutral, punishing).

7. State a behavioral objective for this interview; identify its components.

8. Construct four questions, each a different type, and each dealing with the same topic from one of the units in this course.

9. Cite examples in which this review unit requires you to discriminate and to generalize.

10. There are several ways for determining whether a change in behavior was caused by what *you* did. Which one do you think is most feasible for the teacher in the classroom? Why?

11. Choose three or four of the "rules for managing consequences" and show how they are or are not followed in this course.

12. Name one event that has been reinforcing to you recently, and explain behaviorally how you know it was reinforcing. Do the same for a punishing event.

13. As a teacher, why and how would you collect baseline data? What would you do with it?

14. How could you use the Premack Principle to help you get an A in a course?

15. Choose several current issues in education and show how the way in which one is resolved may affect the resolution of another.

Review Discussion: Unit 14

DATE: TIME:

STUDENTS (identify chairman, recorder):

SUMMARY of Topics, Questions, and Situations Discussed (identify contributors):

Part III

EXTENSIONS AND PROJECTS

NEW PROFILE OF THE AMERICAN PUBLIC SCHOOL TEACHER

Teachers are younger, better educated (but less experienced), and better paid than they were 10 years ago. They still work as many hours a week both in and out of school as they used to and teach as many days of the year, but they spend fewer hours on unpaid work and have fewer extra nonteaching days of duty. They have slightly smaller classes, are less likely to be misassigned, and are more likely to have a duty-free lunch period than in the past. They are less likely to join organizations (although very likely to participate in political elections) and more likely to own or be buying their own homes and two cars.

These are some of the changes in the teaching profession during the 1960's that came to light in a recent study by the NEA Research Division. Every 5 years, the Division conducts a comprehensive survey of the American teaching profession by means of a questionnaire sent to a nationwide sample of teachers in public elementary and secondary schools. Topics covered range from details of the teacher's assignment to facts about his family and outside activities. The latest survey, made in spring 1971, received an 84 percent response from the teachers questioned. This article presents some of the major findings about what has happened to the teaching profession in the 1960's and where it stands at the beginning of the 1970's.

"New Profile of the American Public School Teacher" is taken from *Today's Education*, May 1972. Reprinted by permission.

Who are the teachers of America?

The 1960's have seen some changes in the teaching population, including the following:

• The median age of teachers has dropped from 41 years in 1961 to 35 years in 1971. Men still have a median age of 33, but women have become progressively younger; their median age fell from 45½ to 40 between 1961 and 1966 and to 37 in the last 5 years.

• The percentage of men teachers in the profession has increased from 31 to 34 percent since 1966. More elementary teachers and more older teachers (age 50 or older) are now men.

• More teachers are married, an increase from 68 to 72 percent in 10 years. Four men out of 5 and 2 women out of 3 are married.

• The "old maid schoolteacher" was already a thing of the past in 1961, but single women in the profession have since decreased in percent from 17 to 14.

• The percentage of men with working wives has increased from 32 to 45 percent in the last 10 years, and the percentage of men with wives employed in fulltime teaching has increased from 17 to 21 percent in the last 5 years.

• Women teachers tend to come from families of higher occupational and educational status than men. The percentage of women whose fathers were business or professional men has increased from 38 to 45 percent since 1961, compared with a constant 34 percent of men from such background. The mothers of 3 in 10 women, compared with 2 in 10 men, went to college.

Men and women teachers exhibit different and changing career patterns:

• The experience of men teachers has *increased* from a median of 7 years to a median of 8 years in the course of the 1960's, but the experience of women has *decreased* from 14 to 8 years in median terms since 1961.

• Two-thirds of all women teachers began teaching either within the past 5 years or more than 20 years ago. In contrast, 6 in 10 men began teaching within the last 10 years.

• The percentage of women teachers who have had a break in service has decreased from 53 to 40 percent since 1961, and the percentage of women with a break in service for marriage or homemaking has decreased from 17 to 10 percent since 1966. However, nearly 1 woman in 5 continues to report a break in service for maternity or child rearing, and 5 percent of women teaching in 1970–71 planned to drop out in 1971–72 for homemaking and/or child rearing.

Within the profession, positions held by teachers reflect traditional sex identification of occupational roles:

• Only 1 man in 4 teaches in elementary school and less than 1 percent of all men teach grade 3 or below. In contrast, two-thirds of all women are elementary teachers, and one-third teach grade 3 or below. Conversely, 42 percent of men, compared with 18 percent of women, are senior high teachers.

• In secondary schools, the largest percentage of women teach English, while greater percentages of men than women teach science and social studies.

• The principalship is a male preserve. Two-thirds of all teachers are female, but 89 percent of all teachers report to a male principal. In elementary schools, 84 percent of teachers are women, but 80 percent of elementary teachers have men for principals. In secondary schools, 99 percent of teachers indicate that their principals are men.

Where teachers are

The nation's public school teachers are distributed among different types of communities:

• The largest proportion of teachers, 45 percent, are in school systems enrolling 3,000–24,999 pupils; 28 percent teach in large systems with 25,000 or more enrollment and 27 percent in small systems with less than 3,000 enrollment.

• More than one-third of all teachers teach in urban schools, more than half teach in suburban communities or small towns, and about 1 teacher in 8 is in a rural school. Two teachers in 10 are in large cities with a population of 250,000 or more, about half of them teaching in inner-city schools.

• Three teachers in 8 report that a majority of the pupils they teach come from the lower middle class; 2 in 8 report mainly pupils from the upper middle and upper classes; and 1 teacher in 6 indicates that a majority of his pupils are lower class in socioeconomic status. The rest report mixed economic classes among their pupils.

• Although 8 percent of teachers identify themselves as black and 6 percent report that they have a black principal, 12 percent report that half or more of the pupils they teach are black.

• In large systems, 29 percent of teachers teach in the inner city, 28 percent report that half or more of their pupils are black, and 29 percent that a majority of their pupils are lower class in socioeconomic status.

• Six teachers in 10 live within the boundaries of the school systems that employ them, but only 1 teacher in 3 lives within the attendance area of the school where he is teaching. In large systems, only 17 percent of teachers live within the attendance area of their schools, compared with 36 percent in medium-sized systems and 50 percent in small systems.

Teachers, like the rest of the population, are mobile:

• Only 29 percent of 1971 teachers were living in the communities where they had lived as children, a decrease from 33 percent in 1961. Recent newcomers to their communities increased from 11 to 15 percent in the same 10 years.

• About half of all teachers have taught in more than one school system.

Three teachers in 8 have taught in a different system in the same state where they currently teach, and 1 teacher in 5 has taught in another state.

• Five percent of those teaching in 1970–71 planned to teach in a different school system in 1971–72.

Progress and problems in teaching conditions

Improvement has occurred in a number of areas of teaching conditions, but evidence of continuing problems also exists:

• The percentage of teachers teaching at least part of the time in grades or subjects outside their major field of preparation has decreased from 31 to 23 percent since 1961. However, correction of misassignment has taken place where least needed: Fewer teachers are teaching some but less than half of their time out of field, but 1 teacher in 7 continues to be so seriously misassigned that he is teaching 50 percent or more of the time outside his field.

• The mean size of classes taught by elementary teachers has crept downward at a snail's pace from 29 pupils per class in 1961, to 28 in 1966, to 27 in 1971. Secondary teachers average 26 pupils per class, down from 27 in 1966 and 1961, but the mean number of pupils they teach per day is still over 130.

• Secondary teachers' unassigned periods have increased from a mean of 4 to a mean of 5 per week in the last five years, but 1 secondary teacher in 5, as in 1961, has no unassigned periods at all.

• Data on lunch periods show a victory for teachers in the second half of the 1960's. The percentage of teachers eating lunch with their pupils, which *increased* from 39 to 47 percent between 1961 and 1966, *decreased* to 31 percent in 1971. In 1966, fewer than 4 elementary teachers in 10 had a duty-free lunch period; in 1971, 6 in 10 had a duty-free lunch.

• The mean total working week for teachers is still 47 hours, as at the beginning of the 1960's. However, the mean number of hours spent by teachers on noncompensated school-related activities has decreased from 11 to 8 per week in the last 5 years.

• Teachers still teach a mean of 181 days a year, but their mean number of nonteaching days of contract has dropped from 5 to 4 since 1966.

Teachers' professional qualifications

Academic preparation of teachers has improved greatly during the 1960's:

• Nondegree teachers have almost entirely disappeared from the profession. In 1961, 15 percent of teachers did not even have a bachelor's degree; now 97 percent have at least a bachelor's degree.

• The percentage of teachers with bachelor's degrees increased in the first half of the decade; the percentage with master's degrees, in the second half. Forty-two percent of men and 19 percent of women have a master's degree or 6 years of preparation.

Teachers also show a strong interest in continuing education and professional growth:

• In the last 3 years, 61 percent of teachers have earned a mean of 14 semester hours of college credit beyond the bachelor's degree.

• Six teachers in 10 have participated in workshops sponsored by their school systems during the last 3 years.

• Six percent of 1971 teachers had had sabbatical leave for study, travel, or other purposes at some time since fall 1968.

Outside activities

Teachers' participation in organizational activities has declined in the past decade, but they continue to show a high degree of interest in activities that have professional relevance:

• Percentages of teachers who are members of churches, political parties, youth-serving groups, fraternal organizations, women's groups, men's service clubs, and parent teacher associations have decreased during the 1960's, especially among younger teachers.

• The mean number of hours per week that teachers give to working for organizations during the school year has decreased from 2 to 1 in the past 5 years. The percentage of teachers who do not give time to working for organizations has increased from 33 to 41 percent in the past 10 years.

• A majority of teachers, however, are members of local, state, and national educational associations, and more than half of all secondary teachers are members of subject-matter or professional special-interest associations. Despite the decrease since 1966, a majority of teachers also are still PTA members.

• Teachers are travelers. Apart from 4 percent who have traveled on sabbatical leave in the last 3 years, 26 percent have undertaken other educational travel in the last 3 years, and 35 percent traveled during the 1970 summer vacation.

Data on teachers and politics include the following:

• Formal membership in political party organizations dropped drastically from 31 to 13 percent between 1961 and 1971.

• However, 82 percent of teachers voted in the general election in 1970 and 75 percent voted in primary elections.

• By a ratio of 6 to 4, teachers who classify their political philosophy as conservative or tending to be conservative outnumber those who either are or tend to be liberal.

• Forty-three percent of teachers classify themselves as Democrats and 34 percent as Republicans, but 22 percent report that they are not affiliated with any political party. More than a third of teachers under age 30 have no party affiliation.

From each of the five sections of this article, choose several facts or trends which you consider most significant, and construct your own mini-portrait of the American teacher.

CURRENT ISSUES IN EDUCATION

Past units have introduced you to some of the problems and differing approaches in current education, as they related to the topic of the unit. But there are many other names, methods, and issues you should at least be aware of, and this unit brings together brief introductions to some of the more important of these. Perhaps you will find them important and interesting enough to pursue in greater detail on your own.

Contemporary Spokesmen

James Conant is best known for his 1959 report titled *The American High School Today* in which he advocated that each student be given an individualized program that is carefully planned and supervised to meet his particular needs and capabilities. He voiced strong opposition to the tracking system of placing students into vocational, commercial, or college-bound categories. Individual programs for each student would guarantee minimum competence in such basic areas as English, American problems and government, math, and science, while remaining flexible enough to maximize the potential of each student. Since quality education is paramount in Conant's view, he advocated consolidation of small high schools into schools large enough to be able to provide a broad spectrum of possible opportunities for students.

Harry Broudy, author of *The Real World of the Public Schools,* is a proponent, as is James Conant, of a philosophy of education known as Essentialism or the New Realism. Essentialists believe that the schools should concentrate on quality instruction in the essential skill and knowledge needed to live and compete in the real world.

Robert Hutchins is frequently associated with the phrase: "Since men are everywhere and always the same, education should be everywhere and always the same." In contrast to Conant and Broudy, Hutchins believes that the purpose of education is solely to train the intellect; all other nonintellectual activities (sports, preparing for life adjustment, preparation for citizenship in a democracy, and solving social problems) should be handled by other agencies, such as the home, church, media, or Boy Scouts. Since education should always be the same, the curriculum should be composed of the basic ideas that have reoccurred throughout intellectual history.

George Counts, a proponent of the philosophy of education known as Reconstructionism, advocates an approach to education similar to that of John Dewey and the pragmatists. For Counts, education's purpose is to build a new social order, to foster "frontier thinking" and action groups that would mobilize community forces toward a planned and enlightened democratic society. The curriculum, Counts believes, should stress the development of social concerns, and the anticipation of future needs in training the leaders of the future. Schools are successful when their graduates demonstrate their constructive involvement in rational social planning.

Jerome Bruner is perhaps best known for his research into the nature of concept formation and for his attempts to apply the scientific method to teaching methods. He has stated that "any subject can be taught effectively in some intellectually honest form to any child at any stage of development," provided the teacher translates the structure of the subject matter so that it is tailored to the way in which the student structures his world and explains it to himself. From this point of view, the question is not when to start teaching a certain concept or skill, but how to match it with the student. Bruner is also a spokesman for those who feel that "desire to learn" should be stimulated by the subject matter itself rather than by any arrangement of consequent events.

Jean Piaget is a developmental psychologist who has sampled the abilities and learning processes of many children at different ages and, as a result of these observations, believes that a child's mental growth is genetically controlled. A child, he argues, must pass through several sequential stages or levels, determined by his genetic development in conjunction with experience: the *sensorimotor* level (birth to about age two); the *perceptual* level (ages one to two) in which functional relationships are perceived; a *symbolic* stage (ages three to seven) in which the use of symbols such as language, drawings, and role-playing, is learned; the level of *concrete operations* (ages seven to twelve) in which the child begins to think logically, though not abstractly; and a *formal operations* level in which the child begins to use mental operations that are not dependent on visible concrete cues. Piaget has urged teachers to be more realistic about what children can be expected to do at various stages, to identify each child's current stage, and to individualize his instruction accordingly.

Robert Gagne, like Piaget, is a child psychologist whose research has had tremendous impact on educational design and practice. Gagne also is convinced that a child's learning passes through certain sequential stages, none of which can be bypassed; but Gagne believes that what determines the sequence of these stages is the nature of the skills to be learned—much more so than the child's genetic limits at various ages. Gagne has identified eight conditions for general learning: *signal* learning, in which infants learn useful responses to general cues or signals; *stimulus-response* learning, by which signal learning becomes more precise, controlled, and voluntary; *chaining,* in which the previous responses are put together in appropriate sequences (for example, walking includes a sequence of balance and motor responses); a *verbal discrimination* condition, involving associations between objects and names; *multiple discrimination,* a rote-memory type of learning to make complex chains of responses, and to identify and classify groups of stimuli; *concept* learning, or the ability to identify the important similarities and differences between sets of information, and to respond according to these similarities or differences; *principle* learning, the ability to relate one complete concept to several others in order to form a principle (such as a physics formula); and finally, *problem solving,* in which several principles can be related in the solving of new problems. Gagne is best known for his contributions to the area of programmed instruction, based on Skinner's basic research into the processes of learning. Gagne urges educators to be careful about how instruction is sequenced, arguing that many school failures occur because a student is expected to learn something for which he has not been taught the prerequisite skills.

Benjamin Bloom, in conjunction with several associates, is best known for his two taxonomies of educational objectives, and for his advocacy of the "Mastery Learning" concept of instruction. The two taxonomies (cognitive and affective) begin to specify and sequence the range of general learning tasks, from simple recall of information, through application and evaluation of that information, and from simple attention to stimuli, through degrees of internalizing and acting on a set of values and attitudes. The Mastery Learning approach calls for individualized and self-paced progress through the various levels and conditions of learning, with each student demonstrating his mastery of a given objective before moving on to the next.

Methods

Behavior Modification is the term used to include various applications of operant conditioning, or the experimental analysis of learning, to the problems of classroom learning. Units seven through nine summarize these principles and their applications.

Performance-Based Instruction, sometimes referred to as competency-based or contingency-managed instruction, is an attempt to translate the theory of Mastery Learning (see the notes on Benjamin Bloom) into practical methods. In general, this method involves:

1. Specifying the goals of instruction, in terms of measurable behavioral objectives.
2. Sequencing these objectives according to their interdependencies.
3. Grouping these sequenced objectives into small tasks.
4. Self-pacing each student's progress through these tasks.
5. Requiring that each student demonstrate minimum mastery competencies for one task, before proceeding to the next.
6. Evaluating a student solely on the basis of his mastery of these objectives, and providing whatever immediate remediation is necessary for mastery.
7. Giving each student immediate feedback about the adequacy of his work after each task.
8. Arranging deliberate contingencies of reinforcement for individual student progress and improvement.
9. Using continuous student performance data to evaluate and revise the instructional material and procedures.

Curriculum materials are being devised for use in performance-based instruction systems at all levels (e.g., *Individually Prescribed Instruction* (IPI) *in Math and Reading,* published by Research for Better Schools in Pittsburgh, and a variety of secondary and college texts from several national publishers). Many states and universities are moving toward a performance-based system for preparing and certifying their teachers. Since a teacher's competency as a teacher cannot directly be demonstrated by his college GPA, a performance-based teacher education program requires, in addition to the above characteristics, a field-centered component in which the student is gradually introduced to the real world of teaching and is taught to apply his knowledge and skills in actual classroom settings.

Individualized Contracting is very similar to performance-based instruction, except that greater attention is paid to the formal aspects of the contract arranged between each student and the teacher regarding the task or tasks to be completed, the criteria for this work, and the contingencies in effect if the student does or does not meet the criteria. Usually the student is given some involvement in formulating the terms of the contract, especially in regard to choosing from a variety of elective tasks and choosing the order in which he completes a set of contracts.

Differentiated Staffing is a method of organizing different teacher interests, talents, ambitions, and skills to meet different student needs, interests and abilities. Rather than assigning one teacher to one class of students for a semester or school year, the differentiated staffing plan calls for groups of teachers working with groups of students, each teacher taking responsibility for certain aspects of the instruction for as long as that component is needed with those students.

School systems have implemented this plan in a variety of ways. Some methods call for different levels of teachers: master teachers, senior teachers, staff teachers, and associate teachers. Each level has different degrees of administrative and instructional responsibility and opportunity; a beginning teacher, for example, could work into the profession in cooperation with experienced teachers of proven ability, while experienced teachers of outstanding ability are able to earn prestige and financial reward without having to leave the classroom for administrative positions. All methods of differentiated staffing make considerable use of paraprofessionals as teacher aides, resource-center assistants, and supervisors of various school areas.

Differentiated staffing is a move toward greater individualization of instruction and toward increased professionalism among teachers. The method has, however, experienced difficulty in defining the different levels of responsibility and assessing the competencies required at each level. Many administrators have also been reluctant to involve teachers in policy development and decision-making.

Flexible Scheduling, or modular scheduling, is a procedure by which the school day is organized into varied periods of time for different classes and activities. The basic unit of time, called a module, is used in various multiples. A school may, for instance, use a fifteen-minute module, and various classes, activities, or projects may then be assigned one module per day (fifteen minutes), or two modules (thirty minutes) or five modules (seventy-five minutes) or any other multiple of fifteen. A specific class might have four modules on Monday and Friday, two modules on Wednesday, and not meet at all on the other days.

Flexible scheduling is a procedure frequently used with differentiated staffing and team teaching methods to give the teachers flexibility in dividing their responsibilities, and in arranging for appropriate use of large-group presentations, small discussion groups, and individual work. In this way, flexible scheduling is another device intended to aid schools in individualizing the instruction of each student.

Individually Guided Education (IGE) is an instructional system developed and promoted by the Wisconsin Research and Development Center, which incorporates differentiated staffing, flexible scheduling, some aspects of performance-based instruction, and the use of student tutors. Students and teachers are organized into units of 100 or more students with a three to four year age range, three or more teachers, including perhaps a student teacher or an intern, a unit leader, and instructional aides. Within each unit, the teachers make the decisions about the grouping and regrouping of students according to their educational, social and emotional needs. Frequent unit staff meetings, frequent diagnosis of student performance, and special curricula allow the school to adjust daily procedures and materials to the perceived needs of each student.

Individualized Instruction is, as you may already have discovered, a label that refers either to (a) an unspecified theoretical inclination toward tailoring instruction in some way to the needs of individual students, or (b) one or more of a wide variety of instructional methods which claim to achieve that individualized tailoring. All of the instructional methods described above and most of those that will follow have been described as individualized instruction by their proponents. The term has become so broad, it has lost meaning; and that's an unfortunate abuse of a good idea. Of course, individualization is a relative term; when a teacher answers a question raised by a student, he is individualizing his instruction. In that sense all teaching is individualized to some degree.

One useful way to view individualization is in terms of how frequently the instruction can be adapted to individual needs. Review the components of performance-based instruction and you will notice that each of those components makes it easier and more likely that day-to-day decisions will be made to adjust each student's instructional program to his needs of the moment. And the next time you hear a curriculum or method described as individualized, ask yourself how frequently it allows for decisions to be made to change instruction for a given student.

Nongrading is a philosophy about student evaluation and promotion, and it focuses on individual differences among students, particularly regarding the rate at which each student learns. Instead of retention and repeating of a grade, nongrading suggests immediate remediation at the level of discrete skills; instead of skipping a grade, nongrading suggests that each student's rate of progress be maximized as much as is possible for him. Students are not delayed at a given skill while other students catch up, nor are students moved on to a new skill before they have mastered the last. Evaluation of students tends to be performance-based, and the school records and reports to parents emphasize the achievement of the student relative to the objectives rather than to other students or to the national average grade level.

The Open School (or the Open Classroom) refers to an ill-defined method of unstructured schooling in which students assume major responsibility for many aspects of their instruction. The Open School movement is based partly on a reaction against traditional schools and their oppressive lock-step structure and obsession with rigid discipline. The concept has been popularized by such authors as John Holt, Charles Silberman, and Joseph Featherstone, who have drawn extensively on theory and practices developed earlier in England. The methods for applying this theory to actual school settings are equally ill-defined. In some cases, the teacher's role is simply to provide a vast assortment of resources which the student can use when and if he is inclined, while the teacher tags along offering (but not imposing) guidance and direction. In most cases, however, there is some structure and direction inserted by teachers so that the student's learning is logically sequenced, broadly based, and efficient. The main thrust of the Open School Movement is, however, to guarantee that to a great degree each student can "do his thing with joy."

Computer-Assisted Instruction (CAI) is a logical outgrowth of programmed instruction. Skinner's small, inexpensive teaching machines of the early 1950s have given way to computerized programs, but the theory is essentially the same. In both cases, the material to be taught is broken down into discrete objectives, sequenced, and then presented to the student in small chunks. The student is required to respond to the material frequently enough so that his mastery of each objective can be evaluated. At each evaluation point, the program decides on the next stage, based on the student's performance at the last stage. Computers, of course, can perform these roles more efficiently and effectively than can printed programs, though at a much greater expense. But it is likely that in the future computers will play a much greater role in the individualization of classroom drill exercises, tutorial sessions, and independent study.

Computer-Managed Instruction (CMI) represents an equally probable and important role for the computer in the schools of tomorrow. The various forms of individualized instruction all require an enormous amount of record-keeping and record-accessing, if daily decisions about each student's instruction are to be tailored to the actual needs of the students. Incomplete, occasional, or inaccessible student performance records require the teacher to postpone decisions or to make decisions that only approximate the actual situation. Computers have the capacity to store and retrieve vast amounts of data accurately and quickly, and can be used rather inexpensively to manage the instructional data of thousands of students. It is almost inevitable that the technology of CMI will be commonplace in the schools of the future.

Multi-Media Instruction is a catch-all label used to indicate that instruction can take place through a variety of media including not only books, but also slides and filmstrips, models and transparencies, videotapes and simulations, and manual tools and electronic apparatus. Cassette tapes and videotapes are now being used in some schools to make lectures and demonstrations available to individual students at their request and convenience. Videotaping is also used in allowing students and inservice and preservice teachers to practice a newly-learned skill and then replay the tape to view their performance for its improvable aspects. Cable TV is now bringing special educational programs to local classrooms and, in conjunction with videotapes, CMI, and CAI, may in the future make some forms of individualized and performance-based instruction available to students in their homes.

The danger in multi-media instruction is a fairly common one: we tend to be less discriminate and logical with the novel, mysterious, shiny new tool. Media tools are, first of all, tools. They must not replace instruction, but serve it. There is no doubt however that these tools, and the instructional options they make possible, have served and will serve instruction by making it more efficient, effective and enjoyable.

The Year-Round School is an extended school year schedule, by which instruction is offered during most or all of the summer months, as well as during the regular school months. There are a variety of year-round plans being tried. Some plans involve staggered schedules for different groups or classes of students, in which a student gets one- or two-week holiday periods every two or three months. Other plans schedule three semesters or four twelve-week periods, with one summer month off for all. Still others use the summer months as a time for remediation for some students, and acceleration for others.

Pressure for schedule reorganization comes from community members concerned about having expensive school plants sit idle for a quarter of the year, and from professionals who see year-round schooling as a way of accelerating the pace of students through the basic skills training, leaving more time for an expanded curriculum and a broader educational experience.

Performance Contracting is a procedure by which a school district contracts with a business to carry out a specific instructional program for a specified time; a specified payment of money is promised for specified results in student achievement. Since taxpayers are reluctant to approve higher school taxes, most school districts have not been able to spend any money for research into methods for improving instruction. But some business firms have been attracted to the educational marketplace and have invested in research and development of specialized programs. The most widely publicized performance contract was between a private firm and the Texarkana schools; that, and eighteen other performance contracts analyzed by the Office of Economic Opportunity in 1972 were found to produce disappointing results.

Part of the problem is related to the newness of accountability. The school districts are frequently unable to pinpoint appropriate student performance objectives and select adequate measurement procedures. Private industry frequently underestimates the complexity of the problems. And certain teacher organizations sometimes give the public the impression that any form of accountability in education is worse than the plague. It is clear that performance contracting and its variants are a stumbling first attempt at joining education and private enterprise resources to improve education. Hopefully the quality of education will not become the football in a short-sighted struggle.

The Voucher System is a plan for financing schools through the use of government-issued certificates or vouchers to parents, who transfer the voucher to the particular school they choose for their child, and the school in turn receives a government payment for each voucher received. The value of each voucher within a given area would be the same for all students at each grade level, though some plans suggest that vouchers for disadvantaged children be given greater value. Once a child is admitted to a school, he is guaranteed a place for future years, as are his brothers and sisters. A school would be required to admit all students who listed that school as a first choice. When a school received more applicants than it had places, the school would select at least half on the basis of a lottery, and the rest on any other basis as long as discrimination against minorities was avoided.

Voucher plans were first established in the South during the 1950s to allow parents to send their children to segregated private schools, and this system has repeatedly been declared unconstitutional. Several states have also experimented with voucher systems designed to support parochial schools, and it was questionable whether the Courts would allow this as constitutional; but safeguards against these uses are included in most current voucher plans.

Opponents of the voucher system (especially the AFT) contend that such a plan would be used to encourage publicly-supported segregated and private schools, that it would promote hucksterism by nonpublic operators to recruit students, and that schools would resort to ostentatious teaching rather than professional teaching. In general, they feel that the system is unworkable and would splinter our system of free public education.

Proponents of the voucher system contend that a properly regulated system could inaugurate a new era of innovation and reform in the schools; schools would no longer have to please everybody (as they now do because of diverse backgrounds and involuntary participation) by maintaining a middle-of-the-road type of program. Once parents have a choice, they argue, schools can set up all kinds of alternatives on a take-it-or-leave-it basis. Furthermore, such a plan would provide the same freedom of choice for the poor that is now open to the wealthy.

Career Education, or Occupational Education, (it used to be called Vocational Education), is education that meets the career needs of students and the knowledge and skill required by society. Trade and agriculture schools have been around for a long time, of course; but the needs of society have changed drastically since such education was first designed. Even more important is the fact that since 80 percent of our high school students do not complete a college program, and only twenty percent are getting occupational training of any sort, half of our high school students are being offered a heavy dose of what—for them—amounts to irrelevant general educational pap.

Sidney Marland, as U.S. Commissioner of Education, suggested that we adopt a universal goal, guaranteeing that every high school graduate be ready to enter either higher education or useful and rewarding employment. Some schools are currently developing cooperative training and work experience programs with local employers for disadvantaged youth, and there are several career orientation programs being developed in both secondary and elementary schools to give students basic occupational information, and to develop appropriate attitudes. But Marland's proposal goes much further. He would abolish the snobbish distinction between the academic and the vocational, integrate both directions into a single, strong secondary program, and offer in-depth preparation for a variety of careers for every student.[1]

Deschooling is a label for several radical proposals to do away with most forms of formal schooling, not only because schools fail, but because they cripple minds. The late Paul Goodman, an American social critic, first introduced the proposal early in the 1960s in his book *Growing Up Absurd.* Goodman believed that most secondary and college students do not want to be in school and shouldn't be there. He points out that in all societies, even our own, until very recently, the education of most students has occurred informally and incidentally. Instead of the "delusion of formal teaching" which violates nature and stunts growth, he advocates incidental education taking place in the natural daily activities of society. Instead of the one school path, we should multiply the paths of growing up and provide opportunities to start over again, change focus, take a break, travel, and work separately with no compulsory attendance, no required sequences, and no certificates.

Ivan Illich, in his book, *Deschooling Society,* argues that schools favor the student who starts out earlier, healthier, or better prepared; that they deaden the desire to learn; and that they make knowledge hard to get by making it a packaged commodity to be bought and sold as private property. He believes that the disestablishment of the school has become inevitable, but that its replacement could be a worldwide classroom for correction and conformity, made possible by new educational technology. He argues that culture itself must be deschooled and technology must be used "to make society more simple and transparent, so that all men can once again know the facts and use the tools that shape their lives."

Opponents of deschooling reply that such proposals are hysterical and illogical exaggerations of some real problems with schools, and that they offer

---

[1] See his article on career education in the October, 1971 issue of *Today's Education.*

only vague and propagandistic alternatives. They agree that education involves more than schooling, but they argue that education without any schooling means directionless, helter-skelter hit-and-miss learning that leaves a child's learning to chance.

There are signs that whether or not society is eventually deschooled, schools in the meantime will improve because of the controversy.

1. Be able to define or identify in your own words the persons, methods and issues described in this unit, when given the name of each.

2. Paraphrase the method suggested for determining the degree of individualization in an instructional program.

3. Identify one commonality in the educational theories of:
   (a) Gagne and Piaget
   (b) Conant and Broudy
   (c) Bloom and Gagne
   (d) Bruner and Bloom
   (e) Broudy and Goodman

4. Identify one basic difference between the educational theories of:
   (a) Bruner and Piaget
   (b) Hutchins and Broudy
   (c) Gagne and Piaget
   (d) Broudy and Counts
   (e) Illich and Broudy

5. Identify one basic commonality and one basic difference in the following pairs:
   (a) CAI and CMI
   (b) Flexible Scheduling and the Year-Round School
   (c) Individualized Instruction and Behavior Modification
   (d) Individualized Instruction and Performance-Based Instruction
   (e) Individualized Instruction and Career Education
   (f) Differentiated Staffing and IGE
   (g) The Open School and Individualized Instruction

OBSERVATION AND RECORDING EXERCISE

If you have the opportunity to observe and record data in an actual teaching situation, you should prepare beforehand so that you can use your time as efficiently as possible. Observation opportunities are usually difficult to arrange, and much effort and time will be wasted if you simply observe casually to "get the feel of the class."

You should first of all limit your focus of attention by deciding on what general categories of events you will concentrate on. Will you focus on one student, on just the teacher, or on a small group of students, or on a certain kind of behavior? Perhaps you will have the opportunity for several observations, in which case you might use the first visit to help you make these decisions.

Then you will need a coding system appropriate to the behaviors you will be observing. If you tried to record all the behaviors in longhand, you would spend most of your time writing rather than observing. And you will have to have the code memorized so that the shorthand symbols come to you quickly when you need them.

Table 17–1 is a list of symbols that might be of use in an initial observation of student behaviors and their relationship to teacher responses.

Using these symbols, a portion of your running record might look like Table 17–2.

TABLE 17-1

Symbol	Class of Behavior
X	Gross motor behavior that is inappropriate (getting out of seat, running, turning around in seat, etc.)
N	Disruptive loud nonverbal noise (banging desk, tapping pencil, etc.)
IV	Blurting out, or other inappropriate verbals
A	Disturbing others directly
/	Other irrelevant behavior (not X, N, IV, or A, but no appropriate attention, either)
+	Relevant nonverbal behavior and time attending to task
AV	Proper verbal behavior, including talking and answering, laughing, etc., when appropriate to the teacher's instructions
P	Praise or approval comment
F	Facial indicator (smile, frown, or other nonverbal indication) of approval or disapproval
C	Criticism, scolding, threat, or other nonverbal disapproval

T = teacher; S = student; Ss = several or all students.

You should use whatever shorthand devices you feel most comfortable with. And the list must be appropriate for the specific kinds of behaviors you will be observing and recording. You might, for example, be concerned only with verbal interaction between teacher and students. Or you might narrow your

TABLE 17–2

Time (Min)	Event
00	Ss seated +; Mike, Mary, Jim, IV A; Alex, N T explains workbook task Mike / T—F—Mike
01	T—C—Mike Mike IV Mike + T P—6 Ss for +
02	all Ss +; T circulates among Ss

focus even more and examine how often the teacher asks questions of different types (see Unit 13). Or you might examine the verbal and nonverbal types and frequencies of reinforcing and punishing events the teacher uses for individual student responses. In each case, your shorthand system must be adapted to the situation.[1]

---

[1] You might find the following references helpful for observing verbal interaction: Flanders, N. A. *Using Interaction Analysis in the Inservice Training of Teachers; Journal of Teacher Education* (1963), *14,* 251–60; and *Journal of Research and Development in Education* (1970), *4,* especially pages 23–33.

Instead of recording the elapsed time in the lefthand column, as shown in Table 17–2, you might instead use a time sampling procedure. Prepare a sheet of paper with rows of blocks (six per minute). Using a watch, you can observe the behavior occurring at the beginning of each ten-second period, record it in the block, wait for the next ten-second interval to begin, and repeat the process.

1						2						3	
												etc.	

At the end of the observation period, you can total up the different kinds of behaviors and graph them (see Unit 10). In summary, you complete this unit with these steps:

1. Make arrangements with the principal of the school you wish to visit. Ask his permission and note any procedural details he suggests. (Be sure to check your own school's policy regarding procedures for arranging such a visit before you contact the principal.)
2. Prepare your observation coding and recording forms and outline in as much detail as possible how you intend to use your observation time. Submit your forms and plan to your instructor for approval *before* continuing.
3. Carry out your observation plan during the times arranged with the principal. If your plan involves several observation periods, your instructor may want to review your records with you after each session.
4. Analyze your data in one or more of the ways suggested in Unit 10 and/or as suggested by your instructor. Include all your records when you submit your analysis report to your instructor.

Unit 18

SELF-MANAGEMENT OF STUDY PROJECT

This project is appropriate and tailor-made for you if you find yourself having serious difficulty managing your study time or deciding what, when, or how to study for this or any of your classes.

If you don't see yourself as really needing help in this area, or if you are not very interested in working on the problem at this time, then just skip over this unit. Furthermore, to be of some value to you, this project should be started early in the semester. This is what you do:

Step 1: *Read* through this whole unit carefully and completely, so that you know where you're going and how you're going to get there.

Step 2: Begin to record the following *baselines:*
  (a) Minutes of actual study time per day for each subject
  (b) Pages read per day for each subject

You may think of other baselines that might be appropriate and important in your particular case; if so, begin measuring these also. Keep separate graphs for each behavior, at least during the baseline recording period.

Then write up a detailed description of your current study behavior. This should include answers to the following questions:

  (a) Where do you study? (Describe the places.) What distractors are there?

189

(b) What free time do you have available during the day, after school, at night, and on weekends?

(c) What do you do during each of these free periods when you don't study?

(d) When the thought occurs to you that you should study—but you don't—what activities do you frequently choose instead?

(e) When you do choose to study, which subjects do you choose first? Why? Which subjects or activities do you frequently put off? Why?

Include in your writeup any other factors which add to a description of your study behavior.

Submit the baselines and the writeup to your instructor for approval. If possible, bring along some ideas you have about arranging situations and contingencies for changing your pattern of study. Your instructor will also make some suggestions, based on the data you supply. If necessary, he will also suggest modifications in your writeup or in your procedures for collecting baseline data.

Step 3: The Plan. After you obtain your instructor's approval of Step 2 activities, begin planning the details of your procedures for changing your study behavior. To prepare for this, review Unit 11, and perhaps the several units preceding it. Your plan should, wherever appropriate, observe the following:

(a) Specify full details of the internal chain procedure you will use to increase the probability of self-instruction occurring and being effective; be sure to identify the preceding stimulus, the thought chain, the consequent event, and the times when this process will occur during the day.

(b) List the external control arrangements you intend to make; include details of any contingencies you will arrange for others to impose, how you will arrange your study environments, and how you will graph your progress.

(c) Graph the details of your general planned study schedule for the various time slots each day of the week. Perhaps this can be in the form of a chart, with days of the week blocked horizontally and the time periods of the day blocked vertically, and each block identified as a class meeting, a library study period, lunch, study at home, recreation, etc. The intention is that this time schedule be not an inflexible routine, but a general guide to be followed whenever possible and feasible.

(d) Break down the requirements for each of the courses you are currently taking into small sequential units, divided into relatively equal weekly amounts according to the number of weeks available for accomplishing them.

(e) Continue taking your baseline measurements while developing these plans.

(f) Submit your complete plan, along with your complete baseline records, to your instructor, for his analysis and possible modifications.

(g) Your credit in this course, dependent on your implementation of the details of this plan, should be arranged at this point with your instructor.

(h) After your instructor's final approval of these plans, proceed to Step 4.

Step 4: Implementation.

(a) Begin immediately to implement all the details of your plan as approved.

(b) Report weekly (unless arranged otherwise) to your instructor, with your progress graph for the last week, the list of small units you intend to achieve in the coming week, and any problems that have arisen during the past week.

(c) Near the end of the semester, or as arranged with your instructor, collect your data, graphs, and writeups, add a summary assessment of the procedures and a note as to what you would do differently if you were to do this the following semester, and submit the complete package to your instructor.

(d) Your credit for this unit should be based on criteria established between you and your instructor just prior to implementation.

This Unit, if done as outlined above, will undoubtedly teach you how to change your own study behavior, not only in theory but also in practice. But simply being *able* to do it is not likely to be helpful unless you continue to manage your own behavior. Hopefully, the results of your study-scheduling this semester will convince you that it is worth continuing.

CURRENT EDUCATIONAL ISSUES PROJECT

In Unit 16, a variety of educational spokesmen, issues, and innovative procedures are briefly summarized. This unit gives you an opportunity to more closely examine several of these topics, to develop your understanding of them, and also to receive extra credit for each such investigation.

In order to avoid the usual problems connected with a "paper project" (such as your doubts about exactly what is required, and the instructor's problems about how to fairly evaluate such papers), the following guidelines are suggested.

These steps should be completed for each written project:

Step 1: Choose a topic that interests you from the topics suggested by previous units or design your own and have it approved by your instructor.

Step 2: Locate and study at least three articles that pertain directly to the topic you have chosen. The articles can be taken from periodicals (see the end of this unit for suggestions), or it can be a chapter from a book, or an article in a book of readings, but the article should have been published no more than three years ago.

Step 3: Summarize each article on one side of a 4 × 6 index card, and include:

    (a)   your name, course, section, and date;

    (b)   the article title, author, source, and date of publication;

(c)   an outline of the main points of the article;

(d)   and the conclusion of the article.

Step 4:   *Write* a two to four page paper in which you:

(a)   *compare* (not summarize) the three articles with each other. Show on what points each agrees, disagrees, or expands on the others, regarding (1) the essential components of the topic (2) the values and advantages of the topic and (3) the criticisms and disadvantages of the topic.

(b)   Give your own *definition* of the issue or position and its essential components;

(c)   Give your summary *assessment* of the current and future value of this topic for educational practice.

Despite the above guidelines, it is possible that some misunderstanding might lead to inadequacies in your final report. For this reason, if you intend to do several reports on different issues, you might be wise to get your first report submitted and approved before you begin others, and to get all your intended reports in before the last week of the semester, so that there will be time to remedy any possible deficiencies that might be uncovered. The following is a list of journals that might contain appropriate articles:

American Educational Research Journal
Audiovisual Instruction
Center Magazine
Changing Education
Contemporary Education
Educational Forum
Educational Technology
Educational Theory
Harper's
Harvard Educational Review
Instructor
Journal of Applied Behavior Analysis
Journal of Educational Research
Learning
Peabody Journal of Education
Phi Delta Kappan
Psychology Today
Review of Educational Research
Saturday Review
School Review
Teachers College Record
Today's Education

The Reader's Guide and other such reference sources might also help you in locating appropriate articles. Check with your instructor before selecting an article from one of the more popular nonprofessional magazines not listed above.

WORKSHOP— DEALING WITH FEELINGS

"I never suspected that he felt that strongly about it. Boy, I bet he thought I was hard. I just never got the message."

"I wish I could get my parents to understand how I feel about their nagging, but every time I try we get into a big argument and things get blown all out of proportion."

"Letting your feelings show just buys trouble. When I'm happy and excited, and I show it, I come off looking like some kind of childish nut. When I'm bugged about something and say so, it sounds like I'm uptight and selfish about petty things. I say, stay cool or be a fool."

These are statements of fairly common attitudes. They are said or thought by students and by teachers in thousands of schools. And they represent one important hindrance to effective instruction in the schools and to effective interpersonal relationships everywhere.

Feelings are states of mind or emotion a person has toward someone or something. Of course, we usually are not in a position to measure these states directly. We sometimes even find it difficult to identify our own feelings accurately and are surprised when our actions reveal different feelings. But we can and do identify feelings on the basis of what a person says and does. A person's statements may clearly express his attitude toward someone or something, or they may vaguely hint at such an attitude. On the other hand, a person's actions (including facial expression, tone of voice, and posture) may give nonverbal indication of his feelings. In this sense, feelings—like attitudes—are sets of approach or avoidance behaviors, especially verbal behaviors, regarding the object of the feeling.

Whether we like it or not, the way we express (or don't express) our feelings about people and things has a great deal of influence on the satisfaction and achievement we and others get out of life. You already know how important it is that you, as a teacher and as a human being, exercise care in arranging contingencies and consequences for others and for yourself. Trusting relationships can be developed or stunted, understanding can be deepened or destroyed, self-satisfaction can be nurtured or perverted—all depending to a large extent on your ability to accurately read the feelings of yourself and others, and to respond appropriately.

This unit will not make you an expert in this. But it will probably make you better at it than you are now. It will improve your ability to attend to and interpret the feelings expressed by others or held by yourself, and to respond to others in a way that shows understanding and invites trust, and to express your own feelings honestly, courteously, and productively.

Of course there are times when it is not appropriate or advisable to completely expose your feelings. But you can't really make a wise choice about this unless you have certain judgemental skills. This unit will give you information, practice, and feedback about these skills.

Introduction to Session 1

This unit takes the form of a workshop with other students. The unit's objectives are, in part, social skills and they are best learned in a setting that is, in part, social. To complete this unit you will need at least five other students (total group membership of no less than six and no more than nine) who can all meet at the same time twice a week for fifty to sixty minutes each. When this group has agreed on a schedule for their sessions, submit the names of the members, and the date and time for your first session to your instructor, who may want to make some recommendations to the group. All members should read the Introduction to this unit before the first session, and all should bring the complete unit to each session. The directions for conducting each session are included in the pages for each session.

It might be helpful to learn one definition before beginning Session 1.

> *Empathy:* feeling for and with another person. Putting yourself in the other person's shoes so that you understand exactly how the other person is experiencing something, no matter how superficial or deep his feelings are.

Session 1

Organization

Each member should introduce himself to the group and state several things about himself that he thinks might help the others know and understand him.

Choose a moderator, if you wish. The moderator participates as a member in all the activities of the workshop, but he is also responsible, when necessary, to get a session started, to keep discussion on the topic, to keep track of time spent on each step, and to turn in the record sheets for all members.

Begin with Step 1. Check off each step as it is completed. Do not remain at any step longer than the time allowed for it. During the first session, you will probably not be able to complete all the steps. *Be sure to save 15 minutes for steps 8 and 10.*

Each member should privately and quickly complete steps 1, 2, 3, and 4 by writing a one- or two-sentence response he would most likely make in the following situations:

_____Step 1.   A good friend says to you: "I'm pretty worried. I don't think Joe likes me any
     (2 min.)   more. He hasn't called me all week, and yesterday I think he saw me on campus and deliberately avoided me. I wish I knew what I did wrong." *Write your response on the Session 1 Record Sheet.*

_____Step 2.   A close friend says: "Well, the team I play for finally got an invitation to the
     (2 min.)   NCAA finals in St. Louis." *Write your response on the Session 1 Record Sheet.*

_____Step 3.   How do you feel right now about any or all aspects of this interpersonal work-
     (4 min.)   shop? *Write your response on the Session 1 Record Sheet.*

_____Step 4.   Your professor has just handed you back a term paper you wrote. He marked
     (2 min.)   it C, with no comments. You thought you had done A or at least B work. What would you most likely do or say? *Write your response on the Session 1 Record Sheet.*

_____Step 5.   One member of the group reads his response to Step 1 aloud. The group then
     (after 25   discusses his response in terms of the following questions: (a) Might the re-
     min. on   sponse in some way make the friend feel foolish or unreasonable for being
     steps 5, 6   worried? (b) Does the response avoid the issue of how the friend is feeling?
     and 7,   (c) Does the response show some degree of acceptance or empathy for the
     skip to   friend's anxiety?
     step 8)   Be sure to save 10–15 minutes for Steps 8 and 10.

_____Step 6.   Other members of the group take turns reading their responses to Step 1, and the group discusses the response in terms of the above questions. No member should be required to read his response unwillingly.

_____Step 7.   Each member reads his response to Step 2. After each response the group discusses it in terms of: (a) Does the response belittle the accomplishment? (b) Does it focus on the unstated enthusiasm the friend probably feels, but is hiding? (c) Does the response reflect enthusiasm for the accomplishment and opportunity? (d) Can anyone think of other responses that would do this?

_____Step 8. Each member then reads his response to Step 3, and after each response the
(10–15 group discusses it in terms of the following questions: (a) Does the response
min., but actually express *some* feeling, or is it noncommittal? (b) Ask each other if
be sure to there are other feelings about some aspect of the workshop that were *not* ex-
save 5 pressed. If so, why were they not expressed—out of reluctance, or out of in-
min. for ability to describe them precisely? (Here again, discussion should be voluntary
c, d only.) (c) At this point, the group spends a minute or two in complete silence,
and e) with each member using the time to try to identify more precisely how he or
she feels at this time about the workshop, or the other members. (d) Can anyone think of a clearer or more straightforward response to Step 3 than the one
first made? (e) Did anyone feel uncomfortable with the silence?

_____Step 9. Each member reads his response to Step 4, and after each response is read, the
(if there group discusses it in terms of the following questions: (a) Does the response
is time) include an honest, direct expression of what the student feels are his rights
for information? (b) Does the response show respect for the rights of the professor? (c) Can anyone think of other responses that include both of the
above?

_____Step 10. Preparation for Next Session:
(2–4 min.)   (a)   Agree on a date and time for the next session of the group, and write
it below and at the top of the Session 2 Record Sheet.
Date and Time: _____

(b)   Review the activities and study materials which are expected. Each
member is expected to study some material and complete some activities *before* the next meeting. The worthwhileness of the workshop for
each member depends on each member's preparation and participation.

(c)   Turn in the Session 1 Record Sheets to your instructor.

(d)   Things to do before the next session: (1) Study the Introduction to
Session 2. (2) Learn the 5-point rating scale.

Session 1 Record Sheet

Name: _____   Class and Section: _____

Date: _____   Time: _____

Response to Step 1:

_____

Response to Step 2:

_____

Response to Step 3:

_____

Response to Step 4:

Evaluating Session 1

If your first session included some honest and serious discussion, you may be feeling uneasy right now about your own abilities to understand feelings, express them openly and clearly, give honest reactions, and take them from others. That's understandable and normal after one session—and it's a good sign that your workshop will be profitable for you and the others. The anxiety should pass rather quickly, whereas the improved skills will remain.

Perhaps, however, you feel that your first session was rather superficial, an exercise in the avoidance of the topic of feelings. If so, why not tell the group that you feel this way at your next session. But be prepared to make serious contributions of your own by listening closely, expressing clearly, admitting to your own feelings, and by being willing to try something new.

AVOIDING THE AFFECTIVE

Many people find it very easy to participate in a conversation about things that they do not feel strongly about, focusing on factual information at a cognitive level without revealing their feelings. Many people find it very difficult to talk about and share their real feelings about things that are important to them.

From childhood, most of us have been deliberately taught how to discuss at a cognitive and unemotional level; far less frequently are we deliberately taught to converse on an affective level. As a result, without the necessary skills we feel uneasy with periods of deliberate silence, uncomfortable in dealing with another's expressed feelings, and fearful of expressing our own. We learn to avoid these consequences by changing the topic, by expressing *opinions* rather than feelings, by putting someone down, by pretending to agree, by avoiding periods of silence, and by a variety of other ways. These ways of responding are not always bad or inappropriate; but when they occur so frequently that they become a general pattern in our dealings with others, they prevent us from learning much about ourselves and others, and from relating in helpful ways. Compare this pair of statements:

"I feel uncomfortable in this workshop—I guess it's because this is a new experience for me."

"Everyone can expect to feel a little uneasy in a new situation."

and these statements:

"I'm really happy about my new stereo."

"I think that this stereo was a good buy."

Perhaps you can begin to see how small differences in wording can make important differences in the message conveyed. They can change the focus and avoid the important.

ADVICE

Typically, when a person tells us about a problem, a worry, or a fear, we tend to jump right in with a suggestion that will fix it up, or with strong agreement or vague reassurance. In live situations this might be an avoidance device for closing the topic quickly, avoiding any prolonged discussion of feelings, or even a subtle way of patronizing the other person and putting him down. Often a sense of understanding and empathy is more helpful than "words of wisdom." In any case, it is foolish to attempt advice until you are sure you really understand how the other person feels, and at what level. For that reason, in the remaining sessions of this workshop, try to avoid responding with advice, and concentrate instead on practicing responses that show empathy, acceptance and a desire to understand more completely.

ACCEPTANCE

When you express acceptance of another's feelings, you are, in effect, saying that you sense what he is feeling and that it's all right with you if he feels that way. Whether or not you share or would share his attitude in his situation, you are telling him that his attitude is perfectly understandable and acceptable. And by implication you are also saying that it's okay for him to continue expressing these feelings in his attempt to gain a better understanding of them himself.

For example, if your date says "I don't know if I want to go to this party— I won't know any of the people there," and you respond, "Aw, just relax— they are all good kids and you'll have fun if you just relax," you probably have told your date that the worry is foolish, not worth talking about any more. If instead you had said something like "It can be pretty frightening going into a new situation and thinking you might be ignored all evening," your date would probably have a better chance of understanding and coming to grips with his or her own feelings. Of course, a few people learn to take constant advantage of that device to get attention and sympathy, in which case selective extinction might be appropriate. But, as with the law, a person deserves the benefit of the doubt until proven guilty.

LEVELS AND RATING SCALES

In several of the following sessions (including Session 2) of your group, you will need to know and use the following scale for rating the levels of statements and responses made by yourself and your fellow members. It's about the only memorization that this unit requires, but you will have to know the levels well enough to use them without rereading them during the session.

This is a 5-point scale for rating a statement for its empathy, clarity, and depth of feeling expressed.[1]

Level 1: The statement expresses *no feeling or awareness* of another's feeling, not even the most obvious surface feelings.

> "I don't want to take the test today."
> "Let's get going. Class starts in ten minutes."

Level 2: The statement expresses *some feeling or awareness* of another's feeling, but at a somewhat camouflaged or very *superficial* level. A level 2 response tends to distort the feeling actually felt or expressed by the other person.

> "I feel uneasy about going to the party tonight."
> "Don't be silly. You look fine."

Level 3: The statement accurately expresses the *surface* feelings or responds with an accurate awareness of the surface feelings of another, but *hides* or *misinterprets* the deeper feelings of another.

> "It's starting to irritate me a little that you always borrow my class notes but never return them unless I bug you for them."
> "I'm glad you told me that that annoys you. I'll try to get the notes back sooner in the future, ok?"

Level 4: The statement expresses feelings somewhat *beneath the surface* or, as a response, *adds something* to the stated feelings in terms of either precision or depth.

> "Boy, these students around here are something else—curvebusters, working like crazy for the Almighty A. And if you don't have a 3.5 GPA, they think you're a misplaced half-wit from the hills. Just because you get a couple of Cs doesn't mean you'll be digging ditches for the rest of your life. What a bunch of phonies."
> "The grades and expectations of other students make you furious. I'm sure that makes your school life miserable. It probably also makes it more difficult to socialize with the A students."

Level 5: The statement expresses *deep feelings* with accuracy and understanding or, as a response to another's stated feelings, it *adds much* to the statement and shows accurate understanding and empathy at the deepest level of the other's feelings.

---

[1] Adapted and revised from several levels suggested by Robert Carkhuff in Vol. 1 of *Helping and Human Relations: A Primer for Lay and Professional Helpers* (New York: Holt, Rinehart, and Winston, 1969).

"I can easily sense how furious you must feel because of the grades and expectations of other students; I'm sure that makes your social life miserable also. But I sense that this problem also touches on something in you that you are unsure about—how to handle your relations with these people. I sense that you are perhaps unsure and anxious about who you are in relation to them."

Review these five levels several times until you feel comfortable with them and *able to use them* in your next session. Check the examples to see why they were judged to be at the stated level.

Remember: Just because a level 5 response is the highest type doesn't mean that it's always the best response in any situation. But unless you *can* respond at a higher level, you won't be able to choose the right response for the right situation. In the hypothetical situations you use in this workshop, *presume* that a high-level response *is* appropriate.

Presume also that focusing immediately on *solving* the problem is *not* the best way to respond. In real life, immediately suggesting a solution may be a way of avoiding the issue of the person's feelings. Besides, a good solution may be impossible until the feelings are thoroughly probed and clarified. Finally, in some real situations, empathy may not be the most appropriate initial response, but in these workshop situations it is the best, because the purpose here is simply to learn how.

Questions to consider about your group:

1. Are *all* members participating? If not, what can you do to improve this?

2. Are any members being put down, becoming defensive or fearful? If so, what can you do to make this person more comfortable and able to test his thoughts and feelings?

3. Are any members dominating the discussion, or in some ways frustrating others? If so, consider making these feelings known to the person or the group.

Session 2

Before beginning Session 2, the group moderator should pick up the record sheets for the first session from the instructor and give each member his sheet.

_____Step 1.   The group forms into *pairs* (and one threesome, if the number of members is uneven). Each pair moves away from the other pairs a little distance.

_____Step 2.   Each member rates his own written response to each of the first three situations
(3–5   in Session 1 (Steps 1, 2, and 3). Write the ratings on the response sheet for
min.)   Session 2. Do not share them with your partner at this time; make the best rating you can, simply on the basis of what was written.

_____Step 3.   Each member exchanges his written responses (from Session 1) with his part-
(3–5   ner (do *not* exchange the ratings), and rates his partner's responses to the same
min.)   three situations.

_____Step 4.   Now each pair compares the ratings they gave to each others responses and dis-
(5–10   cusses the agreements and differences in the ratings.
min.)

_____Step 5.   The group as a whole discusses any questions or doubts that pairs of members
(5–10   may have found regarding the empathy and acceptance scales or the ratings.
min.)

_____Step 6.   The group forms into different pairs for some brief role-playing. One member
(10–15   assumes the role of a parent, and says to his partner (in the role of a high
min.)   school-age son or daughter) "Please, can we save your problem until tomor-
                 row? I've got a splitting headache and I've had a very bad day and I'm very
                 upset. Later, okay?"
                 The partner responds, and the discussion continues for a minute or so, or un-
                 til a logical conclusion is reached.
                 Each member writes his rating on the level of his own responding and of his
                 partner's responding on the Session 2 Record Sheet.
                 Then both members analyze the responses for: (a) the stated feelings ex-
                 pressed; (b) the unstated feelings implied; (c) the level of empathy and accu-
                 racy shown by each member's responses; (d) ideas on how the responses might
                 have been improved.

_____Step 7.   One member (one who did not initiate the Step 6 dialogue) assumes the role
(10–15   of a high school student and says to his partner (who plays the role of the stu-
min.)   dent's teacher), just as he or she is about to begin class:

                        "Mr. (or Ms.) _____, I know the deadline for our project is to-
                        day, but our family has had the flu the last several days, and I just
                        couldn't get to the project. I've got part of it done, but could I have
                        a few more days to finish it up?"

The partner responds and the discussion continues for a minute or so, or until a logical conclusion is reached.

Both members analyze the responses for: (a) the stated feelings expressed; (b) the unstated feelings implied; (c) the level of empathy or acceptance shown by each member's responses; (d) ideas on how the responses might have been improved.

_____Step 8.   The group as a whole again discusses questions and ratings coming out of the
(5 min.)   pair dialogues and discussions.

_____Step 9.   Preparation for Session 3
(2 min.)
      (a)   Agree on a date and time for the next session of the group, and write it below and at the top of the Session 3 Record Sheet.
           Date and Time _____

      (b)   Things to do before Session 3: (1) Restudy the introduction to Session 2. (2) Construct several original situations of your own for use during the next session.

      (c)   Moderator collects record sheets for Sessions 1 and 2 and gives them to the instructor.

Session 2 Record Sheet

Name: _____   Class and Section: _____

Date: _____   Time: _____

Step 2: Self-Ratings (check the appropriate level number)

Response to Step 1   Response to Step 2   Response to Step 3

| 1 | 2 | 3 | 4 | 5 | | 1 | 2 | 3 | 4 | 5 | | 1 | 2 | 3 | 4 | 5 |

Step 3: Ratings of Partner's Responses

Response to Step 1   Response to Step 2   Response to Step 3

| 1 | 2 | 3 | 4 | 5 | | 1 | 2 | 3 | 4 | 5 | | 1 | 2 | 3 | 4 | 5 |

Partner's Name: _____

Step 6: Ratings

My Own Response   Partner's Response

| 1 | 2 | 3 | 4 | 5 | | 1 | 2 | 3 | 4 | 5 |

Partner's Name: _____

Step 7: Ratings

My Own Response   Partner's Response

| 1 | 2 | 3 | 4 | 5 | | 1 | 2 | 3 | 4 | 5 |

Partner's Name: _____

Introduction to Session 3

Don't be discouraged if you had trouble responding at a 4 or 5 level. They are fairly rare in the real world, even among trained counselors. If, by the end of the workshop, you are able to express and respond with ease at one or perhaps two levels higher than when you started, your ability to relate to others will have been improved tremendously. To prepare for the next session, you should do three things:

1. Re-read the introduction to Session 2. These brief notes will probably mean more to you now that you've had some live practice. Pay particular attention to the description and examples of the five levels, so that your ratings can be more precise during the next sessions.

2. Construct original situations or initiating statements which can be used in the next session. The statements should express a feeling at some level, and the situation should be a realistic one, that members of the group can easily respond to. Plan to bring at least two different situational statements to the next session. It might be best to write them out for easy memory and easy use.

3. Consider the advisability of asking your instructor to sit in on a session or on a part of one. Consider other procedures that might improve the functioning of your workshop and its helpfulness to each member.

Session 3

_____Step 1.
(15–20
min.)

Members form into groups of three, with each member taking his turn at being discussion initiator, respondent, or recorder.

The discussion initiator gives the opening statement in the original situation supplied by the recorder; the respondent responds to that statement, and while the discussion continues, the recorder rates the level of responding by both discussants.

The situation is repeated twice, giving each member a turn at being discussion initiator, respondent, or recorder.

_____Step 2.
(15–20
min.)

The whole group comes together again, and new groups of three are formed. The procedures of Step 1 are repeated, using new situations.

_____Step 3.
(15–20
min.)

The whole group comes together for a brief discussion of ways in which the group might make its remaining sessions more profitable for all members. This discussion might also give members the opportunity to express their own feelings honestly, courteously and constructively.

_____Step 4.

Preparation for Session 4.

(a) Agree on a date and time for the next session (record here and on Session 4 Record Sheet).

Date and Time: _____

(b) Things to do before Session 4: (1) Read the Introduction to Session 4. (2) Prepare to state your own feelings about a topic of your choice.

(c) Turn in Session 3 Record Sheets.

Session 3 Record Sheet

Name: _____   Class and Section: _____

Date: _____   Time: _____

Step 1: Recorder's Ratings

Initiator's Statements   Respondent's Statements

| 1 | 2 | 3 | 4 | 5 | | 1 | 2 | 3 | 4 | 5 |

Initiator's Name_____   Respondent's Name_____

Step 2: Recorder's Ratings

Initiator's Statements   Respondent's Statements

| 1 | 2 | 3 | 4 | 5 | | 1 | 2 | 3 | 4 | 5 |

Initiator's Name_____   Respondent's Name_____

Introduction to Session 4

During the next two sessions, you will be asked to make a brief statement about your feelings regarding someone or something—a friend, a parent, a brother or sister, your job, an aspect of your school life or social life, a specific event you were involved in, this workshop—whatever you have some feelings about that you want to discuss. Try to be as *clear* and *honest* as you can, but keep your statement brief. You will also be responding to similar statements by other members of your group to test your understanding of the feelings expressed.

Before the next session, give some thought to the topic you want to discuss and also to exactly what your feelings are about it. One way to do this is to get yourself relaxed in an undistracting environment, bring the person, thing or event into your imagination and watch (or feel) what happens, as if you were a bystander.

Remember that *depth* of feeling is not the same as *intensity*. A statement that expresses very intense and strongly felt feelings may not be getting at the deeper, perhaps less clearly identified feelings. Your task as initiator is to express your feelings as clearly and deeply as possible. Your task as a respondent is to probe the initiator's statement for accuracy and depth regarding the feelings. Try also not to talk *about* but *to* another member of the group about his statements or feelings.

Session 4

_____Step 1.
(2–4
min.)

One member of the group initiates a discussion about the feelings that member has toward someone or something. This initiator _briefly_ states how he or she feels about the topic, as clearly and honestly as possible. Each member then rates the initiator's statement for its level of clarity and depth of feeling.

_____Step 2.
(5–10
min.)

The other members discuss the feeling _with the initiator_. They test their understanding of the initiator's feelings by attempting to paraphrase and/or interpret what the initiator expressed and by getting the initiator's reaction about the accuracy of the response. This discussion will, in many cases, also help the initiator clarify more precisely his own feelings toward the topic.

Remember: All discussion should concern _only_ the initiator's _feelings_ toward the topic he or she raised. Any discussion of the person or thing involved in causing the feeling, or of the level of statement should be avoided or redirected. The initiating member may terminate the discussion at any time simply by informing the group that he wishes to do so.

_____Step 3.
(5 min.)

The group as a whole briefly discusses the following:
(a)   to what extent was the statement clear and perceptive.
(b)   did the discussion focus only on the initiator's feelings.
(c)   did the discussion tend to put down, embarrass, or give advice.
(d)   did the discussion help to clarify the initiator's feelings.

_____Step 4.
(10–15
min.)

The procedures in Steps 1 and 2 are repeated with a new member expressing his feelings, and the other members checking their understanding and, helping to clarify.

_____Step 5.
(10–15
min.)

Repeat the procedure with another member.

_____Step 6.

If there are ten or more minutes left, repeat the procedure with another member.

_____Step 7.

Preparation for Session 5:
(a)   Agree on a date and time for Session 5 and write it below and at the top of the Session 5 Record Sheet.
Date and Time: _____
(b)   Activities for Session 5: (1) Do some thinking about the statements and responses you made this session, and about the comments of the other members. Consider how you could improve your statements. (2) Prepare to repeat Session 4's procedures next time, with new topics.
(c)   Turn in the Session 4 Record Sheets to your instructor.

Session 4 Record Sheet

Name: _____   Class and Section: _____

Date: _____   Time: _____

Step 1: *Rating of Statement of Feeling by* (*name*): _____ | 1 | 2 | 3 | 4 | 5 |

Rating of my response: | 1 | 2 | 3 | 4 | 5 |

Step 3: *Rating of Statement of Feeling by* (*name*): _____ | 1 | 2 | 3 | 4 | 5 |

Rating of my response: | 1 | 2 | 3 | 4 | 5 |

Step 4: *Rating of Statement of Feeling by* (*name*): _____ | 1 | 2 | 3 | 4 | 5 |

Rating of my response: | 1 | 2 | 3 | 4 | 5 |

Step 5: *Rating of Statement of Feeling by* (*name*): _____ | 1 | 2 | 3 | 4 | 5 |

Rating of my response: | 1 | 2 | 3 | 4 | 5 |

Session 5

_____Step 1. Repeat the procedures in Session 4, beginning with members who were not ini-
(10–20   tiators in expressing a personal feeling during Session 4.
min.)

_____Step 2. The initiating member verbally rates each of the other members on: (a) the
(5–10   accuracy of each member's paraphrases of the feeling; (b) the degree of em-
min.)   pathy expressed.
         The group discusses the initiator's ratings.

_____Step 3. The procedures in Steps 1 and 2 are repeated, with a new member introducing
(15–25   his feelings.
min.)

_____Step 4. If there are 10–15 minutes left, steps 1 and 2 are repeated again, with another
         member initiating.

_____Step 5. Preparation for Session 6
(2 min.)   (a)   Enter date and time for Session 6 both here and on Session 6 Record
                  Sheet.
                  Date and Time: _____
            (b)   Things to do before Session 6: (1) Study the Introduction to Ses-
                  sion 6. (2) Construct several original statements calling for assertive
                  responses. (3) Decide on how you want to use Session 7.
            (c)   Turn in the Session 5 Record Sheets to your instructor.

Session 5 Record Sheet

Name: _____   Class and Section: _____

Date: _____   Time: _____

Step 1: *Rating of Statement of Feeling by* (*name*): _____ | 1 | 2 | 3 | 4 | 5 |

Rating of my response: | 1 | 2 | 3 | 4 | 5 |

Step 3: *Rating of Statement of Feeling by* (*name*): _____ | 1 | 2 | 3 | 4 | 5 |

Rating of my response: | 1 | 2 | 3 | 4 | 5 |

Step 4: *Rating of Statement of Feeling by* (*name*): _____ | 1 | 2 | 3 | 4 | 5 |

Rating of my response: | 1 | 2 | 3 | 4 | 5 |

So far we've concentrated on developing the ability to express feelings honestly and clearly and to respond to another's expression of feelings with understanding and acceptance. We've avoided any direct focus on the causes of those feelings. But as you know, sometimes the causes of your feelings are important, and an attempt must be made to change those causes in some way. In these cases, the cause is usually another person's behavior.

One way you can attempt to change that behavior is by telling the person his behavior is bad and he should change it. This method doesn't often change the behavior unless you include an effective threat. And when it does work, the relationship is usually a little less open than before.

When someone tells you to change your behavior because it is bothersome, you are probably tempted to justify your behavior and to attempt to make him stop showing his feelings. The next easy step is an argument in which the discussion can get off onto many irrelevant tangents, with exaggerated references to every irritant ever experienced.

On the other hand, your chances of improving both the situation and the relationship are better if your statement states *your* feelings about the behavior. For example:

"It's insane the way you try to get even with other drivers."

or

"I really get frightened when you take after another driver."

In the first statement, you are accusing the other person; this focuses on *his* behavior and is more likely to lead to a nonproductive argument. The second statement focuses on *your* feelings, invites him to do the same with your feelings and his own, and is more likely to lead to an honest and better understanding of each other. A behavior change is more likely here than if he is put on the defensive, but whether or not he changes his behavior, you are both better able to understand each other's behavior.

An accusation implies that the other person's behavior must change. You are implying that he must change if you are going to continue liking him. On the other hand, when you state your feelings, you are avoiding the implication that you are blaming him; instead you are making it clear that you are talking about yourself and your own feelings.

Of course we usually try to avoid arguments, but the method we choose is to avoid the problem all together—not mentioning it at all. That usually avoids an argument all right, at least temporarily. But denying your own feelings in order to avoid a disagreement is frequently a big price to pay; and you don't have to pay this price. You can learn how to express your negative feelings without arguing or accusing.

ASSERTIVENESS

Often a person wants to and should express his feelings about another person's behavior because his rights are being violated in some way. If he avoids such an assertion, whether deliberately or not, or if he expresses his feelings indirectly and vaguely (perhaps in a nonverbal way by his tone of voice or facial expression), he is being *nonassertive*. But if he asserts his own rights in a way that does not violate the rights of another, if he gives honest and direct expression of his feelings, while showing respect for the other person, he is being *assertive*. Notice that assertiveness does not imply respect for the other person's behavior, nor does it mean deference or indecisiveness.

If a person asserts his rights in a way that violates the rights of others, or if he attempts to dominate, humiliate or verbally attack the other person with a hostile outburst, then we say that person is being *aggressive,* not assertive. For example: A fellow student asks to borrow your class notes, something he has done regularly for most of the semester, and you don't like it. You might say:

1. "Well, all right, but I wish you would do your own work." You put a scowl on your face and march off.

2. "I've become very irritated by your borrowing my notes all the time. I hate not being able to study them when I want to, and I don't like the condition they come back in. I'm sorry, but I don't want to lend you my notes anymore. I hope you'll understand."

3. "Who was your slave last year? I've had enough of your parasitic behavior. Get lost!"

The first response is a mild, somewhat deferential indication of the person's feelings about the note borrowing. Notice that most of the bad feeling is expressed nonverbally. This response is clearly a nonassertive response.

The second response is an assertive one. The focus is on the person's feelings, and even though there is some properly implied criticism of the other person's behavior, the speaker talks mostly about *his own feelings* and his own reactions.

The third response blasts the borrower and violates his right to be free from abusive personal attack. The focus is almost entirely on the other person and his behavior. This is clearly an aggressive response.

Assertiveness, like most behavior, is a learned behavior; so is nonassertiveness. Nonassertiveness is primarily avoidance behavior; on the basis of painful experiences in past attempts to express our feelings and assert our rights (perhaps with some aggression), we decide that we would rather live with the bad personal feelings. Often a tendency to nonassertiveness is situation specific;

that is, we experience difficulty in asserting ourselves only in one or a few situations (e.g. with one's spouse, or boss), but not with other people.

To become assertive, we must first of all learn how to express ourselves assertively without aggression and without minimizing our feelings; that is, we must first learn how to do it. But we must also learn that it is worth doing; that is, we must learn that in the long run we are better off being able to exercise our rights, express our feelings, and have honest and open relationships with our friends, even though we run the risk of displeasing some people on occasion, or being called selfish.

Of course there is no guarantee that in every case, asserting your rights and expressing your feelings honestly and openly will improve your relationships with other people. Remember, again, that sometimes it is wise to be cautious and keep your feelings to yourself. But until you have the appropriate skills and have learned to value openness, you do not have the choice of being flexible, depending on the circumstances.

In the sixth session, you will be able to practice making assertive responses to hypothetical situations. To prepare for this session, you should construct several original situations of your own, ones which might be familiar to the members of the group, and ones which call for an assertive response if one's rights are to be exercised. Be sure to come prepared with these situations, written out for easy recall and use.

At the end of the sixth session, your group will spend a few minutes deciding on the topic and procedures for the final session. This is intended to allow the group itself to decide on which aspect of the workshop the members feel they would like more practice in. To prepare for this mutual decision, you might want to review the previous units and evaluate your current skills and needs. Once you have decided the area in which you want more practice, then decide whether one of the methods used in the previous sessions might be the best way of proceeding, or whether a modified procedure would best serve the purpose. If it happens that the group comes to no decision about the seventh session, then by default the topic and procedures of the sixth session are repeated.

Session 6

Step 1.
(15–20
min.)
The members form into threesomes. Each member takes a turn at attempting an assertive response to *each* of the following situations. The other members score the response as nonassertive, assertive or aggressive. Then the group briefly discusses the ratings.

(a)   You've had your car in twice this week to the local mechanic because it stalls out at about 40 mph. The first time he said it was the tuning and he adjusted it, the second time he said it was the carburetor and he fixed it. But it still stalls out. You drive in the next morning and say: (your response)

(b)   A good friend calls and asks to use some of your records for a party. Records are the one item you are definitely not willing to lend out to anyone. You say to your friend: (your response)

Questions to consider: 1. Did the response assert honest feelings (not just a decision)? 2. Did the response avoid or soften the feelings? 3. Did the response focus on the other person's actions? 4. Did the response show respect for the other person (not necessarily for his behavior)?

Step 2.
(5 min.)
The group then discusses other assertive but nonaggressive ways of responding to the above situations. Refer to the Introduction to Session 6, if necessary, for clarification and examples.

Step 3.
(15–20
min.)
Different groups of three are formed, and steps 1 and 2 are repeated, using original situations suggested by the members. Be sure to save ten minutes for Step 4.

Step 4.
(10 min.)
(a)   The group as a whole decides on the topic for Session 7: (1) expressing understanding and empathy for another's feelings; (2) understanding and expressing one's own feelings clearly; or (3) asserting one's rights without violating the rights of others.

(b)   The group selects the procedures for Session 7: (1) using a format from a previous session; or (2) using a format especially designed by the members for their topic.

(In either case, the emphasis should be on individual practice of a skill, with feedback from the others.)

(c)   Turn in Session 6 Record Sheets to your instructor.

Session 6 Record Sheet

Name: _____   Class and Section: _____

Date: _____   Time: _____

Step 1:   Assertive Rating

Respondent _____

_____Nonassertive   _____Assertive   _____Aggressive

Respondent _____

_____Nonassertive   _____Assertive   _____Aggressive

Respondent _____

_____Nonassertive   _____Assertive   _____Aggressive

Respondent _____

_____Nonassertive   _____Assertive   _____Aggressive

Respondent _____

_____Nonassertive   _____Assertive   _____Aggressive

Respondent _____

_____Nonassertive   _____Assertive   _____Aggressive

Respondent _____

_____Nonassertive   _____Assertive   _____Aggressive

Respondent _____

_____Nonassertive   _____Assertive   _____Aggressive

Session 6 Record Sheet—(Continued)

Step 3:   Assertive Rating

Respondent _____

_____Nonassertive   _____Assertive   _____Aggressive

Respondent _____

_____Nonassertive   _____Assertive   _____Aggressive

Respondent _____

_____Nonassertive   _____Assertive   _____Aggressive

Respondent _____

_____Nonassertive   _____Assertive   _____Aggressive

Respondent _____

_____Nonassertive   _____Assertive   _____Aggressive

Respondent _____

_____Nonassertive   _____Assertive   _____Aggressive

Respondent _____

_____Nonassertive   _____Assertive   _____Aggressive

Respondent _____

_____Nonassertive   _____Assertive   _____Aggressive

Session 7

_____Step 1.   The group uses the topic and procedures decided on at the last meeting, reserving the last 10–15 minutes for Step 2.

_____Step 2.   Each individual member writes the response he would most likely make to the
(10–15   following statements: (*Write on Session 7 Record Sheet*)
min.)

    (a)   A good friend says to you: I'm pretty worried. I don't think Joe likes me any more. He hasn't called me all week, and yesterday I think he saw me on campus and deliberately avoided me. I wish I knew what I did wrong."

    (b)   A friend says: "Well, the team I play for finally got an invitation to the NCAA finals in St. Louis."

    (c)   How do you feel right now about any or all aspects of this interpersonal workshop?

    (d)   Your professor has just handed you back a term paper you wrote. He marked it C, with no comments. You thought that you had done A or at least B work. What would you most likely do or say?

_____Step 3.   Turn in the record sheet for Session 7. Also turn in your personal reaction sheet.

Session 7 Record Sheet

Name: _____   Class and Section: _____

Date: _____   Time: _____

Use this page to record ratings and names, as appropriate to topic and procedures used.
   Use the next page to record Step 2.

Session 7 Record Sheet—(Continued)

Step 2:

Response to statement (a):

Response to statement (b):

Response to statement (c):

Response to statement (d):

Personal Reaction

We would appreciate your reactions, comments or suggestions regarding any or all sessions of your workshop—anonymous if you wish—using this sheet.

YOU-NAME-IT PROJECT

In this unit you will design and carry out a project (study, research, or other activity) tailored to your own educational interests or needs. The project may be on any topic that is in some direct way related to the basic objectives of this course.

For example, the project might involve in-depth study of a specific and well-defined topic; or it might be some first-hand analysis of an educational innovation in practice; or it might involve your own practice at applying some of the skill or knowledge of the course, or an attempt to test some of the principles of the course; You might even arrange to tutor another student in the material of this or another course. Whatever the topic, you may carry out the project via any medium that you think appropriate (paper, audio or video tape, demonstration, data charts and graphs, etc.)

Before you begin your project, you must submit your plan to the instructor for approval. This plan should normally include:

(a)   A *precise statement* specifying the limits of the topic or activity

(b)   A list of the *resources* you will use

(c)   A complete statement of your *objectives* for the project

(d)   A procedure for *measuring* your achievement of these objectives

PERSONAL PROGRESS GRAPH

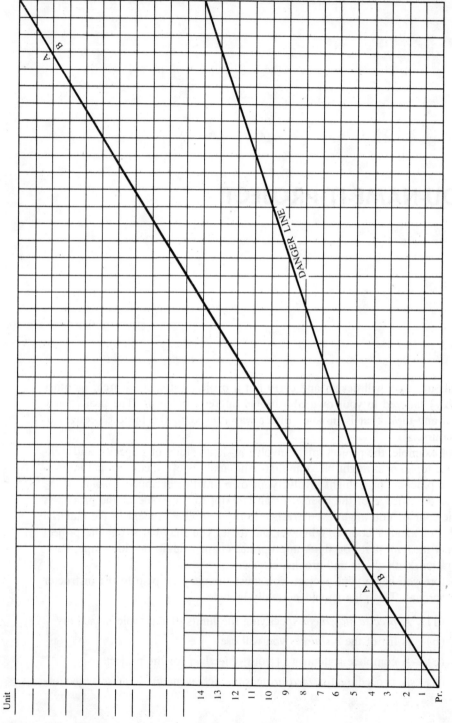

Class Days

PERSONAL PROGRESS GRAPH

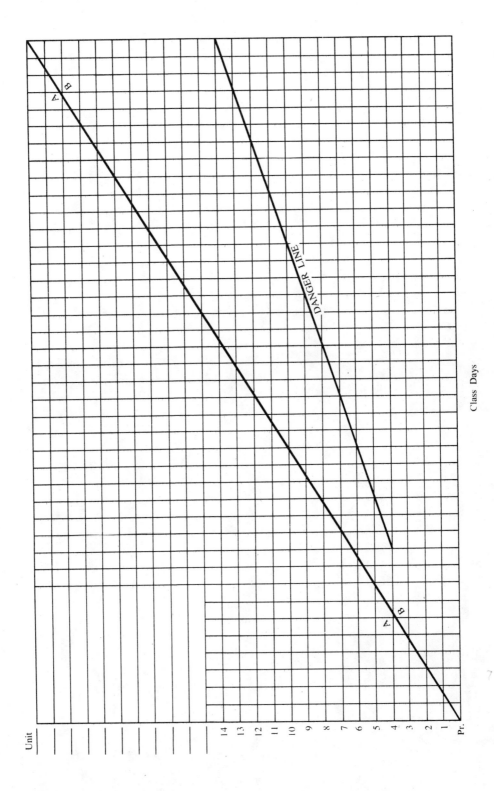

Class Days

INDEX

INDEX